TWO BOYS

Divided by Fortune—United by Tragedy
A True Story of the Pursuit of Justice

ROBERT ZAUSNER

CAMINO BOOKS, INC.
Philadelphia

Manufactured in the United States of America

1 2 3 4 5   11 10 09

LIBRARY OF CONGRESS CATALOGING-IN-PUBLICATION DATA

Zausner, Robert, 1953–
Two boys, divided by fortune, united by tragedy : a
true story of the pursuit of justice / Robert Zausner.
p. cm.
Includes index.
ISBN 978-1-933822-15-0 (alk. paper)
1. Trials (Products liability)—Pennsylvania—Philadelphia. 2. Kline &
Specter (Law firm) 3. Mahoney, Tucker—Trials, litigation, etc. 4. Daisy
Manufacturing Company—Trials, litigation, etc. 5. K-Mart Corporation—
Trials, litigation, etc. 6. Hall, Shareif—Trials, litigation, etc. 7. Hall,
Deneen—Trials, litigation, etc. 8. Southeastern Pennsylvania
Transportation Authority—Trials, litigation, etc. I. Title.

KF226.Z38 2008
346.7303'8—dc22   2008024412

Cover design: Jerilyn Bockorick
Interior design: Rachel Reiss

This book is available at a special discount on bulk
purchases for promotional, business, and educational use.

Publisher
Camino Books, Inc.
P.O. Box 59026
Philadelphia, PA 19102

www. caminobooks.com

To Eve and Jackie, my two girls

Contents

PREFACE

John "Tucker" Mahoney and Shareif Hall lived less than an hour away from each other. Yet they were worlds apart.

At 16, Tucker, as his family and friends called him, was tall and handsome, with sandy hair, blue eyes, and a crystalline personality. He was Mr. Popularity. Everyone liked Tucker—his parents, his sisters, his friends at New Hope–Solebury High School, his teachers. Seeing that Tucker was still growing and could already dunk a basketball, his coach figured he had a good shot at a college scholarship. Not that Tucker needed one. His parents were well off—his father was an executive at a computer company—and years earlier the Mahoneys had settled into a large stone house in an affluent, wooded community north of Philadelphia.

College wasn't in the plan for four-year-old Shareif, a quiet, somewhat introverted little boy. There was no plan. His mother was struggling to raise him and his four siblings in a second-floor apartment in North Philadelphia, a notorious, pockmarked part of town, where the streets were strewn with debris, both material and human. Drug dealers were a common sight in the area. So was violence. College grads were not, even though Shareif's home stood in the shadow of nearby Temple University, whose campus the Hall family passed every day. It seemed to be an oasis that was forever out of reach.

Tucker was an upper-middle-class kid with a large, loving family and a bright future. Shareif was poor and lived without a father—

his had wandered away a few years before. Shareif's future was near-term and filled with questions: Would his mother have a job to-morrow? Would food stamps be enough to put food on the table?

But these two boys had something in common. They would share similar experiences, freakish occurrences that would leave both struggling for their physical well-being and against formidable foes—one a large government authority and the other a widely known U.S. corporation.

Each family would seek redress by turning to members of a pro-fession much maligned in modern society—trial lawyers. In these two cases, the lawyers were partners in a Philadelphia firm. They would become, as often happens, the victims' remedy of last resort, called on to win not only a measure of compensation but also a broader justice.

The following story is true. It is based on official documents, trial transcripts, and interviews with those who were involved.

CHAPTER 1

DROPS OF BLOOD

IT WAS A LAZY, NOTHING-TO-DO KIND of afternoon. Maggie, a college student and the oldest of the Mahoney kids, was napping on the couch in the family room. Tucker Mahoney, who was 16, was out by the pool with his best friend, Ty, doing, well, what teenage boys do. Becky, their mother, could hear them cackling through the sliding glass door. She surveyed the scene and decided this was a good time to make a quick trip to the supermarket.

It took barely an hour to buy her groceries and return home, her Volvo coursing easily through the country roads of Solebury Township, an affluent, suburban–rural community bordering horse farms and corn fields nearly an hour's drive north of Philadelphia. Becky pulled into the garage of the Mahoneys' large stone and stucco house. She grabbed her shopping bags and stepped out of the car. She took only a few steps when she noticed a reddish spot "the size of a nickel" on the garage floor. It looked like blood. Stanley must have stepped on something and cut himself, Becky thought. Stanley was the family dog, a floppy springer spaniel prone to misadventure.

"Maggie," she called out as she entered the house.

Nothing.

"Tucker?"

Nothing.

Becky took a few more steps and noticed another drop of blood. Fresh blood, still a bright red against the white stone floor. Then another drop, and another. As she walked toward the counter to put her bags down, she saw a strand of droplets in a curved row on the floor, like red pearls on a string. More drops were in the sink, some spilling down the drain. Becky, a tall, willowy blonde with a relaxed nature, felt a rush of anxiety.

She ran to the other side of the house and shouted up the stairs. "Maggie!"

She ran to the back door and thrust it open.

"Tucker! Tucker!"

No one was home. Except Stanley, and Stanley was fine.

CHAPTER 2

A BANGING NOISE

I N A SMALL SUBTERRANEAN WORKROOM with a heavy stainless
steel door that thousands of commuters walked past every day,
Bill Kinkle and Ray Mosley, employees of the Southeastern
Pennsylvania Transportation Authority, sat eating their lunch. The
two men were SEPTA millwrights, mechanics who worked on the
mass transit authority's machinery, including its escalators and elevators, installing and repairing and replacing parts as warranted.
Kinkle and Mosley, dressed in their blue coveralls, were virtually
invisible to the people who hurried on and off the trains in the un-
derground of the Broad Street Line, a subway system that stretched
from North Philadelphia to Veterans Stadium, home to the Phillies
and Eagles, in the south part of town.

The workroom that Kinkle and Mosley occupied was located
just beneath the escalator leading to the subway at the Cecil B.
Moore Station, named for the late Philadelphia attorney, city
councilman, and civil rights leader. A constant groan emanated
from the underbelly of the mammoth escalator rumbling overhead, with the sweep of its steps and constant clatter of its chains
creating a monotonous drumbeat. But the workmen were accustomed to the sounds, and the room offered sanctuary in a public
train station.

Kinkle was peeling the plastic wrap from a ham sandwich when he heard a commotion from above. Unusual sounds. First he thought he heard someone running on the escalator. Then a banging noise. Loud. Mosley would later recollect it as a "boom, boom, boom, boom." Both men dropped their lunches and ran for the door, Mosley a few steps in front of Kinkle. They ran to the bottom of the escalator and saw people standing at the top. Then they heard shrieking, harsh screams. Mosley bounded up the escalator, while Kinkle smacked the emergency stop button at the bottom of the escalator. Only one of the 27 working escalators in the SEPTA system had an automatic emergency stop, one that tripped at the slightest sign of something jamming in the escalator. This was not that escalator.

Kinkle ran up the escalator after Mosley, the huge cluster of keys that hung from his belt loop jangling like tiny alarm bells. When he got to the top, he saw Mosley standing still, staring. Kinkle looked down and saw what had halted Mosley in his tracks, what all the screaming was about. The sight paralyzed him as well.

"Oh, shit," Kinkle yelped. "Oh, shit!"

CHAPTER 3

THE GUN

He was the golden boy. A friendly kid with a ready smile, Tucker Mahoney had grown from a cute, white-blond tot to a handsome 6-foot-2 teenager. As a freshman he'd been his high school's Homecoming prince, and now he was vice president of his sophomore class. "The girls were just starting to take notice," said his father, Jay. In the six years since his family had moved to Solebury, Tucker's upstairs bedroom had become a testimonial to a flourishing adolescence—the ubiquitous Michael Jordan poster, framed pictures from his many Little League teams, trophies topped with tiny golden men hitting baseballs, kicking soccer balls, shooting basketballs. Tucker had outgrown his twin bed long ago, his feet hanging off the end when he stretched out. He had been MVP of the junior varsity basketball team as a freshman and now played on the varsity, even occasionally prevailing in games of one-on-one against his coach, who saw him as a sure shot to play college ball.

Tucker, a middle name he got from his fishing buddy and grandfather, Becky's father, who never had a son of his own, was one of three children in the Mahoney family, the middle child and the only boy. He was everyone's favorite, on his teams, in school—where in both 6th and 8th grades he had won the Humanitarian Award voted by teachers and students for the most admired

5

student—and nowhere more than at home. He was a big, sweet kid
with a happy-go-lucky demeanor.

And why not? He *was* lucky. He was popular without trying to
be. He was living the American dream, at once an exceptional kid
with every benefit life had to offer—loving parents, a pretty home
on three acres shaded by towering pines, a future filled with sunshine—and yet a typical kid, one who got good grades and enjoyed
just hanging out with his friends. In many ways, Tucker was like
any boy you might find shooting hoops in his driveway in a shel-
tered corner of suburbia.

Which made what happened all the more scary.

It was May 24, two days after Tucker's 16th birthday. He had just
come home from school. With him was Ty—actually Ellsworth
Weatherby IV—who lived across the road and was one of the first
kids Tucker had met in Solebury. Ty and Tucker, Tucker and Ty.
They were buddies, inseparable. Ty's picture was all over Tucker's
wall among the team photos. There was one from when they were
10, smiling after a game, both dressed in the red uniform of the
New Hope Phillies. Tonight, they were going with Ty's parents to
see the Phillies, the major league version.

The boys wolfed down a couple of pieces of leftover birthday
cake in the Mahoney's kitchen. Later, when Tucker's mother left for
a short shopping trip, Tucker and Ty were standing in the backyard
near the kidney-shaped pool, talking. Maggie, Tucker's older sister,
who was home for the summer from Vanderbilt University, was
sleeping on the couch in the family room. She didn't feel well. It
was almost 5 o'clock. "I'm going to Doylestown. Maggie's asleep
on the couch," Becky yelled out to Tucker, then added about the
Mahoney's youngest, "I'm taking Abby with me. Be back soon."

Tucker and Ty stayed outside. Tucker had his birthday present in
his hand, a Daisy PowerLine 856 airgun. It was the only thing he
had asked for this year. He'd had BB guns before. But this was no
ordinary BB gun, not the Red Ryder that Daisy had made for generations of boys, the one that used a spring to propel BBs and
barely had the power to reach—much less kill—a bird in a tree.

No, this newer version could be pumped to propel a BB or pellet 780 feet per second, a speed faster than a bullet fired from a 38-caliber police special, a real gun.

A few days earlier, Tucker and his father had gone shopping for a new BB gun at Kmart. Tucker wanted a new gun, this particular gun, because it came with a scope. "We had no idea about its power. We never even looked at the specs, just that it had a scope," Jay would recall. The BB guns were located at the rear of the store, in sporting goods, near the fishing rods and tennis balls and just past the toy shelves, a few dozen feet from Barbie, Betty Boop, and GI Joe. On either side were hunting knives and hunting guns, rifles and shotguns, with bullets and shells. With one difference: the knives and guns and ammunition were locked behind plate glass. The BB guns were not. At first, Tucker and his father couldn't find them.

"I don't see any," said Tucker.

"No, I can't find them either," said his father. "Tuck, let's go."

They had turned to walk out when Jay spotted some boxes standing vertically on a floor shelf. He reached in and turned one around.

"Hey, look, Tuck. Here they are."

"Yeah."

"This one has a sight on it. That's what you want, isn't it?"

"Yeah."

"Is this OK?"

"It's great, Dad."

The only requirement for purchasing the rifle was that the buyer be 18 years old. In neighboring New Jersey, where BB and pellet guns (the 856 shot both) were considered weapons, buyers had to have a Firearm Purchase Card, which could be obtained through the police after a three- to ten-week waiting period. Not so in Pennsylvania. Jay plunked down two $20 bills, and he and Tucker walked out with the gun.

Tucker's old BB guns were the spring-fired Red Ryder he had gotten when he was 13 or 14 and an old wood-handled pump-action rifle that took one BB at a time. The 856 could hold as many as 100.

Ty had three BB guns. The boys had shot together plenty of times before, at targets, mailboxes, trees, birds. On this day, Tucker took his new gun from a cabinet behind the washing machine, and he and Ty went out back to see if they could finally rid the property of that damned crow that had been camping out around the pool. They lay in wait and, sure enough, before long, there he was, cawing overhead and settling onto the branch of a tree. Ty aimed and fired the gun. He missed, and the crow left in a hurry. They fired at a few more birds but kept missing. "The sight must be off," said Tucker.

The boys walked to Ty's house to see if they could fix it. Ty grabbed a screwdriver and fiddled with the gun's sight. They fired the gun, adjusted the sight, fired and adjusted, until they had it just right. Tucker used the Weatherbys' metal mailbox as a test target. He stood across the road and took aim. *Ping!* The sound of metal striking metal. The sight appeared to be fixed. *Ping! Ping! Ping! Ping!* Tucker hit the mailbox with five straight shots. There was no pinging sound on the sixth shot. He fired again, and again nothing.

"You missed from here?" chided Ty.

"Nah, must be out."

"Must be."

"Let's go back to my house. I've got more BBs," Tucker said.

As they walked to the Mahoneys', Tucker pumped his gun and fired into the trees five times, maybe more. "It's funny," said Ty, "You notice how the birds only fly away when you actually shoot BBs? It's the BBs cutting through the leaves and the branches, not just the sound of the gun that scares them off." Tucker shot a few more times into the late afternoon sky. Then he did something neither of the boys had done before, not with this gun. As Ty walked in front of him, Tucker pumped the gun again, leveled it, aimed at the back of Ty's head and pulled the trigger.

"What the . . . ?" Ty was stunned for a second. He felt the strong burst of air on the back of his head, low and right in the middle, a few inches up from his neck. The sensation was weird, scary but kind of cool at the same time. He was surprised but not mad, even though he knew you were never supposed to aim a gun at anyone, that you were supposed to treat every gun as if it was loaded. But, of course, he knew it wasn't loaded.

They kept walking. When they reached the Mahoneys' driveway, Tucker saw his weekly chore awaiting him. He had to bring in the emptied trash cans from the side of the road.

"Here," he said, handing Ty the gun and bending down to pick up the barrels.

Ty pumped the gun three or four times, then shot it at Tucker.

"Whoa . . . ," said Tucker, raising his eyebrows. He too was surprised by the strong burst of air on the back of his head, puffing up his sandy hair.

As Tucker started to put the trash cans down, he heard Ty pumping the gun again—one pump, two pumps, three pumps. He knew what was coming. He smiled. "I'm going to do you as many times as you do me," he warned Ty. Four pumps, five pumps, six pumps.

Pop!

Tucker stood up slowly.

"Ouch." He felt a stinging near his left ear. "I think I'm hit."

"Yeah, sure," said Ty. Tucker was such a joker.

"No, really. I think I'm hit."

"C'mon . . . ."

"Really, see if I'm bleeding." Tucker ducked down so Ty could get a look.

"Jesus, Tucker . . . ."

CHAPTER 4

THE ESCALATOR

SHAREIF HALL COULD NOT HAVE been brought into the world under worse circumstances. He was the fifth of five children living in a small, second-floor apartment in the poorest and most perilous part of Philadelphia, North Philly. A lot of kids never made it out of the neighborhood, a jumble of trash-strewn streets, vacant lots, and brick rowhouses, many of them empty and with plywood over their windows. They didn't shoot hoops in this neighborhood; they shot guns. Tough-looking teens gangsta-walked the streets. Survival here was a goal, not a given. Shareif had no father, at least not the kind who lived with the family and provided an income. His mother was home but she had her own problems, not the least of which was paying the rent and feeding five kids.

Yet somehow, Deneen Hall found the resolve to help herself, even though it meant leaving Shareif and his siblings—Sherrod, Sherrell, Shaneen, and Shaheed—with her own mother for a spell. She earned a high school equivalency diploma and got a job. Although too poor to leave the neighborhood, she found a decent apartment in a row of scrubbed, brick-faced buildings, many occupied by families like her own.

By the time Shareif, the baby of the family, turned four—Sherrod, the oldest, was now 13—things had been starting to look

up. Deneen, 32 and never married, was working at a small construction company that paid her $7.50 an hour to do a variety of
odd jobs—paint, mix cement, clean up debris at job sites, cut the
weekly payroll checks. She liked her job and the people there liked
her. The work wasn't always steady, sometimes 40 hours a week,
sometimes as few as 8, but she was off welfare. Together with food
stamps and government-paid health care, she could put food on the
table and pay the rent. And once in a while she had enough for an
extravagance, like the $65 she had spent on Shareif's black leather
Fila boots. It took a full day's work to earn that much money, but
it was worth it to see his wide smile when she brought them home
and flipped open the cardboard box.

On this day, November 27, about a month after Shareif's fourth
birthday, Deneen was in a good mood. So were Shareif and Shaheed,
who was the older brother by nine months. The boys had no school
the Wednesday before Thanksgiving, and so Deneen had taken them
to work with her. She was scheduled to work a half day. Her boss had
told her she could skip the day, but she wanted to show him she
cared enough to come and help out. The boys played in the office,
while Deneen did the weekly payroll. She finished by 11 a.m. and
grabbed her coat, looking forward to the next four days off.

This would be a busy afternoon. She and the kids were headed
to Super Fresh to buy their Thanksgiving turkey. A trip to the supermarket was a big deal for the Halls, especially after payday. By
tomorrow afternoon the family would be sitting together around a
roasted turkey. Tomorrow there would be sweet potatoes and corn-
bread and cranberry sauce, apple pie and ice cream. Tomorrow
would be a great day.

The boys were excited as they stepped off the orange and stainless steel car of the Broad Street Line (or Orange Line) subway at the
station. The Halls' apartment was five blocks from the station. The
subway here wasn't like most of the others in North Philly. Thanks
to Temple's proximity, it wasn't dark and dank or polluted with
garbage and the pervasive odor of urine. The Cecil B. Moore Station,
packed day and night with students and faculty, was brightly lit,

with high ceilings and shiny ceramic-tiled walls of white and soothing shades of green. The brown tiled floors were routinely mopped,
and the whole place had a fresh, ammonia smell to it.

Deneen took each boy by the hand as they stepped off the train
and into the station. She was always careful, always grasping her
children by their hands, especially the younger Shareif. It was part
of her routine. As the three of them walked through the station,
Shaheed holding her left hand, Shareif her right, the boys looked up
at their mother and smiled. Deneen, a heavyset, strong-looking
woman had a round face framed by close-cropped black hair. Hers
was a stern face upon which smiles surfaced hesitantly. But not today.
She smiled back at her boys, their eyes bright with optimism.

It was 11:30 a.m when they exited one by one through the huge
metal turnstiles that separated the train platform from the main
station. There weren't many other people here today. It was a chilly
morning, so Deneen had made Shareif wear his winter parka over
his usual uniform of jeans and a T-shirt. And Shareif had on his favorite shoes, his black Fila boots.

Up ahead, the huge escalator led to the street level and the
nearby Super Fresh. They would pick out a big turkey, a 20-
pounder. They'd enjoy that turkey for days, maybe a cold drum-
stick for lunch on Friday or open-faced sandwiches with gravy on
Saturday night. The escalator was a giant, riding 24 feet to the surface. It was also very narrow, with no room for all three of them to
stand on one step. Deneen nudged Shaheed onto the step ahead of
her. She and Shareif stood together one step behind, Deneen to the
left and holding Shareif's hand. Shareif put his right hand onto the
black rubber handrail. Both boys looked straight ahead, not moving, certainly not clowning around. They knew better. Mom didn't
stand for it.

As the escalator carried them toward the summit, Deneen
alerted her boys to step off. "Get ready, Shaheed," she said. She
was careful to make sure he stepped off at the right moment. Not
too early, not too late. "OK, Shareif. Let's go." She'd give his little
hand a tug and off they'd go.

But not this time.

Shaheed stepped off the escalator and as Deneen started to step off herself, she heard a sound coming from the escalator that she'd never heard before, a sharp *click, click, click*. She got one foot off the escalator step. Still holding Shareif's hand, she began to step off with her right foot as well, but Shareif didn't move with her. She tugged him a little harder but he still didn't budge. *What was going on?* Deneen started to lose her balance. She looked down. There was a space, she noticed now, between the highest step and the top of the escalator, the stationary plate that resembled a large steel comb. Regaining her balance, she tugged at Shareif again. But the boy was just standing there even though the escalator was still running, still moving. Shareif didn't look panicked or scared. He just remained in place. *Why wasn't he coming?*

Then Shareif started to holler.

"Owwww! Momma!"

She looked down and finally understood what was going on. Now Deneen started to scream, too.

"Oh my God! Oh my God!"

CHAPTER 5

TOUCH AND GO

Maggie Mahoney was still on the couch, awake now, the TV on, when Tucker came into the house. Not running, not yelling, but seeming, as Maggie would say later, "a little bit scared."

"Maggie?"

"What?"

"Maggie!"

She hopped over the small wooden fence that kept the dogs out of the kitchen and saw Tucker standing at the sink. He had wadded up three or four paper towels and was holding them by his ear. She could see blood on the towels.

"What happened?"

"I got hit with a BB."

"You got stung by a bee?"

"No, a BB. I got shot by a BB."

"How?"

"Ty . . . ."

"Ty? I can't believe you did this!" Maggie shouted, whirling to face Tucker's friend.

"Don't blame Ty . . . ."

"Ty! You moron!"

"No, don't be mad at Ty," Tucker insisted. "He thought the gun was empty."

"Come with me," Maggie ordered. She hustled Tucker out to the driveway to her 1992 Grand Am. She gave Ty a sharp look. "Go home and tell your dad I'm taking him to the hospital. Tell him to call my mom on her cell."

"Tucker, get in the car. We'll get you to the hospital for some stitches," Maggie said, thinking he'd gotten nicked in the ear. Tucker looked a little nervous but hardly overwrought. In the car he sat up to adjust the radio, switching from Maggie's country and western, which he despised, to a rock station. He turned up the volume.

A few drops of blood trickled through the paper towels that Tucker held to the back of his head and onto the gray leather headrest of Maggie's front passenger seat. During the ride Tucker told her what had happened: He and Ty had been shooting in the yard when the gun ran out of BBs. Bursts of air fired from the gun. At one point, Ty fired into the back of his head and he felt a twinge of pain.

Hearing this made Maggie nervous. Tucker hadn't been hit in the ear at all but in the head. As they drove, he sat up and twisted the rear-view mirror to try to get a look at where he'd been shot. He saw the blood and became a little panicky. Soon Tucker began to feel a tingling sensation in his fingertips. Then in his toes. "My left eye is getting fuzzy," he said. Maggie got on her cell phone and dialed Ty's father, Ted Weatherby, Dr. Ted Weatherby, who worked at Doylestown Hospital.

"What should I do?"

"Recline his chair and get him to put his feet up."

Tucker did it.

"Don't worry, Tuck. Everything'll be all right," Maggie reassured, trying to keep her little brother talking.

"OK. Just don't blame Ty."

"You'll be all right ... don't worry ... you'll be fine ...."

"Maggie, don't blame Ty."

A minute or two went by. Suddenly, Tucker shouted.

"Oh my God!"

"Don't worry . . . ."

"Oh my God! My eyes are starting to get fuzzy!"

"Tucker . . . ."

"I can't see anything!"

"Tucker, hold on . . . ."

"I can't see!"

And then he uttered his last words: "Maggie, please hurry up!"

MAGGIE KEPT TALKING to her brother. But as her Grand Am rounded a turn on Mechanicsville Road near a farm that grew flowers, she realized Tucker had grown silent.

"Tucker! Tucker!"

No answer. He was unconscious. It hadn't even been 10 minutes since they had left home, though it felt like much longer. Maggie could see that her brother was still breathing. Then he choked, suddenly and violently. He had aspirated a piece of his birthday cake, it would turn out, a few chunks moving into his lungs.

Maggie pushed her foot down harder on the accelerator. Her car zoomed along a two-lane country highway past local roads with cute and curious names—Ash Mill, Lace Leaf, Byro, Fieldstown, Burnt House Hill, Church School, Chubb. Maggie came to a red light, slowed down a bit, then leaned on her horn and breezed through it. Then the next red light, and the next.

She called 911. Busy.

She called again. Busy.

Finally it answered. The words rushed out of Maggie.

"Hello. My name is Maggie Mahoney. I'm on my way to Doylestown Hospital. My brother's been shot in the head, with a BB in the skull. He's gone into shock! He can't feel his arms or his legs!"

"Is he awake? Is he able to talk to you?"

"No, he's not talking to me. No, he's not awake."

"Pull over to the side of the road and wait for assistance."

"No!" said Maggie, both worried and angry now. "I'm only two or three minutes away now."

"Are you sure you don't want to pull over?"

"No, that's ridiculous. Don't waste my time! Just have someone waiting for us at the hospital."

She raced along Main Street in Doylestown, past its quaint shops and outdoor cafes. Maggie held her foot down on the accelerator, roaring through red lights one after another. Other drivers shouted behind their windshields. One gave her the finger.

An army of nurses met her car at Doylestown Hospital's emergency room. It took four of them to wrestle Tucker's long body out of the bucket seat and through the car door. Once he was whisked away, Maggie fell apart. She began sobbing. Her knees felt weak and she thought she would collapse as she saw her baby brother whisked inside. She just stood there for a while and cried.

Becky Mahoney arrived 15 minutes later. Tucker was in the emergency room. When the doctor came out, he had one question: "Are you sure a BB did this?" It was hard to believe.

Tucker needed to be transferred to a hospital better equipped to help him. They decided on Abington Memorial Hospital. Before Tucker was moved, Becky was allowed to see him. A tube had been placed down her son's throat. His eyes had rolled back into his head, only a sliver of white showing between his eyelids. His shorts, the khaki American Eagle shorts Becky had given him only two days earlier as a birthday gift, had been sliced from his body. He was in a hospital gown.

Minutes later, Tucker was in an ambulance, its sirens blaring and lights flashing as it sped down Route 611 to Abington. Local police, alerted, had closed off the intersections of the usually congested four-lane road. The trip took just 12 minutes.

Maggie and Becky arrived also, as did Ty Weatherby and his mother, and several other concerned neighbors. Becky had left Abby at a neighbor's house. Jay Mahoney, an executive with a computer information storage company in New Jersey, had called Becky from his cell phone, something he didn't usually do but for some reason had felt compelled to do that evening. He was on his way.

Outside the emergency room, people greeted one another with hugs as they awaited word on Tucker. Ty stood off on his own, crying.

When a neurosurgeon emerged, he said that Tucker had been brought to an operating room. "We need to see if the BB penetrated the brain," he told Becky. "I'm not going to lie to you. It could be serious."

The Mahoneys waited. Becky, teary-eyed and exhausted, sat in a chair. Jay, his shoulders sagging, blue eyes soggy and reddened, paced the halls sick with worry.

Midnight came. As they passed the hours in the large, sterile waiting room, shock and panic gave way to hushed anxiety. The first one to break the silence was not a doctor but a cop. He was carrying a small vial. In it was the BB that, he announced, had been removed from Tucker's head.

The officer, a veteran from the Solebury force named John Kenderdine, wanted to talk to the Mahoneys about what had happened. He had already spoken with the Weatherbys back at Doylestown Hospital, getting Ty's account of the incident. To Jay Mahoney, it sounded dubious, but Ty was the sole witness to what had happened, except for Tucker, of course, who was unable to speak. Had Tucker really fired first at the back of Ty's head? Tucker was a responsible, cautious kid. He'd never aim a gun at another person, let alone pull the trigger. Ty, on the other hand, Jay had always found to be "impulsive," a little more on the wild side. He believed Ty had shot at Tucker, but not Tucker at Ty. He couldn't swear to it. Besides, it hardly mattered at this point.

Becky and Jay had just sat down with the policeman when Dr. Stephen Barrer stepped out of the operating room. "We were able to get the BB out, and the brain looked good," he said. But any relief the Mahoney's felt was fleeting. The BB had nicked an artery, and there had been a great deal of bleeding in Tucker's brain.

"It's going to be touch and go," the doctor told them. "I can't tell you if he's going to make it."

CHAPTER 6

STEEL TEETH

DENEEN HALL CONTINUED TO pull at Shareif, yanking him by the arm to free him from the metal monster. Then suddenly, the escalator let go of his leg. Deneen was holding her little boy in her arms now, but she knew all was not right. She knew a terrible thing had happened. She turned and saw a man in work clothes, a large, burly man, run up the escalator and stop as he reached her. His eyes were wide. "Oh shit!" he said. "Oh shit!"

Shaheed looked back at Deneen, confused and worried. Deneen clutched Shareif tightly in her arms, her face wet with tears. Bill Kinkle would recall later: "... I saw this, a lady holding her baby and she was holding the baby around the waist with the child facing her, and I just saw the bottom of his leg, the bone protruding from the bottom of where the foot used to be."

"I'll go for help," said Kinkle, and he dashed back down the escalator.

Now Ray Mosley approached Deneen, who was screaming, clutching Shareif. The child's foot had been sheared off. His toes, the bottom of his foot, the heel—all gone. Only a nub remained, with the bone sticking out from the ankle area. Blood was dripping from his leg, forming a small puddle that nearly matched the red-brick pavement. Mosley was worried the boy might bleed to death.

"Give me the boy," he said, holding his arms out to Deneen.

"Oh, God!"

"Ma'am...."

"Dear God! What's happening? Oh my God!"

"Ma'am, give me the boy. Let me help."

Deneen was hysterical. Mosley, a big man of about 250 pounds, tried to pry Shareif loose from his mother's grip. She was sobbing and screaming, holding the boy tightly. Mosley pulled harder and was finally able to take Shareif from her. He placed the child down on the floor near the top of the escalator. Shareif seemed so small. And brave. He wasn't hollering or even crying much. He just made tiny whimpering sounds, barely audible. Mosley looked down at him with horror and admiration. *This is one tough little guy.* Thoughts of his own grandkids came to mind. His youngest grandson was five, not much older than the child looking up at him from the ground. Shareif was awfully quiet now. Mosley figured he must have fallen into a state of shock. The child was there, but not really there.

Now what? Mosley wasn't sure. He wasn't a doctor, hadn't even finished high school. Kinkle had gone to call for help, but none had arrived. Just then, a SEPTA policeman arrived. The transit cop thought quickly. He spotted a street vendor nearby, his stand filled with cheap umbrellas, hats, 76ers T-shirts, scarves, gloves. *Scarves!* The officer ran to the stand and grabbed a scarf, ran back to Shareif and tied it tightly around the child's calf to stop the bleeding.

Mosley watched the scarf become a tourniquet. Then he ran out onto the sidewalk and darted across busy Broad Street to the Shanghai Chinese Restaurant next to the Barnes & Noble Temple University Bookstore. "Give me some ice! Fast!" he yelled to a man behind the counter. "Please, I need ice! A kid's been hurt in the subway...."

In the meantime, Kinkle had run to the cashier's booth, where a SEPTA employee sat behind inch-thick glass. Kinkle used the phone there, shouting into it. "We need an ambulance.... It's an emergency.... A kid's had his foot amputated in the escalator....

Hurry up!" He hung up and headed back to the top of the escalator. Kinkle saw the blood, an awful lot for a little kid. He saw Deneen standing there with another boy, another son, he guessed. She wasn't screaming anymore, just sobbing.

Deneen suddenly felt very alone. A small crowd hovered around Shareif, most of them kneeling, staring at her son. There were two police officers, some SEPTA workmen, a few other people she didn't recognize. Commuters, she figured, just taking it all in. One man, the policeman, had tied a scarf around Shareif's leg. Another man arrived, running and out of breath, carrying a plastic bag filled with ice cubes. Deneen looked at Shareif's foot, where his foot used to be . . . and all that blood spattered on the pavement, on the steel teeth at the top of the escalator, on his pants. She began to feel faint. Her legs trembled. But she made herself stand there without collapsing. She had to be strong for Shareif, who now seemed in a state of tranquility. There was an odd look on his face.

Where was the ambulance? What was taking so long? Finally, it arrived. What felt like an hour had only taken 12 minutes since the call was made. By now several people surrounded Deneen, trying to calm her. Someone offered her a cup of juice, which she shoved away. A woman she didn't know put an arm around her shoulders and offered encouragement. "It'll be OK," the woman said in a soothing voice. "It'll be OK." Deneen wasn't so sure.

The rescue workers examined Shareif briefly, then hustled him onto a gurney and out to the street to the waiting ambulance. Inside the vehicle, its lights flashing as it raced through city traffic, they removed Shareif's winter clothes quickly, not bothering with buttons or zippers but using scissors to cut right through them, slicing up the middle of his gray and green winter parka and his brown woolen scarf, then through his blood-spattered gray jeans, his black belt and the multicolored "Kids' Animals" T-shirt that bore pictures of baby dinosaurs—a brontosaurus, stegosaurus, and allosaurus—hatching from their eggshells. The scissors sliced through his little boxer shorts and his white waffle–weave undershirt. Ruined clothing was the least of Shareif's problems. The rescuers needed him ready for the triage nurses and doctors they knew were waiting at the hospital.

Kinkle had returned to the gruesome scene in time to see the rescue squad depart. After they took the boy away, SEPTA workers began cleaning up the splotches of blood from the station floor. A few transit cops were talking. It was quieter now, but Kinkle knew that one more terrible task remained. He lifted a cover plate on the escalator and hit the main power button. Now the contraption was completely turned off. He noticed that a comb-plate—one in a series of steel plates that attached to the landing under which the moving steps disappeared—was missing. The square opening that remained led down into what the millwrights called the "pit," a small area maybe three feet deep and just as wide. Kinkle removed several other plates and crawled into the pit, planting first one foot and then the other into dirt and residue nearly an inch thick.

The first thing he saw was the dislodged comb-plate. He scrunched down so that his fingertips reached the plate. Then he found the two screws that had held it in place. He put the items onto the pavement. Right next to where the plate had been he spotted a black shoe, Shareif's right shoe. With a sense of dread, Kinkle reached down for it. The shoe was mangled, the leather on the arch side raked with a row of gashes where it had been clawed by the steel teeth of the comb-plate. It looked as if an animal had gotten at it. The rubber sole was torn from the shoe on the same side. The tongue and the lace portion at the top of the shoe had been sheared off.

Mosley saw the shoe and immediately devised a theory to explain how the accident had occurred, though SEPTA never made such a conclusion officially. Shareif's foot, he believed, had become caught in a space between the top step and the comb-plate, a space that wasn't supposed to be there but, nevertheless, sometimes was. The space, perhaps, had been large enough to catch the sole of a small child's shoe. As the force of the escalator motor continued to move the step, it pulled the front of the comb-plate, the teeth, down into the boy's foot. The continued force of the escalator then pulled out the two screws holding the plate in position. When the plate was pulled into the pit, it took the boy's foot with it.

The shoe still contained most of a blood-soaked sock and a piece of Shareif's foot when Kinkle removed it from the pit. Mosley was waiting with his bag of ice, hoping that the child's foot would be in the shoe, intact. Perhaps doctors could reattach it. He'd heard of such operations. But when he saw what was there, what was left of the foot, he gave up hope. Whatever piece of a limb was in the shoe, it was tiny and badly mangled. Mosley gave the shoe to the ambulance crew. He also gave them the ice containing the small, mangled piece of Shareif's foot, though it appeared to have little purpose now.

CHAPTER 7

"GRIM"

TUCKER MADE IT, BUT HE WAS in awful shape. Unable to move, unable to speak or swallow nourishment, he just lay on his back in Abington's trauma unit, with only the lights and noises of hospital machinery giving any sign that he was alive. A ventilator controlled his breathing. Two days had passed since the shooting.

"Show me something, Tuck," Becky implored, standing by her son's metal-frame bed. "You have to show me *something*."

Nothing.

"At least wiggle your toes."

And with that, Tucker's toes moved ever so slightly. Becky saw it. The nurse saw it. A sign, at least, that Tucker was with them, that he had some awareness. "They moved!" Becky was thrilled. Hope had returned, even if just a glimmer.

The doctors, told later of Tucker's physical response, dismissed the notion. The movement, they said, was most likely involuntary. Typical in such cases.

Four days later, at 7:30 a.m. on a Friday, the Mahoneys were told that their son's condition was "grim." The doctors said it was doubtful that Tucker would ever improve, that he would remain in essentially a vegetative state.

"Let me tell you a few things," Becky said to them, her pretty face flushed now with anger. "Tucker is very hard to wake up . . . and he doesn't test well. We're not giving up. You hear me? We're not giving up!"

Family and friends continued to offer support. Becky's parents flew up from Florida. Her sister came from Chicago. Stuffed animals and cards and letters streamed in, most from kids at school who liked, even idolized, Tucker, whether they knew him well or not. Like Melissa Moyer, who sent a card and wrote: "You've never been anything but nice to everyone. The world needs more people like you. Come back to us soon." Becky memorized the words and would recite them, like a prayer, every time she sat alone in a sterile hospital room waiting anxiously while Tucker underwent a CAT scan or a spinal tap or myriad other tests. *You've never been anything but nice to everyone. The world needs more people like you. Come back to us soon.*

In the days and weeks ahead, family and friends would talk to Tucker as they entered his room. "Hey, Tuck, how are you, honey? You're looking much better today!" said one neighbor, a large smile on her face. She tried to be animated and upbeat, her voice loud and cheery. Tucker seemed to recognize the woman, or at least her voice. His eyes looked off somewhere in the distance, but he was smiling, or he seemed to be. "It's so good to see you! You'll be getting better soon, Tuck. I just know it!"

When the woman turned away to speak with Becky, Tucker's smile faded. Had it really been a smile or only an involuntary motion? Now he seemed to be staring off into space. It was as if Tucker had gone away, his spirit lifted to another place. He was there, physically, but his being had evaporated. He would appear to look at visitors, but then his eyes, looking right past them, would focus on another part of the room. He seemed one moment to be watching the television in his room, but the next, merely drawn to its light. Tucker was there, but he was gone.

———————

AMONG THE MANY visitors was Stan Travis, a doctor and family friend, and his wife, Louise. They could sympathize with the Mahoneys because their son had been through something similar. He had suffered brain damage in a car accident. A week after Tucker's injury Louise asked Becky something she hadn't thought of before.

"Do you have a lawyer?"

"Why would we need a lawyer?"

"Believe me, you'll want a lawyer."

"Jay's medical will pay the hospital bills."

"Trust me," Louise said, "you'll want a lawyer."

Tucker eventually did begin showing improvement. Minor, nearly imperceptible improvement, but improvement. A few days after Becky's conversation with Louise, Tucker squeezed one of his doctor's hands. For the first time in days, Becky felt a joyful warmth. But the good news faded fast. "Within 10 minutes," she remembered later, "the social workers came down and said Tucker was going to go." If he was well enough to squeeze a hand, he was well enough to leave the hospital. The social workers departed to a nearby cubicle, a space no bigger than a closet—and without room for Becky—to discuss Tucker's transfer out of Abington to an institution that primarily offered "maintenance," rather than medical attention directed toward getting him better. Warehousing, not therapy. Becky did not want her son put into storage. She wanted him to stay in the hospital where he would receive more intensive care. Alarmed and feeling helpless, she pulled out a phone number Louise had given her and punched it into her cell phone.

CHAPTER 8

PHANTOM PAIN

"HE HAD A LOSS OF SKIN . . . and muscles and tendons and everything was shredded," said Shareif's doctor, John Gregg, an orthopedic surgeon at Children's Hospital of Philadelphia.

There was no chance of reattaching the foot. The small amount of flesh and snarled tendon that remained below his ankle was too damaged. What was left of Shareif's severed foot was imbedded with what doctors termed "debris," bits of shattered bone along with dirt and grime from the escalator. Gregg had the limb cleaned and realized that even some of what remained would have to be cut away. He inspected the parts that arrived on ice, the slice of the child's heel and the severed front part of the foot that held his toes. They were tiny toes. Gregg saw immediately that it was all unusable.

The only thing the doctors could do was to determine how much of the existing limb they could save—basically, at what point to end the amputation. "Injury patterns" extended to Shareif's ankle, but Gregg at first thought he might have a chance of saving the back half of the foot if there was enough muscle and viable skin. It was risky. For one thing, some of the skin had suffered shear injury, meaning that, though not ripped, it was damaged in a way that gave it a tendency to "bead up." Without enough healthy skin to cover the remaining part of the foot, the tissue and muscle beneath it would die, then rot. Such decay produced toxins that could lead to infections, even death. Also, the bone leading up to Shareif's ankle was fractured, as was the bone in his heel. Still, Gregg decided to give it a try. If he could save half the foot, it would be worth it. Working in his favor was Shareif's age. Younger patients tended to have better skin, better tissue, better blood supply. The metatarsal part of the foot, the front of the foot, was removed, the skin used as a drape over the back part of the foot and sutured into place.

Two days later, Gregg examined Shareif's foot. It didn't look good. There was more dead tissue, and some of the skin below his ankle appeared damaged. Gregg cut away more tissue and remained hopeful that enough healthy material remained to save Shareif's heel. Again he stretched skin over the boy's foot and sutured it closed. The procedure, with the heel remaining, was called a Bier's amputation. It offered benefits to a patient, including greater stability when compared to removing the entire foot. If it worked, Shareif would find walking easier and less uncomfortable.

Operation No. 3 came a few days after the second. It was Shareif's third surgery in six days. The foot had more dead skin, more dead tissue. The heel bone, Gregg decided, had to be removed. That would leave an inverted U-shape at the base of Shareif's leg, but now Gregg would have good, healthy tissue and skin to work with. The thick skin that had formed on the back of the heel was pulled underneath the ankle bone and sewn into place. The skin was thick enough to bear weight without tearing. The remaining bone also provided a broader surface at its base, an "end-bearing stump," which supported weight better than bone that came to a sharper point. Gregg was also able to leave the growth plate in the remaining part of the ankle so that portion of Shareif's leg would continue to grow some as he got older. Gregg knew that other parts of the leg also would show stunted growth, particularly the calf muscle, which works the foot. Because Shareif would no longer have a foot, the calf would atrophy and become much smaller than the same muscle on his left leg.

Another operation was performed to change the stitching and fit Shareif with an intermediate prosthetic device so he could begin placing weight back on his leg. In all, he underwent four operations in eight days.

All of this exacted a terrific toll on Shareif, who was a bit on the skinny side and stood just 3-foot-8. The physical pain alone that he endured was more than most people, even grownups, could have tolerated. Pain-killing drugs dripped constantly into his thin arm from an intravenous tube. Still, at all hours Shareif would shriek in pain, sudden yelps emanating from his hospital room in the middle of the night.

What made Shareif's pain worse to watch, even for some of the hardened hospital staff, was that he didn't understand it. He didn't know yet that his foot was gone. No one had told him. The doctors and nurses felt it was Deneen's job, and she hadn't had the heart. Shareif couldn't see that his foot had been amputated because the heavy bandages formed a large bulb at the base of his leg, resembling a foot. He couldn't feel that it was missing because he still had pain there, what the doctors called "phantom pain," a common occurrence among amputees. Severed nerve endings leading to a removed limb registered pain as if the limb were still attached.

A note from a social worker written two days after the accident and placed in Shareif's medical file read: "Spoke with mother about the importance of being honest with Shareif. Offered social work assistance to tell him of the loss of his foot. Mother said she is not yet ready to tell him."

Deneen finally summoned the courage she needed. She walked into Shareif's room at Children's Hospital. He looked so small lying in that huge hospital bed in his blue pajamas, surrounded by white bedsheets and propped up by a mountain range of white pillows. Shareif had a teddy bear next to his left leg, the brown and white one he liked so much. At the end of his right leg was the large, bulbous bandaging. In black magic marker it bore the words "Big June & Valley Gang." Big June was a boyfriend of Deneen's at the time. When Shareif saw her walk in, his big brown eyes looked up at her. He smiled, a small smile.

"How you feelin', son?"

"My foot hurts."

"I know, Shareif."

"It hurts. Momma, my foot really, really hurts."

"Honey, the foot isn't there," she said, sitting down by the side of his bed. "It was hurt too bad in the accident."

"What do you mean?"

"Listen to me, Shareif. Your foot, it's gone. The doctors had to do what they call an amputation. They had to amputate your foot."

"No, it hurts. I can feel it . . . ."

"Shareif, your foot is gone."

"But it hurts! I can feel my foot!"

"Your mind just thinks it hurts. The doctors, they say that will pass. The doctors say the pain will go away. But your foot is gone."

"When will the pain go away?" Shareif asked, his mouth down-turned, the way it always seemed these days.

"Soon, I hope. Soon."

For days after that, Shareif kept asking the doctors and the nurses for something else.

"I want my foot back."

He thought the doctors could simply fix the problem—that they could get his foot and put it back on. Doctors were like gods. They wore ties and white coats and spoke softly but with an authority even young Shareif could sense. If he had "lost" his foot—that was the way the nurses put it—couldn't one of these doctors just put it back on?

When he was told that was impossible, Shareif had a new de-mand: "I want a new foot. Can't I get a new foot?" He was told that after he went home for a while, he could come back to the hospital and he would get a prosthesis. A fake foot, a plastic foot, one that would enable him to walk again. But Shareif wanted a real foot! "Don't worry," the doctors told him, "You'll get used to your pros-thesis. It won't be as good as before, but you'll get used to it."

Shareif was released from Children's Hospital on December 5. After eight days, his doctors felt his pain could be controlled with pills. Shareif was moved back to the small apartment in North Philadelphia with his mother, now out of work and back on welfare, as his main care provider. A visiting nurse stopped by from time to time. Deneen had sent her three older children to stay with her mother, who lived in another part of the city.

Deneen was to take her son twice a week to Children's Seashore House, a wing of Children's Hospital that specialized in treating injured and handicapped kids. The place tried to be cheery, with colorfully tiled floors and bright paintings by patients adorning the hallways. One floor had a mosaic floor showing objects from the sea—a yellow and blue fish, a blue and green beach ball, an orange sailboat. Seashore House, as the name implied, had once been on the sea, in Atlantic City, where its founder, Dr. Louis Holt, believed that the salty ocean breezes had a therapeutic benefit. Children in the late 1800s would sit in rocking chairs on the large, white painted porch and breathe in gulps of fresh air.

Later bought by Children's Hospital, Seashore House was now a six-floor building in the part of Philadelphia known as University City and adjacent to the Hospital of the University of Pennsylvania. Much of the therapy was conducted in a large room with stationary bicycles, rubber mats, and a long moving walkway with handrails. Children, some as old as 18, strained to do leglifts or took slow, pained steps while holding the handrails, their legs often supported by metal and plastic braces. This was where Shareif would learn to use his prosthesis. He would need to continue to get training throughout his childhood. Because he was still growing, Shareif would need to get a new prosthesis every year, sometimes twice a year, until he was an adult. The first device he was fitted with was hard and extended up over his shin almost to his knee. It was dark brown, a clumsy attempt at matching his skin color.

Shareif now had an awkward gait, and always would. He found it hard to walk up the stairs to the family's apartment. He found it difficult to put on his own prosthesis and impossible to take it off.

Deneen did both for him. She also had to bathe him, since Shareif was unable to climb in and out of the bathtub, and putting on his clothes, especially his pants and underpants, took Shareif great time and effort. He'd get frustrated. His brother, Shaheed, would get dressed in a few minutes. For Shareif, it was a daily struggle, so much so that Deneen usually just did it for him. When Deneen's mother and sister visited, she would ask them to help Shareif, but they found it hard to even look at the fleshy stub that existed where a foot once had been. The bottom of the stump was white and callused. Deneen would catch them flinching at the sight. She just hoped Shareif didn't see the looks on their faces.

Shareif, the doctors said, would never be able to run well. Though he could bend his knee, he would always be somewhat stiff-legged. He faced the persistent risk of skin breakdown—he'd already had infections in several spots—and the forming of bone spurs, which could necessitate more operations in the future. The years ahead would be marked with discomfort and pain.

Yet the surgery had been considered a success. Shareif had good feeling in the stump. The skin at its base, though sometimes damp or dry and cracked, had healed thick and strong.

It was not the same for Shareif's psyche. Not long after getting him home, Deneen noticed him behaving oddly. Quite suddenly, he would start banging his head against a wall or a piece of furniture. It could happen anytime or anywhere. He also would hit his prosthesis, either with his hand or another object, hit it as if he was mad at it. He had trouble eating and sleeping. Nightmares would awaken him in the middle of the night. His moods swung from anxiety to depression. Other times he would become frustrated and angry. His behavior was often disruptive.

While other kids went to prekindergarten, Shareif was picked up each weekday morning by a paratransit van that dropped him off at the Children's Crisis Treatment Center. He was entered into the center's Intensive Trauma Assistance Program, where he was diagnosed as suffering emotional trauma. Even at the center the head banging continued whenever Shareif started to feel frustrated or, to use the clinicians' word, "thwarted." While other kids in regular preschool programs played with clay and cars and crayons, the children at the CCTC took turns role playing, acting out incidents that had caused traumatic injuries. One day a little girl might act out a scene in which a fire surged through her apartment building. Or a little boy would tell about how his parents got shot when a thief broke into their house. Shareif, noted one report from the center, had "play scenarios [that] were permeated by themes of people losing their feet and sustaining physical injury." Some days were better than others. Sometimes a child, often Shareif, would throw a tantrum, and the counselors would go along with it, letting the child release pent-up energy and expend his frustrations. At other calmer times the kids would take a walk or play in the yard. They often drew with pencils or crayons to express their feelings, though Shareif preferred to play alone, isolating himself from the others.

A psychiatric exam conducted at the center in June 1997, seven months after the accident, found Shareif to be "tense, hyperalert and often appearing sad." One doctor noted: "He fidgeted a great deal when required to sit and tore holes in his stocking, poking at his prosthesis.... He also preferred to play with other office equipment such as the computer where he again impulsively hit the keys repeatedly, not seeming to stop and plan. It should be noted that he had a great deal of difficulty even tracing over the letters of his name."

Shareif was diagnosed as having prolonged post–traumatic stress disorder, an ailment not different from that suffered by combat soldiers returning home "shell shocked" from a war. It was an ailment still afflicting veterans from the Vietnam War.

PTSD had only recently, around the last decade or so, been diagnosed among children. Shareif obviously suffered from what was known as Type 1, the result of a single traumatic event. Experts noted that this resulted in feelings of intense fear, helplessness, even horror. Agitated behavior was common. Child and adolescent sufferers were alternately aggressive, then socially withdrawn. Sometimes they had awful dreams about their traumatic experiences;

sometimes they acted them out. One doctor who examined Shareif saw this exhibited when Shareif was given toy figures. He tore their legs off.

Visiting the center daily was draining for Shareif. When Deneen met his van outside their rowhouse at 4 p.m. each day, she usually found him curled up on one of the bench seats, fast asleep. She would pick him up and carry him up the stairs to their apartment. Although he didn't get actual homework, Deneen would make something up and have Shareif work at the kitchen table while she made dinner. Some days she wanted to take him to the playground on the next block, but he looked too tired. Besides, his inability to climb on the jungle gym or push off on the seesaw would just frustrate Shareif. And Deneen constantly worried that he would get hurt.

In the meantime, Deneen was suffering along with her son. Post–traumatic stress disorder, according to the experts, affects not only the victims of a horrible event but also those who witness the trauma. Deneen had been reliving it every day since November 27, 1996, the day before Thanksgiving. The center counseled her as well in sessions with Shareif.

When autumn came, Deneen, whose monthly welfare check barely covered her $427 rent, could not afford private school for Shareif. Her boyfriend moved in with her and the two younger boys, but, even so, money was still scarce. She sent Shareif to public school. He was five years old now, and it was time for kindergarten. Shareif was excited about going to school. He wanted to go. For the first time in ages, Deneen sensed a thin ray of hope. For the first time in a long time, Shareif was happy about something.

She had concerns, though. His behavior was unpredictable, often unruly, even with the doctors who observed him. The doctors had also found that Shareif, whether because of the escalator accident or not, had learning difficulties. He was hyperactive and had an attention deficit. His verbal IQ tested in the low-average range. His learning skills were already far behind those of Shaheed, who was in first grade and beginning to read. Shareif would hold a book and mimic his older brother, but he was only pretending to read. Up to this point, approaching his sixth birthday, Shareif had trouble reciting the ABCs.

Deneen's concerns, it turned out, were well founded. Shareif's glee at being able to attend George Meade public school only two blocks from his home, close enough for his mother to walk him there, soon turned into agony. It wasn't the light assignments that bothered him, or the teacher's discipline. It was the other children. Kids can be cruel, goes the saying. It was especially true in the case of a boy with a plastic foot and wounded self-esteem.

The other kids noticed right away, from the first moment Shareif ran in the schoolyard to chase a ball. He was able to run, but it was clumsy, "stupefied," as his mother described it. Shareif wore a sneaker over his prosthesis, but the other kids noticed his peculiar gait and the way his pants fit so tightly over his plastic shin. They wanted to see his fake foot, wanted to touch it. Within days, Shareif had a nickname: "Hard Leg." And the teasing became relentless. One girl in particular took delight in ridiculing Shareif. Deneen complained to the school administration and was promised that the girl would be kept away from Shareif. Yet two days later she was seated directly beside him in class, and the taunting continued: "Hard Leg! Hard Leg!" When Shareif told his teacher, she dismissed his complaint. "Oh, Shareif," she said, "someone's always messing with you."

The embarrassment and anger would well up in Shareif until he finally exploded. Once he picked up a yardstick and began swinging it wildly at his classmates and his teacher, who had scolded him for not paying attention. He swung that stick and kicked his legs and balled up one little hand into a fist and swung as hard as he could. Security had to be called to the classroom. When one of the guards tried to grab Shareif, he bit the guard. Only when Deneen arrived—she'd been phoned by the school and ran all the way there—did Shareif calm down. When she got him home, she saw that he had scratches on his arms and chest and neck, wounds apparently suffered during the classroom scuffle.

Other times Shareif would be brought to the principal's office and told to call his mother to come and get him. He would become hysterical at first, crying so hard he could barely catch his breath, the words stumbling out in a torrent. Deneen would calm him, her own eyes welling up on the other side of the telephone line. Then she would run to the school.

At home she would try to talk to him about what was bothering him. She had to coax out the words.

"Shareif," she would say gently, "what's going on at school?"

"Hmmm," he would say, not answering.

"Huh, Shareif? What's the matter?"

"I don't know," he would say. Sometimes he just shrugged.

"You have to tell me. What's wrong?"

"Don't nobody like me."

"Now, Shareif, that's not so . . . ."

"I don't have any friends at school."

"That's not so . . . ."

"Uh-hum."

"You don't know every kid. I'm sure there's some you could make friends with."

"Don't nobody like me."

"Now why do you say that?"

"Because that girl, she says stuff about my foot. And this boy, he says it too."

"What do they say?"

"Hard Leg! They say that I got a hard leg."

Deneen knew her son would not last much longer at George Meade Elementary. But she lacked the money to send him to another school. Medical assistance paid his doctors, the psychiatrist at the center, the orthopedist who fitted his prostheses. But there was no money for private school, no money to free Shareif from his tormentors. Money couldn't solve all of Shareif's problems, but it would make things easier.

There was one way to get it. Sue. But Deneen was not from a world in which people had lawyers. She didn't know any lawyers.

She opened the *Yellow Pages* and dialed the number in one of the small ads. She told the lawyer what had happened to her son, related the details, still painful to her after some time. The lawyer said he would look into it. Deneen waited.

And waited.

Nothing.

A few weeks went by and still nothing. Deneen wasn't aware of how busy lawyers were. And she didn't care. She only knew her son had been hurt, that he was still in pain, that he—and she—needed help.

CHAPTER 9

SPECTER AND KLINE

SHANIN SPECTER LIKED ORDER. He liked being in charge. And generally he was. Generally.

"Not Daddy's stinky cheese! I don't want stinky cheese," protested Lilli Shanin Specter. She was a precocious four year old, named for her great-grandmother (whose maiden name was Lillian Shanin). Dressed in a red plaid dress with a white collar and ready for preschool, Lilli had already turned down sliced strawberries for breakfast and was fretful that her father would next give her Camembert or Liederkranz or one of those other smelly cheeses that he liked. And that she hated.

"No stinky cheese!"

"Careful, you'll spill it," Specter said, turning toward Silvi, at eight the oldest of his four daughters, as she slid a bowl of cereal along a granite countertop. She was seated on a stool between Perri, 6, and Lilli. Specter warmed a bottle for Hatti, his youngest. In the background, TV's *Earthwatch* delivered the day's weather forecast: unseasonably warm. Soon, the two oldest children, still in the kitchen, had electric toothbrushes buzzing in their mouths while Specter's wife, Tracey, loaded sandwiches and juice packs into purple and pink Power Puff lunch boxes lined up in order of age on the counter, a modicum of organization amidst the morning bedlam.

Specter finally delivered a waffle to Lilli, and she pronounced the waffle acceptable. "Daddy's a little angel," she said in sing-song fashion, poking fun at her father. And the three other lasses all cracked up. A four year old had just manipulated one of Philadelphia's top trial lawyers.

"We have to leave. C'mon. I'm getting in the car," said Specter, trying to regain the upper hand. He drove the children to school on non-trial days. He started walking briskly toward the front door. "C'mon, I'm going now." The lasses giggled as they trotted behind him.

This was as hectic as life got for Specter. At work he was steady and controlled, rarely allowing sentiment to leak onto his face, staying away from the edges of emotion, good or bad. Admittedly, he could be brusque, a trait he inherited from his father, the veteran Senator Arlen Specter, along with his intellect. That was not to say that Shanin Specter had no funny bone or that he felt no passion or emotion. He felt strongly about things. Just didn't show it.

Tall and thin, almost skinny, Specter glided into a room, walking lithely, without effort or sound, almost ghostlike, an effect exaggerated on rainy days when he donned a sleek black raincoat that draped to his calves. Specter was an avid and aggressive squash player, arranging for games and opponents even when he was on trial overnight out of town, sometimes penciling in a local club pro. (In a future year he would compete in the Maccabi Games, the Olympic–style event held every four years in Israel, and win a gold medal as part of a team of 45-and-over players.) It was on the courts at the University of Pennsylvania that Specter met his wife, a varsity player there. Asked if he beat his wife at squash, he replied in typical to-the-point fashion. "Yes." At 44, Specter had hazel eyes and a boyish face that resembled his mother, Joan Specter, the long-time Philadelphia councilwoman, more than his famous, jowly father. He presented a calm, soothing exterior. Pleasant, as if to say, "I'm a pushover."

Nothing was further from the truth.

Once, in a relatively minor medical malpractice case, a defense attorney offered $500,000 as a settlement but let it be known that his client was willing to offer $1 million.

"Providing you'll take it. You will take $1 million, won't you?" he asked.

"In fact, I won't," Specter replied, noting the client's insurance covered him for twice that amount.

"Oh, you'll take $1 million."

"I certainly will not. I'll get $2 million."

"You'll never see $2 million."

Hearing that, Specter withdrew a pen from his shirt pocket, took hold of the other lawyer's tie and wrote his initials—S.S.— on the back.

"When I get the $2 million, I'll take that tie, too," Specter said with a smile. "Remember my initials."

"You won't get $2 million," responded the other lawyer, also smiling but not so confident now.

Specter, telling the story later, said that he hadn't been sure he would get $2 million, though he thought he might. But that wasn't important. What was important was to put his opponent in a "subservient position," and he did that with one simple action—writing his initials, in indelible ink, on the other man's necktie.

(Later, after he settled the case, Specter took the tie that he himself had worn during that conversation, one of his favorites in shades of blue and green, and mailed it to his adversary.)

Specter was in many ways the polar opposite of his partner, Tom Kline. The two left a well-established firm together in 1995 and started their own practice. James E. Beasley Sr., the legendary plaintiffs attorney who had been their boss and colleague, did not want either of the younger lawyers to leave. Beasley had been a litigator in Philadelphia for more than 40 years and had won many multi-million-dollar verdicts. He warned Kline and Specter that they would never make the money they had made at his well-established firm.

After they had given notice, Beasley called Kline, who was older than Specter by 10 years, to his office for a private chat. Beasley had been Kline's mentor since the first day he had arrived at the prestigious firm. Over 16 years, Beasley and Kline had handled major cases together, shared many long laughs and late dinners. Kline had sat beside Beasley in many of his seven airplanes as the older lawyer wildly—at least in the estimation of Kline—soared and swooped over the Pennsylvania countryside, sometimes to take photos as evidence for cases, sometimes just for kicks. When Kline decided to go out on his own, Beasley was more than disappointed. He was hurt. Now, as Kline walked the long walk through Beasley's ornate office to a chair in front of his boss's antique mahogany desk, he did so with fragile emotions. Beasley did not make this last meeting easy. "He tried to make me feel bad," Kline recalled, "and he succeeded." Afterward, Kline walked back to his office, sat at his desk, and wept, feeling that he had let down his boss and his old friend. Beasley had reminded him, "Tom, you've been like a son to me." But Kline did not change his mind. With slight trepidation, Kline and his new partner left The Beasley Firm to form Kline & Specter, P.C.

Few people might have anticipated this partnership. Kline and Specter were, particularly in demeanor, a strange pairing. Specter was more formal, a fellow who got to the point right away, who could be pleasant enough when he wanted to—he just didn't always want to. He had little time or enthusiasm for small talk. His phone conversations occasionally ended not with a good-bye but with a click, and sometimes before the caller was aware the conversation was over. Kline dawdled in conversation, floated around in it like a warm pool. He would ask where you lived, what your wife's name was, how old your kids were. And he was interested in the answers. He kibitzed with assistants, secretaries, the receptionist. He seemed more interested at times in how many points the 76ers had scored the night before than the case a young attorney was bringing to his attention, or trying to. Kline would work the phone, while one or two or three associates vied for his time and attention. Specter was tidy and focused on one piece of business at a time; Kline delighted in always having three balls in the air at once.

Kline, with grown–up children (Hilary, a teacher, and Zac, a high school student), was a child of the 1960s, his dark hair flecked with gray, worn long, brushed back and a bit over his collar. Kline was a confirmed "Bobcat," meaning a devout follower of Bob Dylan. When Dylan was in town or even in concert farther off—Atlantic City, New York, Poughkeepsie, Boston, Reno, even in Dublin, Ireland—Kline would be in the audience, as close to the stage as he could get. Whereas Specter quoted Churchill, Kline borrowed lines from Dylan for his courtroom speeches.

Specter grew up in big and bustling Philadelphia, where his father was a lawyer, district attorney, candidate for mayor, and, finally, U.S. senator. Kline was raised in a three-story, asbestos-shingled "double" on busy West Diamond Avenue in Hazleton, an old, stoop-shouldered Pennsylvania city in the heart of the anthracite coal region. His father, Isadore, managed one of the many small dress factories that replaced coal upon its abdication as the region's leading industry.

Specter attended the William Penn Charter School, an exclusive private school in Philadelphia. He went to Haverford College, then attended law school at the Ivy League's University of Pennsylvania and at Cambridge University in England. Kline was a product of Hazleton's public school system and attended Albright College in Reading, Pennsylvania. Kline didn't go straight to law school after college but went back to public elementary school, where he taught sixth grade. After six years he enrolled at Duquesne University School of Law in western Pennsylvania. In his first year, he worked diligently and got good grades, though just missing Law Review. But when Kline graduated, he did so with Duquesne Law's Distinguished Student Award in hand.

Kline might have spent his life and career in law back in rural Northeast Pennsylvania if not for his wife, Paula, who still worked as a teacher at the same elementary school Kline left to attend law school. After graduating, he obtained a clerkship with a Pennsylvania Supreme Court justice, and then took a job with a small, local law firm in Pottsville. Kline was there just nine months, but Paula wanted to move on to a better life.

"Why aren't you trying to get another job?" she asked her husband one Saturday morning. "What are we still doing here in Pottsville?"

Kline could see the frustration in her face. He knew he could do better. Sincerely he asked, "What do you want me to do?"

Paula had a ready answer. "How about that great lawyer in Philadelphia who appeared before the Supreme Court when you were a law clerk?"

There had been more than a few newspaper accounts in recent years about James Beasley. The lawyer had won the first million-dollar verdict in Philadelphia, and then several more after that. Beasley had compiled an impressive list of highly publicized courtroom victories. He had become the city's top trial lawyer.

"Why don't you send him a resume?"

"I'll tell you what," Kline said. "I'll sit down and write him a letter."

"Today?"

"I'll do it right now," Kline said to pacify his uncharacteristically assertive spouse.

Kline rose from the breakfast table, walked to a closet, and reached for the case that contained his old reliable Ultronic, an electric typewriter he'd bought "reconditioned" at the nearby Balas Tire Supply and Gas Station. He kept the letter short and to the point.

> Dear Mr. Beasley:
>
> I am a former law clerk to Pennsylvania Supreme Court Justice Thomas A. Pomeroy, and am currently practicing law in Pottsville. I am interested in practicing in a large city and in a plaintiffs' personal injury practice and especially with you. Please contact me if you have an interest. My resume is attached.
>
> Sincerely,
> *Thomas R. Kline*

The letter would alter Kline's career and his life.

Beasley's firm was where Kline and Specter would meet and become close. With adjoining offices, they often sought each other out for advice. One was often impressed by the other's take on a case.

Although Kline and Specter consulted almost daily, the first time Beasley formally assigned them to a case together it happened that they served as his personal attorneys. The suit involved a three-foot penis. The giant plastic phallus, which lit up and shot confetti into the air, stood near the entrance of The Catacombs, a nightclub (and reputed S & M parlor) that resided in the basement of the building at 1125 Walnut Street in Philadelphia. Beasley had purchased the building for his new offices. The operator of The Catacombs and the discotheque above it, appropriately dubbed The Second Story, was a tenant Beasley had inherited with the purchase. Frequently cited and padlocked by city inspectors for various violations, the tenant had simply broken the sheriff's department locks and continued operating, serving drinks and playing loud music. Beasley wanted the tenant out, but the tenant had a lease and didn't want to leave. So Beasley gave Kline and Specter the job. Since they didn't have much of a case on zoning or ordinance grounds, they employed an old, seldom-used Pennsylvania statute against the tenant. The theory was that since the tenant was not putting the property to a beneficial use, it was being laid to waste, thus devaluating the property, much the way a tenant farmer would harm a parcel of land if he chose not to seed and farm it. The approach was novel—and in vain. Kline and Specter lost the case. They appealed to Superior Court, the second highest court in Pennsylvania. They lost again. The tenant, and the nightclubs, remained until the lease ran out.

Of course, the two attorneys collaborated on their "real" cases, those involving medical malpractice and product liability, bodily injury and death. A mutual respect grew between them, and they became fast friends.

When they decided to start their own practice, Tom Kline and Shanin Specter began by designing office space with an interior adjoining door, one important thing they hadn't had at their old firm. They moved easily from office to office, discussing their cases. Specter, crisp-looking even at day's end, tie still tight to his throat, suit jacket on, shoes shined, would stand erect in the middle of the room. Kline, always well dressed in black—black suit, black shoes, black tie with maybe a small white or silver dot or stripe—would plop, almost collapse, on Specter's leather couch and do a slow downward slide until he settled in, his back almost down to the seat, his head cradled near the armrest, his long legs akimbo. He'd let escape a few drawn-out, delectable yawns. Specter never yawned in public.

They had plenty to discuss. Within a short time they attracted plenty of good cases, which necessitated not only hiring additional lawyers—they had begun with just one associate in 1995—but also making decisions on which cases to take and which to reject. Both had a penchant for taking cases that seemed to have little chance of victory and, even if they could be won, less opportunity for a large award. They both enjoyed challenges, lived for them. Once they had turned the tide in a tough case, with a defendant looking for an escape, they hated accepting a settlement, unless it was too good to refuse or the client insisted.

After several years and many victories, their firm had grown to more than a dozen attorneys. (In a few more years, it would expand to more than 30.) They were in a position now where top cases, the good cases, came to them. They didn't, in the popular negative put-down of the day, "chase ambulances." They rejected most—98 percent—of the cases that came through the door. But both still took cases that many, perhaps most, other lawyers would have rejected out of hand.

Even in its early years, the two won cases with huge damage awards—a $24.25 million award for a three-year-old Philadelphia girl severely brain damaged in a swimming pool accident while a lifeguard was sleeping; a $19.9 million federal jury verdict against a hospital for not preventing a fifteen-year-old patient from being assaulted while at the hospital, an incident that resulted in catastrophic nerve damage; $49.6 million awarded to a young man who died after a tube was mispositioned in his throat, leaving him in a near-vegetative state; $33.1 million against doctors who failed to detect cancer in a middle-aged woman, until it was too late. In none of those cases did they collect the entire verdict, but big verdicts made for big post-trial settlements.

Kline and Specter took on cases in which people suffered unspeakable injuries due to negligence: a patient who had the wrong leg operated on by a doctor who had committed his third "wrong-site" surgery; patients hurt and killed by inattentive nurses and doctors; employees injured at hazardous worksites, including one who was killed when working near a leaking fuel tank that exploded; a young wrestler who died during a nose job procedure; people who suffered heart attacks from taking prescription drugs later recalled because of dangerous side effects; a young boy killed by a truck with defective brakes; patients injured or killed when they were given the wrong drugs. So many cases, so many horrific injuries. And for all these plaintiffs the attorneys were powerless to repair an injury or restore a life. They could only get monetary compensation for the victims and their families. They could make the culprits pay.

In taking cases, Specter and Kline sought more than money. At a time when lawyers were held in such low esteem, they believed in what Specter's father termed the "social utility of what a lawyer does." The elder Specter, once addressing a trial lawyers' dinner held in his honor, spoke of the days when there were far fewer lawyers. They were not good days for regular folks. He told of how his own father, Harry, who owned a junkyard in Russell, Kansas, was injured in the 1930s after a defective wheel sprocket in his Chevy pickup gave way and caused the truck to flip over. Harry lost partial use of one arm for the remainder of his days. "For this," Specter recalled, "my father received the princely sum of $500."

Tom Kline's father got nothing, never even knowing he was likely a victim. He suffered from a rare bone marrow cancer, an illness his son always suspected had been environmental and possibly related to the older Kline's job as manager of a dress factory in McAdoo,

Pennsylvania, which he held from the time he returned from World War II until the late 1960s. Isadore Kline succumbed to cancer in 1981. Only decades later did Tom Kline learn from a newspaper article that toxic waste had been dumped into a stream that ran beneath the Rival Dress Company factory.

CHAPTER 10

"LOOK AT THE GUN"

Shanin Specter believed in order, precision, and cold, hard facts. That was what won cases. Yet he did something at the start of every case that was somewhat unusual for many lawyers, especially for partners in larger plaintiffs' law firms. Specter visited with every client, spending some time with them and their families. He knew that Tucker Mahoney couldn't talk. He knew the teenager might not hear him or see him, probably wouldn't understand what he had to say. Specter had represented many clients like Tucker, alive, but only in the sense that they were breathing and their hearts were pumping. They were "there," nothing more.

Specter and Andy Youman, a young yet experienced lawyer who had left another top Philadelphia firm to join Kline & Specter only a few days earlier, met Jay and Becky Mahoney in the waiting room of Abington Memorial Hospital. "I'm so sorry," Specter said as he grasped Jay's hand. And he was. Becky's pretty, tear-stained face showed pain and worry. Still, she forced a smile. Neither Specter nor the Mahoneys had any clue as to the unusual journey on which they were about to embark together. The Mahoneys had no idea if they even had a legal case, never mind how protracted and combative it would become. In truth, neither did Specter.

He was immediately struck by two things. First, the Mahoney family was educated and well spoken. That would be helpful to a legal case.

Second, there was Tucker himself. Specter found the teenager's injury "unspeakable." To see this handsome, athletic-looking young man lying there, immobile, his face contorted slightly, was upsetting. Specter thought of his own children, his four little girls, and he felt a peculiar, almost metaphysical pain deep inside. He decided on the spot to take the case, even though he didn't think he could get the Mahoneys much more than $1 million, which, he guessed correctly, would be the limit of the homeowner's policy held by Ty Weatherby's parents. Specter assumed that Ty Weatherby would be liable since it was Ty who had pulled the trigger. Ty would be insured under his parents' insurance policy. The Weatherbys' insurance company might give him a fight, but probably not much of one. Specter knew that $1 million wasn't much, not for someone who might need specialized care for the rest of his life, not for someone who would have pain for the rest of his life, whatever kind of life that would be. But it would be a help.

Youman, though, had an additional thought. "We ought to look at the gun," he said, suggesting that perhaps its manufacturer might shoulder some of the blame for the tragedy. Youman was just 31, full of youthful energy and exuberance. Privately, Specter didn't agree with the notion of pursuing the Daisy Manufacturing Company as a possible defendant. People too often insisted there was something wrong with a product when they had actually just misused it. But he was wary of discouraging a new associate from pursuing his own legal angle, even if it was a long shot. Specter was smart enough to know that he didn't have a monopoly on smarts or ideas.

When Youman started examining the records, he found other lawsuits against Daisy in the past. There had also been complaints to government agencies about its products, particularly about the new line of powerful air rifles like the one owned by Tucker Mahoney. Youman discovered that the U.S. Consumer Protection Safety Commission had fielded some of the complaints and conducted a two-year investigation of Daisy products. The CPSC, though, did not find a serious flaw in the BB gun—partly because it did not know what to look for at the time. It took no action against Daisy. It did, however, suggest that Daisy alter its warning label to read, "Warning: This gun can kill you." And it recommended that Daisy "change the design of the magazine so that it is possible to verify that no BBs remain in the gun."

Curious. Youman mulled it over, rolling that last phrase around in his head—"verify that no BBs remain in the gun."

Daisy did not make either of the changes.

Youman found another source of information, ABC TV. Its news show 20/20 in 1996 aired what Barbara Walters had termed "an investigation that may shake the foundations of a boyhood tradition." It was about three boys badly injured by high-powered Daisy BB guns.

"I thought he had just got hit with a BB and it bounced off," said Wayne Hill, grandfather of eight-year-old Tony Hill, who was left brain-damaged by a Daisy gun fired by his older brother. ". . . I told him, 'Quit crying, everything will be all right.'" But the BB fired from the powerful gun had torn through the boy's skin, through his skull, and penetrated his brain. *The same as with Tucker Mahoney,* thought Youman. ABC reported not only on the force of the rifle but also on an apparent defect that made the gun appear empty when it in fact was not. Again, the same as with Tucker and Ty. ABC had also gotten a gun expert to check a Daisy PowerLine air rifle. The expert found that a BB had lodged in the magazine, making a loaded gun appear empty. Nevertheless, Marvin Griffin, president of Daisy at the time and now the company's chairman, denied any problems to 20/20's Brian Ross.

> ROSS: *Is there a design flaw in the way these BBs are loaded?*
> GRIFFIN: *I do not think it is, not at all . . . . This expert has learned how to manipulate our gun. He and an attorney asked the Consumer Product Safety Commission to investigate our 880. They spent two years researching this and found the gun was not defective.*

ROSS: *Isn't it true that BBs can get stuck inside here in the nooks and crannies of this gun?*

GRIFFIN: *That's possible, but it doesn't happen often in our opinion or we would correct that.*

ROSS: *(later) How many times does that have to happen before you fix the gun?*

GRIFFIN: *The gun is fixed. The gun is not defective. We would not sell a gun that is defective.*

Lawsuits and complaints had been lodged against Daisy for injuries incurred after someone thought one of its rifles was unloaded. As far as anyone could tell, Daisy had paid out millions, but the most potentially damaging cases had been, as *20/20* put it, "quietly settled out of court" without Daisy having to publicly admit any fault or wrongdoing.

Youman logged onto the website of the Association of Trial Lawyers of America, a sort of clearing house of information for plaintiffs' attorneys. He hit pay dirt. He found one case, the Tony Washburn case from Michigan, in which an eight-year-old boy suffered a brain injury after an older child shot him with a Daisy PowerLine rifle. BBs had somehow lodged in the gun, with the shooter thinking it was unloaded when it wasn't. It was tailor-made for the Mahoney case. Though more precise details of the Washburn case were not spelled out, the outcome was—Daisy had paid $5 million to settle.

Youman knew he had the basis of a case, but from that point on things got tough. To his surprise, when he called the lawyer whose name was listed on the case, he got no cooperation at all. Nick Simkins, in Novi, Michigan, wasn't in a sharing mood. He would not disclose his file, which included depositions taken in the case and, presumably, the key—whether testimony or critical corporate documents—to why Daisy had decided to pay off. For the company to cough up $5 million, Simkins must have had something juicy. Simkins's unwillingness to share upset Youman, not simply because he wanted the information but because it ran counter to his own firm's policy. Kline & Specter had an "open file policy," meaning that anyone who asked to look at their files got to do so. They could even make photocopies.

Youman tried another source, Bob Cearley, a lawyer from Arkansas, Daisy's headquarters state, who had been brought in to work with Simkins (over him, really) in the Washburn case. Cearley had handled several cases against Daisy. When Youman got him on the phone, Cearley said that, yes, he would be happy to help and to send along relevant documents. Youman felt a sense of relief. There was just one hitch: Cearley, as Youman put it in a memo to Specter, was "interested in a fee–sharing arrangement on the case." Youman responded that his firm was quite competent to handle the case alone, but that he would still like to review Cearley's case documents. They never arrived. Another stone wall.

On August 26, 1999, two months after meeting the Mahoneys, Specter filed suit in federal court in Philadelphia against Daisy. "We knew that BBs got stuck in the guns. We knew it to be true, based on what people had told us; they just wouldn't give us the information," Youman recalled.

They knew; they just had to prove it. Youman kept digging, looking at other suits filed against Daisy. He found and spoke with Dave Townsend, the gun expert who had testified against Daisy in other cases and who had appeared on 20/20. Youman watched tapes of the show's 1996 episode about the dangers of high-powered Daisy guns.

One case stood out, the case of Justin Wild, a seven-year-old Tennessee boy shot in the neck. He had not been as severely injured as Tucker Mahoney, not nearly so, but the case had striking similarities to Tucker's. For one, Justin was shot by a friend about his age, who, according to one court document, believed "that the Daisy rifle was unloaded when in fact it was not.... Patrick Warden shot the Daisy air rifle several times. No BBs fired from the Daisy air rifle. Patrick Warden, thinking the Daisy air rifle was empty when it was not, then pointed the Daisy air rifle in the direction of Justin Wild and pulled the trigger."

Youman got the court docket and immediately flipped to the opening pages listing the names of the plaintiff's lawyers. He would call Justin Wild's lawyers in the hopes they would lend some information. When he saw the first attorney's name listed, his shoulders slumped. It was Bob Cearley from Arkansas. Bob Cearley from the Washburn case. Bob Cearley who didn't like to share.

Another dead end? Not yet. A lawyer named Bill Leader, hired as local counsel in Tennessee, had been brought in to serve as co-counsel to help Cearley. Maybe he would help. It was worth a phone call.

"So, Bill," Youman said after he had introduced himself, "Look, we have this situation with this boy who was horribly injured . . . ."

"Uh-huh."

"Our firm shares information with anybody who asks . . . ."

"Uh-huh."

"But Bob Cearley is refusing to share his documents with us . . . ."

"Uh-huh."

"I don't think that's right. I was hoping you'd lend us a hand."

Leader's response was direct and blunt and final.

"I'd be happy to share," he said.

More than happy, in fact. "This Daisy is a bad company, and they need to be taken down," Leader said, his drawl seeming to disappear as his anger rose. "I'll give you everything I can within the law to help you do that."

"What about Bob Cearley?"

"I don't work for Bob Cearley."

What Youman had no way of knowing, though, was that time was running out. At that very moment, Daisy was in the process of settling the Wild case, an agreement that would seal the case records, making them forever unavailable to future potential plaintiffs. The company knew that the Wild case was a blueprint for more lawsuits and was hustling to close it out and cover its tracks. The case did settle, with the Wild family accepting an offer and a judge ordering records in the case sealed—one day after Leader had sent them off to Kline & Specter. One day too late, for Daisy. Recalled Youman, "I was lucky I called the day I did, real lucky."

CHAPTER 11

OBSTACLES

I T WAS DECEMBER 18, TOM KLINE'S 51st birthday, when he drove down a residential street in North Philadelphia littered with food wrappers and beer cans. Kline noticed that some of the buildings had been abandoned, their windows covered with planks of wood, then painted with graffiti. But the red brick rowhouse that Kline parked in front of had a washed look, a look that said the people who lived there were trying. The inside had been recently renovated, with smooth white walls in the small foyer and hallway. Kline climbed the stairs to the apartment on the second floor and knocked on the door. He didn't know much about the family inside, only that a little boy had lost his foot. He hadn't decided yet whether he would take the case. Deneen Hall opened the door, a crack at first, then all the way.

"C'mon in," she said.

Kline sat on a couch in the small living room. Shareif was nearby, playing with his brother, Shaheed, who was running all around the tiny apartment. Shareif stayed mostly in one spot on the floor, concentrating on the plastic toys in front of him. He seemed, at least for a moment, to be able to ignore his injured leg, the end of which was covered with white bandages.

"How's he doing?" Kline asked.

54

Deneen twisted her face. Her look said, Not so good.

Though she hardly spoke, Kline understood her quite clearly. He could read the concern in her eyes, feel Shareif's pain through her expressions. She had quit her job and was now back on welfare, collecting $201.50 every two weeks from the government. She stayed with Shareif as much as possible, mostly in this small apartment, which, Kline noticed, was remarkably tidy for a home with small children.

"I worry about him," Deneen said.

"I understand," Kline said.

"I worry how's he going to fend for himself."

"I understand."

"I worry, I worry about a lot of stuff."

Deneen told Kline about Shareif, starting from the day he was born and ending with the horrid events of three weeks ago. For two hours, Kline listened, watching Shareif and Shaheed playing nearby as he did. He listened for about two hours, though making a decision didn't take him long at all. He would take the case despite uncertainties that still existed. For one thing, he knew SEPTA would have its side of the story—every defendant did—which he didn't know anything about yet. Initially, he also thought the financial benefit could be minimal. This case would hardly swell the coffers of Kline & Specter.

Suing SEPTA presented a problem. Pennsylvania law gave SEPTA, a public agency, sovereign immunity and limited its liability to just $250,000. Some lawyers liked this type of case, which was known in the trade as a "laydown"—a serious and lamentable injury that could force an agency to quickly hand over its maximum $250,000 limit (which included the attorneys' usual one-third fee)—but there was no guarantee of easy money. Time and expense were involved, and uncertainty. If the plaintiffs did not win, there would be no fee at all.

Also, if SEPTA fought the lawsuit, it had no limit on what it could spend on defending the case. It had about 40 in-house lawyers and the agency also regularly contracted out for hired guns, some of them from the city's best and biggest law firms. The cost would be passed along to commuters and taxpayers. In fact, SEPTA was accustomed to defending itself. With some 1.2 million daily passengers and 10,000 employees, SEPTA's lawyers and its 52-person claims department resolved about 2,000 complaint cases annually, many before they became lawsuits but plenty afterwards. The agency was used to people claiming injury, many of them falsely. (It was a standard joke that after a bus accident there might be 70 or 80 claims even though a bus seated only about 40 people.) Only a small minority of cases made it to trial, and an even smaller number ever saw a jury verdict, particularly one that SEPTA lost. Faced with all these obstacles, most plaintiffs' lawyers wouldn't have bothered with Shareif Hall's case.

But Tom Kline grabbed the case, not simply because he was both intrigued and outraged by what had happened to little Shareif, a sweet-faced youth with big, innocent eyes and an adorable smile, when he could muster one. Kline also concluded that the case had financial potential after all.

Kline had a strategy that he thought might result in a large jury verdict, or a sizeable settlement. He would examine the liability of not just SEPTA but also the escalator manufacturer. Kline had no proof, not yet, that there had been anything wrong with the escalator, but he knew that they weren't supposed to chop off little boys' feet. And if the manufacturer, which would turn out to be a major company called the Schindler Elevator Corporation, was at all responsible, Kline knew that the law would now work on his side. Whereas SEPTA was protected by Pennsylvania's sovereign immunity statutes, Schindler could be left highly exposed by another law known as Joint and Several Liability. The law stated that in cases in which more than one defendant was found negligible and liable, both or either—and either was the operative word—could be held responsible to pay damages. In other words, if a jury found two defendants liable and awarded damages of, say, $5 million, but one defendant had no money or no insurance coverage, the second defendant could be held responsible to pay the full award. In the case of Shareif Hall, if SEPTA's liability was limited to $250,000, Schindler by law would have to pay the rest of any damages awarded, even if it was found to be only partly responsible. It was one way to get the child enough money for what Kline knew would be a lifetime of large medical bills, anguish, and pain.

Still, suing Schindler (which years earlier had taken over the Westinghouse Elevator Company) was an iffy proposition. Making a case, a product liability case, against a manufacturer was always difficult. It was expensive, necessitating in-depth research and discovery, the hiring of investigators and experts, the conducting of tests and studies. Even if solid evidence could be found, big companies contested lawsuits aggressively—often with a litany of maneuvers and motions intended to derail or dismiss a case. Only after all this played out, maybe a jury—if such a case got to a jury—would find a product defective and a company negligent. Maybe.

In this case, proving such a case was doubly difficult because Schindler could claim, and most certainly would, that it was not responsible for an escalator it had sold more than a decade earlier to the city and the transit agency, the Southeastern Pennsylvania Transportation Authority, which was responsible for its maintenance and safety.

Kline tapped Rob Ross, a new associate in the firm, to help him with the case. Ross, an African American who stood a foot shorter than Kline, would assist in filing a lawsuit in Philadelphia Common Pleas court against Schindler and SEPTA.

Kline knew that Schindler was the largest supplier of escalators in the world (and the second-largest manufacturer of elevators) and boasted that its devices moved "more than 700 million people per day" globally. It had roughly 40,000 employees and operations in five continents. The company's operating profits had reached almost $179 million the previous year, enough to convince it to boost its dividend by 50 percent. Schindler, the archives showed, had lost some cases and settled others, although never for terribly large sums.

Kline figured he could get SEPTA's $250,000 limit, though he'd have to fight for it. Kline also planned to double that amount by suing on behalf of both Shareif and his mother, Deneen, who had experienced emotional pain and suffering. The Pennsylvania Supreme Court had cleared the way for such claims by a mother or another relative in a 1979 case titled *Sinn v. Burd*. In that case, a girl named Lisa Anne Sinn had been standing with her sister, Deborah, at the front of the family's home near their mailbox when a car came careening up the road and directly at them. Lisa Anne was struck, her body sent hurtling into the air, and she was killed. Deborah was not hurt, but the family sued on her behalf for psychological damages suffered from witnessing the accident. Though uninjured, Deborah, by law, had been in the same "zone of personal physical danger" as her sister. Their mother, JoAnne, who was further away and not endangered personally, also sued for emotional damages she suffered in witnessing her daughter struck and killed. In its landmark decision, the state Supreme Court ruled that she also could collect damages. Certainly, Deneen Hall's case was similar. The tragedy on the SEPTA escalator had unfolded before her eyes, while she was holding Shareif's hand. Seeing this happen to her son had traumatized her. How could SEPTA argue otherwise?

As for Schindler, discovery and legal preparation for that case would take time and cost money. It was not unusual for Kline & Specter's out-of-pocket costs to reach well into six figures to properly prepare a product liability case in which a large corporation was involved.

THE ESCALATOR WAS sold to SEPTA—technically, the City of Philadelphia bought the escalator and leased it to the transit agency—back in 1984 for $86,000. Over the years, Schindler had sold upgrades to make its escalators safer. SEPTA didn't purchase them.

Kline would later determine that two upgrades could have prevented Shareif's injury. One was a step-level device that automatically shut down an escalator when its steps were out of kilter, which happened if one or two of the rubber rollers upon which a step rested became chipped or flattened on one side. This would cause a step to "dip" down, creating a small space between it and the steel comb-plate when it reached the top of the escalator. The coincidence and timing had to be just right—or terribly wrong—for Shareif to have been on that very step resting on a broken roller and for the dip to have occurred at the precise moment the step reached the comb-plate. If that was what trapped Shareif's foot, a step-leveler would have prevented the accident.

Schindler also had what it called a comb-plate impact switch that automatically stopped an escalator when jamming occurred at an escalator's apex. Such a device, had it been installed in the escalator at Cecil B. Moore Station, also might have prevented Shareif's amputation. The same automatic shut-off was required under city codes on escalators in subway systems in New York and Washington, D.C. Not optional, required.

Kline took the view that if such upgrades could have prevented accidents, they should have been installed. And that it wasn't only SEPTA's responsibility. Schindler, he believed, shared in the responsibility to make its existing products safer, even if it no longer maintained them. The suit against Schindler claimed that the escalator was in a defective condition because it lacked adequate safety mechanisms. It cited Schindler with "failing to recall and/or retrofit the subject escalator with adequately designed safety devices after the defendants marketed the subject escalator."

Kline thought the escalator manufacturer was no different from another type of company that made a potentially dangerous product—automobiles. When improvements were made that rendered older models less safe—and thus relatively unsafe—car companies sent notices to dealers and owners. Sometimes cars were recalled to make changes or repairs. Why shouldn't escalator manufacturers do the same? Sure, Schindler had advertised its new safety devices, but as though they were glitzy extras, not as needed upgrades to ensure riders' safety. To Kline, these automatic escalator shut-off mechanisms were akin to auto seat belts, not sunroofs. Necessities, not niceties. He thought he could convince a jury to see it that way as well.

But first, Kline filed suit against SEPTA. He needed to know exactly what SEPTA had done wrong and, along the way, build a case for joining Schindler in the lawsuit. He needed to know what SEPTA knew and what it had done. Discovery would be conducted to get to the bottom of things. He would make SEPTA come clean. It would not be as easy as he thought.

CHAPTER 12

"A Boy Is a Boy"

Daisy Manufacturing didn't see its BB gun as a dangerous weapon nor itself as a malicious corporate entity. In fact, its success over the years was anchored largely in the public perception that it was the maker of harmless, child-friendly products. Daisy, though begun in the cowboy era of the late 1800s, was not a typical gun company; rather, it catered to kids. Boys, specifically.

Originally the Plymouth Iron Windmill Company incorporated in Michigan in 1882, it first made air rifles not for sale but as a promotional giveaway for the sons of men who purchased windmills. Clients loved the guns and their demand grew. Before long, people who had no intention of ever buying a windmill wanted an air rifle. And before long, the company's directors began changing their marketing emphasis from windmills to the increasingly popular guns. The transformation was largely completed by 1895, when Plymouth Iron Windmill changed its name to match a popular expression of the era meant to convey that something was excellent or superior: "It's a daisy!" (In later years the phrase morphed into "It's a doozy!")

By 1958, when Daisy moved its corporate headquarters to Rogers, Arkansas, it was a toy company well known nationally to generations of boys. When many of those boys grew up—drawing on their fond memories of shooting at tin cans and squirrels (the latter, usually futilely)—they bought guns like those they had owned for their sons. Daisy was the first manufacturer to advertise its product in comic books, and it also acquired the rights for comic strips published in newspapers in order to reach its customer base.

In "A Boy Is a Boy," an essay copyrighted by Daisy in 1966 (parts of which appeared in *Sports Illustrated*), the company traced the history of air guns back to Greece in 200 B.C. and then made this point: "There is a wide variety of air weapons being advertised and sold today...some are only powerful enough to kill small birds and rodents, but others pack as much wallop as many small caliber weapons which use conventional bullets. But a Daisy BB gun is not a weapon. It is a *toy*...."

Daisy took pride back then in having created the ideal plaything. It boasted: "...It does take a deal of ingenuity, know-how and experience to produce a toy that pleases a boy because it looks like a gun, feels like a gun, and, with rigidly proscribed limits, even performs like a gun, and still has an absolute maximum of safety." It went on to say, "One of the secrets of Daisy's success is that it has always carefully regulated its BB rifles to shoot at a speed of 280 to 340 feet per second. And there is no way for a Daisy to go haywire and suddenly start shooting with awesome velocity because it is mechanically impossible."

Daisy promotional materials featured photos and illustrations of children who looked no more than 10 or 12 years old, sometimes younger. Some years the package included literature produced by the National Rifle Association with illustrations of tots. Not only that, Daisy lectured mothers on the importance—the importance—of allowing their offspring to have a Daisy. In "A Boy Is a Boy"—which began with a five year old named Mike make-believe shooting at his father, grandfather, "and the plump little family dachshund named Strudel"—Daisy warned mothers against being overprotective and interfering with their sons' "normal development." Getting their sons a BB gun was showing respect for their "masculine drives," it said. What's more, "Learning to handle a gun is just as much a part of his American birthright as learning to fish, swim, ride a bike or bat a baseball."

"Oh, I had one when I was eight years old," says Darrin McGavin, the actor who plays the father in *A Christmas Story,* the 1983 movie classic that immortalized not only the Red Ryder but the notion that BB guns were harmless. The movie opens with nine-year-old Ralphie Parker, his round little face pressed against a toy store window, longing to own a Red Ryder. The idea that someone can get hurt by a BB gun is a joke strung throughout the movie as characters from Ralphie's mother to his teacher to Santa Claus himself deliver the gag line: "You'll shoot your eye out!" When Ralphie finally gets a Red Ryder on Christmas morning, his first shot ricochets off a tin target and hits him near his eye. But it does little harm, leaving a only small red mouse under his eye and not even breaking his eyeglasses. That happens when Ralphie steps on them.

Daisy literature reinforced the idea that BB guns were risk-free. With the proper handling, said Daisy, a BB gun was no more dangerous than anything else boys played with, even less so. Sure, said "A Boy Is a Boy," a BB striking someone at close range "can sting like blue blazes" and even do damage to vulnerable spots such as an eye.... "But there aren't many sharp or pointed objects that a growing child encounters that don't have the capability of inflicting more damage than a Daisy.... A thrown baseball is far more dangerous." And handled improperly, nearly anything can be a dangerous weapon. Heck, the literature noted, "Cain slew Abel with a rock."

Daisy BB guns, the company said, were especially safe because they were, after all, toys. Daisy, its essay noted, could easily make a more powerful gun—"It would be no trick at all"—but it simply didn't want to. Daisy cared about kids. "And, as most people know, the Daisy company itself is one of those rare firms which is not merely considered a business. Daisy long ago attained the status of an American institution, and if you don't know why, ask the man in the hardware or sporting goods store. Or, better yet, do as Daisy suggests: 'Ask Dad; he owned one.'"

However, near the beginning of the 1970s the company set out to manufacture a new line of guns, and these were no toys. While Daisy was not a publicly traded company and was thus able to guard its production and revenue figures as secrets, several intra-company memos from the early 1970s showed that the new guns were created to hike profits.

Sears, one of Daisy's biggest buyers, wanted an airgun with more firepower, along the lines of those made by Crosman, Daisy's chief competitor. Sears "stated they could sell 25,000 per year," said Hank Waring, Daisy's head of research and development, in an August 3, 1971, memo that followed his meeting with a Sears buyer.

Another memo several weeks later from William H. Cole, a Daisy executive involved with sales to Sears, was more explicit. It said that Sears wanted a powerful new gun "to replace the Crosman 760" and noted that a Sears buyer "accepted our proposal and we have a firm appointment with him on October 21 at 9 a.m. to submit our 'total package' in time for his line review for 1972 merchandise." That proposal review was set for only a month away.

The memo went on to set out a series of deadlines Daisy had to meet if it was to make the sale:

1. Oct. 21, 1971—Present Sears with a total "Power Pump" package including name, package, accessories and prototype gun.
2. April 1972—Present Sears with working models for lab tests.
3. June 1972—Begin production and initial shipments.
4. July 1972—Continue production and shipment approaching a capacity of 2,000 pieces per week minimum.

This didn't give Daisy a lot of time. But three days later another Daisy memo was sent from company executives to the research and development staff expressing the company's "complete commitment" to making the gun and telling them "our continued efforts will produce a Daisy product that will fulfill the commitment and bring in the dollars."

R & D had already been working on something more powerful than Daisy's current line of air guns. A memo dated the previous July said the new multistroke Daisy gun—officially Project Number 69-138—had a 15 percent greater velocity than the Crosman 760.

The prototype was made by the deadline Sears had given: October 21, 1971. The presentation went well, and, reported Cole, the Sears buyer was "very impressed." Cole noted that the process would continue and that "baring [sic] an 'act of God' we will assure him that we can and will meet his beginning delivery date of June." And so the company trusted by generations to make harmless toys for kids began the mass production of a BB gun that would fire with greater velocity than a .38-caliber revolver, the real gun used by most of the nation's police officers. Several countries, including Canada, Denmark, and Sweden, banned airguns that powerful.

Nearly two decades later, it took a herculean effort by Shanin Specter and Andy Youman simply to obtain documents about the PowerLine guns from Daisy. The process was like a dance, which grew familiar after time. Requests would be made of Daisy for information, and Daisy would ignore them, for months on end. Then a Motion to Compel would be submitted to the judge assigned to the federal case, U.S. District Judge J. Curtis Joyner. And the judge, almost perfunctorily, would grant the motions. The process became something of a full-time job for Youman.

He had started by serving Daisy with an initial discovery request containing 70 interrogatories for information. In its responses, Daisy said that some of the materials sought, such as certain research or studies, did not exist. Other answers noted: "To be supplied." Daisy's lawyers refused to provide answers to some of the requests, objecting that they were "overly broad" or "ambiguous" or contained "vague phraseology." Typical was Daisy's response to Interrogatory No. 48 seeking minutes from various corporate meetings at which there may have been discussion of BBs potentially jamming in guns. The company wrote back: "Objection, overly broad and not reasonably calculated to lead to the discovery of admissible evidence. Further, the interrogatory may seek attorney work product and attorney–client privileged communications." Daisy also refused to provide some answers, lest it expose trade secrets. After getting some but not all of the answers and documents he had sought, Youman filed a second motion, which brought a list of "first supplemental responses" from Daisy, but still not everything he wanted. A third motion brought "second supplemental responses." A fourth brought "third supplemental responses." It was a tug of war, but Youman finally got enough to proceed to trial.

ONE THING HE wanted was to take testimony from three Daisy employees, the president and now chairman Marvin Griffin, draftsman Theresa Wrazel, and Ronald Joyce, who had worked for Daisy nearly 40 years and was the project engineer who had designed the PowerLine guns. Joyce was retired when the Mahoneys' suit was filed, but he still helped out at the company in the defense of lawsuits. Daisy fought the depositions. The company came up with various excuses for why they should not or could not appear. Mr. Griffin "has no personal knowledge of facts relevant to the subject," Daisy argued in one motion. Another claimed that to depose Griffin would be "oppressive" or "harassing." Also, one of Griffin's Arkansas attorneys, involved only peripherally, was not available for various proposed deposition dates. Specter was on a fishing expedition, Daisy claimed. And so on.

"This is not a fishing expedition," Specter wrote in one reply to Daisy's legal maneuvers. "Marvin Griffin is a witness whom Daisy knows to possess devastating information going directly to the heart of the case. In a desperate attempt to keep plaintiffs from getting this information on the record, Daisy is asking this court to preclude plaintiffs from exercising their right to take his deposition." After all, Griffin was the guy who had volunteered to defend Daisy on national television and had admitted on 20/20 that BBs got stuck in the guns—just that it "doesn't happen often." The court agreed with

Specter and ordered that Daisy produce Griffin, Wrazel, and Joyce. The company filed a motion for the court to reconsider in Griffin's case, contending that "lower level" employees could provide the same information. But Specter wanted Griffin in the hot seat, and the court agreed he could be forced to testify in a deposition.

Specter was able, in part, to get the information he wanted because he knew what to ask for. From exhaustively studying information about the guns and material from previous cases against Daisy, he had a good idea of what existed in Daisy's own files. His firm had spent a great deal of time, nearly eight months, and money researching what was available. In one instance, he had found a university professor in Michigan who had sat on the American Society for Testing and Materials (ASTM International) Non-Powder Gun Projectiles and Propellants Group (which met ostensibly to set voluntary manufacturer standards); the professor had saved every document that had ever passed through the panel during his tenure. The cost to pay a Kinko's in Michigan to make photocopies and mail all the documents was $5,533.85.

Specter was fastidious in his casework. He prepared so completely that when trial dates finally arrived, he generally had nothing left to do. "I do almost no work outside of court during the trial of a case," he once said. At the end of trial days, rather than do further research into the wee hours like a college kid cramming for finals—which so many other lawyers, including his partner, Tom Kline, often did (and even enjoyed)—Specter would go home, have a Yuengling's Black and Tan, and spend time with his wife and children. The difference in how the two partners worked had become a recurring joke in the office, a difference once put on display during a firm Christmas Party in a PowerPoint that read: "Tom during trial: Necco Wafers, soft pretzels, Diet Coke, out of the office by midnight. Shanin during trial: Play squash, eat dinner, out of the office by 5 p.m."

Specter could relax when trials got underway because his material was so well catalogued and memorized beforehand. He enjoyed demonstrating an uncanny ability to locate even minute details from stacks of files. With mechanical precision, he was able within seconds to reach his hand into dozens of boxes containing hundreds of manila folders and thousands upon thousands of pages and extract the specific quote or detail he needed. Put to the test, he once demonstrated this ability in the midst of a case against General Motors. It was something to watch. "Hold on . . . wait 'til you see this . . . ," he said, both hands riffling through a voluminous file, a few seconds later withdrawing a folder, then sifting through pages with passages marked in various colors. What he exhumed—like a magician holding up a rabbit—was one page of a handwritten memo from a GM executive discussing seat belts. The part Specter had highlighted in yellow was an apparent recognition by the mammoth company of a problem with one of its vehicles, and a potentially costly one at that. The handwritten phrase read simply: " . . . [We] will pay for [these] decisions in the courts eventually."

Still, GM, like Daisy, had decided it would be easier and cheaper in the long run not to fix the problem but to pay off only when and if lawsuits arose. What was not factored into that equation was that there was another price to be paid. People—often children—got hurt, sometimes killed. In his years of practicing law, Specter had never met a client who would rather have the money, no matter how many millions, than get his health back. Or a family that would rather have cash than the life of a loved one.

Having little to do on trial days was not a problem for Specter. He still rose at 5 a.m., read over his materials for perhaps an hour, then scanned the daily newspapers or one of his many volumes of the writings of Churchill, his favorite. "Churchill was the best at putting a complicated set of ideas into easy–to–understand and inspiring language," he said—something Specter himself tried to do in a courtroom.

Once he got the information he needed from Daisy, Specter felt that he had not only a case against the company, but also a winner. Among other things, he found evidence of the internal dilemma Daisy faced in making the new, more powerful air rifles. There was also apparent proof of the company's rush to production and its disregard for safety concerns by one of its own engineers. And, perhaps most important, official memos detailed changes made to the guns in 1998 and 1999 for "safety" reasons—a seeming admission by Daisy that guns manufactured before the changes were not safe, or not as safe as they could have been. Yet the company had issued no recalls or warning notices to the general public. This information had not been revealed in previous cases against Daisy. It was new.

The information showed, at least in Specter's mind, that from early on in the creation of the PowerLine there was a debate at Daisy over whether the company with the homey, safe-for-kids reputation should make such powerful guns.

The Bloom Agency, a Dallas-based marketing group, seemed to love the idea. And it told Daisy as much. It made these remarks (with underlined emphasis by the firm) in its proposed advertising and promotion program for Autumn 1972: "The strategy for maximizing consumer sales is founded on positioning the Daisy as a real gun . . . this positioning will maximize the appeal of Daisy guns to the youth market, categorically inherent is the assumption that youths (boys 8 to 12) are the primary target."

Later, however, some concerns were voiced over Daisy's making "real guns" for kids. In 1975, an executive with the Ackerman Agency, a Tulsa advertising firm, had this to say to Daisy: "Due to the fact that the Daisy PowerLine range was designed for the adult market, a question has emerged in marketing of whether the Daisy name [which was known for the traditional lower velocity guns] should be associated with the PowerLine brand. To date advertising has used the term: PowerLine by Daisy. Buyer research has disturbed Daisy because the median age purchaser for the PowerLine range was 12 years old—precisely the wrong market for which the guns were designed and intended."

Indeed, Daisy's own surveys had turned up some bothersome information. Its survey using gun registration cards, a one-page questionnaire owners were asked to fill out and mail back to the company, showed that many PowerLine guns were being bought for young children. Survey data showed that almost half the owners were younger than 16 and that one in every eight was not yet 12 years old. Thousands of guns were in the hands of kids younger than 10. Some of the owners had filled out the registration cards in crayon.

(Another Daisy study, this one using in-store interviews conducted in four cities—Tulsa, Dallas, Milwaukee, and Rockford, Illinois—asked, "At what age do youngsters develop a serious interest in air guns?" In the northern cities, that age was between 10 and 11. In Tulsa and Dallas, the answer came back: 9 years old.)

In fact, relatively few owners were among Daisy's intended age group, or at least what the company stated was its intended age group, children in their later teens. The gun had great appeal not only to younger kids but also—as testament to its real-gun look, feel, and power—to older folks as well. In two surveys of Daisy owners, many of the owners were quite young, but many were also older than 30.

Clearly, these powerful guns were not turning up in the intended hands. The data coming in from the registration cards had to have been daunting, even a little scary, for Daisy, not to mention a potential liability. Daisy evidently recognized the problem because it acted quickly to do something about it. It stopped using the registration cards. No more negative information.

Further, one study found that PowerLine's "association with the Daisy name" was a main selling point—and perhaps a problem. The study concluded by suggesting that Daisy consider splitting the Daisy and PowerLine names because of "the legal ramifications of potential liability." In March 1978, a memo from the Ackerman agency used by Daisy noted concern on the part of one of its executives, partner Marvin McQueen, over new packaging that tied in Daisy's name with the PowerLine guns. "Mr. McQueen pointed out that he was concerned about the consumer confusion that could arise by the Daisy name's association with PowerLine, particularly in packaging where parents could be misled by Daisy's name being synonymous with less powerful spring type air guns."

THERE SEEMED TO Specter little question that Daisy knew what it was doing, and what it had done. Daisy knew who its customers were. It knew the power of its guns, and the power they had over young minds, over adolescents keen not only on shooting at targets but also on stepping into manhood. It knew there were dangers involved. The company also knew that some questioned whether a person who was 16—Tucker Mahoney's age—was mature enough to use a weapon with a velocity tested to be as great as that of a .38 caliber revolver and a .22 rifle. Yet that very teenager was Daisy's intended customer. A 1984 ad in the magazine *Boy's Life* touted a new PowerLine rifle this way: "Sixteen isn't just another birthday. It's a turning point in your life. A time when you put away the kid stuff and move on to more mature activities. Like driving a car, for instance. And, shooting a more powerful airgun...With a sizzling muzzle velocity of 650 fps [feet per second], the dual-ammo 860 is definitely a gun for shooters sixteen and over...when you're ready to handle the responsibility, this is the gun you'll want to get your hands on." Originally, the Daisy packaging contained no recommended age for use of the PowerLine guns, which fired both BBs and pellets. Then it labeled the rifles for users 14 and older, and, later, changed the labeling again to recommend use for shooters 16 or older. Still, Daisy knew that many of those who got their hands on the PowerLine guns would not be 16, or even 14. Daisy knew; evidently it just didn't care. Sales were booming.

Daisy had an inkling early on that there were safety problems with its newest line of guns. And how could there not be, considering what the company had set out to do? Essentially, it was building a gun with the velocity and feel of a real gun at a toy price. A man's gun for a kid's allowance money. An 856 PowerLine Rifle, for example, cost $15.66 to manufacture and carried a suggested retail price of just $38.95. Yet in comparisons to the Crosman 760, the gun from which Daisy hoped to wrest a significant share of the market, the PowerLine products were more like real guns in many ways. Unlike the Crosman, which was a mere 3/4 scale, the Daisy was similar in size to a real rifle. And when it came to power, the

Crosman was no match for Daisy, not anymore. No matter that increased power did not also provide greater accuracy at most dis-
tances for target shooting, which was supposedly the intended
purpose of the BB gun. (In fact, after five pumps the gun's accuracy
generally decreased over 500 feet.) It was power that people
wanted and Daisy wanted to give it to them. In side-by-side tests,
the Power King 880, the original PowerLine rifle, fired after six
pumps at a velocity of 600 feet per second, while the Crosman BB
reached only 523. At eight pumps, the Daisy hit 652 fps, the Crosman 569. At ten pumps, the comparison was 695 to 599, or 16 percent greater velocity. These were numbers Daisy proudly
advertised. Less promoted but perhaps equally impressive (or dangerous), was that the Daisy air rifles proved in lab tests to be far
easier to pump, requiring little more than half the effort of the
Crosman to pump six, eight, or ten times.

But in making such a gun—powerful, real-looking, and yet relatively inexpensive—and doing it fast enough to make its deadlines,
Daisy seemed to have cut some corners. One of them, apparently,
was safety. On November 2, 1971, just 12 days after Daisy's successful unveiling of its prototype at a meeting with the folks from
Sears, Guy E. Braughler, Daisy's director of Product Evaluation,
sent a three-page memo—a memo Specter managed to get his
hands on—detailing a variety of safety concerns. It began: "With
the availability of an assembly drawing on the Multi-Stroke, I have
noted that the safety systems need review. At the present time,
there is little safety mechanism available to the shooter, and there
is an open invitation to improperly handle the gun in its operation." Among "areas of concern" Braughler listed was that "the
feeding and loading of BBs is not well defined and the BBs are hidden from view throughout the cycle." He suggested "the addition
of a loading slot would add to the safety, as well as assist him [the
shooter] in proper handling of this gun."

Daisy executives were unmoved by the comments from Braughler, whose role was considered to be more that of a devil's advocate
than a quality-control supervisor. He was, in the view of some com-

pany executives, a crybaby. One company official, Earl Fisher, sent
a memo to his superiors dismissing Braughler's concerns and
Braughler himself, making him out as sort of a kook and terming
him "unqualified" to make certain mechanical assessments. The
memo concluded, "I don't believe we need any assistance from Mr.
Braughler to correct any of the items mentioned in his memo."

Months later, after Braughler was able to examine new working
models made by Daisy, he was still unsatisfied. In a memo dated
February 4, 1972, he mentioned "several points that still concern
me related to safety." One was the problem of "rolling pellets" and
"areas of jamming" in the gun's magazine. "In reviewing my safety
memo of Nov. 2, 1971, none of these safeties have been accomplished, and none of the problem areas have been corrected...."
Braughler could not have sounded the alarm bell any louder. His
memo could not have been more unambiguous. While trying to remain a solid company man, Braughler nevertheless made it clear he
was worried about the PowerLine guns being readied to reach Sears
store shelves within months. He wasn't merely concerned, he was
afraid. His memo read like a prophesy:

> This is a dangerous gun, it is not a controlled velocity play
> gun for which we are noted. I am not contradicting the di-
> rection and the objective of this unit, but this gun, with its
> absence of proper safety procedures and mechanisms, in-
> vites a dangerous condition, both in plant and in the con-
> sumer's hands. With the presentation of an unsafe
> product that has the energy capabilities such as this gun,
> we could lose the immunity to criticism that we have en-
> joyed in the Toy Market... Whereas we can now injure
> an eye or irritate the skin, we will be able to inflict a dan-
> gerous wound with the high velocity 880. High velocity is
> the objective of this gun, and it should not be changed,
> but we do need to have the unit handled as safely as pos-
> sible. I do not feel we have succeeded at this requirement
> in the latest design review.

The problem Braughler was explaining was simple: Instead of designing a separate and distinct magazine for the PowerLine guns, Daisy, presumably to keep costs down, merely made a hole through which 100 BBs or more could be poured into the inner workings of the gun. Using only the power of gravity, BBs traveled inside the gun until they reached a magnetic bolt tip. Once on the tip, a single BB could be locked, loaded, and fired. The gun did not have a contained magazine to hold the ammo in a specific chamber. Instead, it allowed BBs to move freely inside the gun, some near the loading point, some in the magazine area, some falling down near a small opening where the smaller, inner gun barrel through which BBs were propelled was joined to the gun's larger outer barrel. In places where some could get stuck.

This was not good. The problems were not part of the plan. Sears wanted to have a working model of the gun in its hands by the following April and wanted production to begin by June. Sears wanted to start receiving 2,000 pieces per month by July. And Daisy wanted to give Sears what it wanted. There was no room for delays on Daisy's end. There was a schedule to meet, and Daisy planned to meet it.

Daisy went into production on time and its new, more powerful guns proved an instant hit. Before long, Daisy estimated, the PowerLine would outsell its older and weaker spring-fired BB guns. Over the years, the company would sell millions.

But as sales took off, so did injuries. The PowerLine was leaving dead and wounded children in its wake. On April 7, 1973, before the gun had been on the market a year, Daisy received a report about a 14-year-old boy from Pittsburgh named James Sherk, who was killed by a PowerLine gun, shot by a friend who thought the safety was on. (Daisy, unlike some other higher-end air rifles, did not use an automatic safety in its guns.) Two months later another boy, also 14 and from Pittsburgh, suffered a brain injury after he was accidentally shot by his brother with a BB. Then a 10-year-old was shot and brain–injured in Tennessee in 1974. And these were just the injuries reported to Daisy. Internal Daisy documents obtained by Specter showed numerous injuries more serious than those ever inflicted by a Red Ryder. Some were fatal. There certainly had been enough evidence early on to suspect something was wrong.

In all, at least 127 deaths and injuries were reported to Daisy until May 24, 1999, the day Tucker Mahoney became the latest injury victim. Some occurred not long after the PowerLine was introduced, which was well before Tucker was even born. More than a dozen were brain injuries, disquieting proof of the gun's power. Ten of the injuries resulted in death, and, again, those were only the cases reported to Daisy and retained in the company files. There were likely more, many more. The U.S. Consumer Product Safety Commission, for one, had recorded tens of thousands of BB-gun injuries and 37 fatalities overall over the 10 years since 1985. All but a few of those children who died were younger than 16 and most were killed by high-powered, multipump air rifles.

The causes listed in the complaints the company had received should also have raised eyebrows at Daisy. Many contained a common word—"defective." And many cited a specific apparent problem—that people had been injured or killed by a gun that was believed to have been unloaded. Empty. Daisy's own records revealed an emerging and alarming pattern:

- 4/5/74 Jenkins, Steve, AR; Eye; "Thought gun was empty."

- 9/18/78 Carr, Mark, CA; Eye; "Thought gun was empty."

- 11/24/82 Shaffman, Raven, FL; Toe; "Thought gun was not loaded."

- 12/26/82 Rewis, Joshua, MI; Brain; "Defectively designed and manufactured; could be loaded but BB not expelled when fired, then later the projectile would be expelled when gun was fired."

- 9/11/84 Stavely, David, FL; Head; "...Thought gun was empty."

- 12/19/85 Offield, Richard D., MO; Eye; "... No way to tell if the gun was loaded ...."

- 2/28/86 Wajer, Kimberly, MI; Hand; "It was thought the gun was not loaded but after several pumps and firings a BB was discharged from the gun."

- 1/18/87 Foucheaux, Ethel, LA; Eye; "BB jammed, causing gun to discharge a BB."

- 3/8/87 Campbell, Ricky, IL; Nose; "Shooter picked up gun, pulled trigger and nothing happened; then pointed gun at Campbell and pulled trigger; Campbell was struck in nose by a projectile."

- 9/16/87 Lake, Edward J., PA; Eye/Brain; "Cannot tell if loaded ...."

- 2/17/87 Diaz, Eunice, TX; Brain; "Too powerful; can't tell if loaded ...."

- 3/18/88 Crawford, Scott, AZ; Head; "Thought gun was empty."

- 7/18/94 McDuffie, Shane, LA; Nose; "Unloaded rifle dislodged a pellet."

- 11/28/94 Hinderhofer, Steven Jr., NY; Eye; "Couldn't tell if loaded; failure to give adequate warning of defect; defective design."

- 7/25/95 Jackson, Christian, TX; Head; "... Unable to tell if loaded .... Defective design and manufacture ...."

- 1/27/96 Wild, Justin, TN; Neck; "... Unable to tell if loaded .... Sale of defective or unreasonably dangerous rifle."

- 3/14/96 Hall, Brandon, NM; Stomach; "Did not know gun was loaded."

- 10/24/96 Papadakis-Schneider, Nicholas, WI; Eye loss; "Thought gun was empty."

- 5/24/99 Mahoney, John, PA; Death; PA; "Thought it was empty, unreasonably dangerous."

Daisy's final entry was, of course, wrong. Tucker Mahoney was not dead.

Some of the most damaging information Specter turned up came from a lengthy, often contentious, and excruciating deposition given over two days by Ronald Joyce, the engineering father of the PowerLine guns. Joyce acknowledged in that testimony that he had seen BBs become lodged in these air rifles—once while he was inspecting the gun from the Wild case and again after his deposition in that case, when he and Theresa Wrazel randomly inspected "four or six" guns and witnessed BBs get stuck in two of them. Joyce maintained that those two guns had been "manipulated," their barrels slammed hard by someone's hand. Still, Daisy's design change was made not long after that sample test. In Specter's mind, Joyce's admission that he had seen BBs get lodged in several guns proved two things: There was definitely a defect in the gun. And Daisy knew about it.

Worse, Daisy had acknowledged in two intracompany notices—officially titled "Engineering Change Notices"—that there were safety problems with its guns, specifically the powerful 856 and its sister 7856. Changes were delineated in writing. One example: "Item #3—PIN153763-001—was reversed in the outer barrel to eliminate possibility of interference w/BB and outer barrel." The change was made so that BBs would not get stuck in the gun, a condition Braughler had alluded to some 17 years earlier. But the most important aspect of the form, at least where it concerned the Mahoney lawsuit, was a small square box in the bottom left-hand corner of the notice, titled "Reason for Change." The preprinted form listed 12 possible reasons and in both cases, the engineer, Theresa Wrazel, had checked "Safety" among the reasons. Wasn't that tantamount to an admission that the guns were not safe before the fixes were made?

Given the choice of buying a gun that included a safety change or one that didn't, who would buy the one without the changes? Nobody.

So Daisy didn't tell anyone. While making the safety changes, the company never issued a recall for the unfixed guns that were already sold with safety problems. It never issued a notification to the millions of people who had owned the guns for years. It didn't recall or send notices about the older, flawed guns that were still on store shelves, in people's homes, in kids' hands. In fact, Daisy continued to use up its inventory of old and potentially defective rifle parts. It also did not clearly inform the U.S. Consumer Product Safety Commission, even though federal regulations required such a notice anytime safety changes were made. Daisy kept the problem to itself.

CHAPTER 13

BROWN PAPER BAG

FIVE MONTHS AFTER THE TRAGEDY in the subway, Tom Kline filed suit in the case of Shareif Hall. He sued SEPTA first, hoping to elicit information he could use against Schindler. He needed to see SEPTA's contract with the escalator manufacturer and to gather other basic information. He also sued on Deneen Hall's behalf, claiming she had watched the accident "in great horror and agony" and that she had suffered as well.

According to the suit, the escalator was in a defective condition when Shareif was injured. SEPTA was blamed for poor upkeep. Kline didn't have all the proof. Not yet. But common sense said that escalators were not supposed to maim people. The incident surely wasn't Shareif's fault. The blame had to lie with the entity that was supposed to have maintained the escalator. It had to lie with SEPTA.

Kline assigned his associate, Ross, who had drafted the complaint, to now conduct routine discovery. As was typical, a formal request was made from SEPTA for all pertinent documents regarding the accident. What he got wasn't much, just some general information and SEPTA's preliminary report completed two days after the accident. There was a list of materials found in the escalator pit, including Shareif's shoe, the steel comb-plate from the top of the escalator, two screws, a piece of a sock, and a torn white shoelace. There were also some photographs, including those taken in the aftermath of the accident. One showed a piece of a torn white shoelace lying atop Shareif's mangled shoe. Part of SEPTA's defense was that the shoelace may have gotten caught in the escalator and pulled the child's shoe into the machinery. That might make the accident the fault of whoever didn't tie his shoes, not SEPTA's.

In all, SEPTA turned over 44 pages of documents, precious little for such a bizarre tragedy. When he learned this, Kline suspected there might be more, but SEPTA, he knew, had a notoriously bad records and claims department. Kline also saw a potential upside to not getting more information from SEPTA, since the brunt of his case was against Schindler Elevator, and to defend itself Schindler would be trying to extract pertinent documents from SEPTA. If Kline wasn't getting such documents, neither was Schindler. And if a lack of information would make it harder for Kline to make his case against SEPTA, it would also make it harder for Schindler to blame SEPTA and defend itself.

There were other ways to get around a stone wall. A series of depositions would find the facts, and the truth.

A number of things came to light. First, SEPTA's inspection of all of its escalators was so far behind schedule that the agency had basically surrendered any notion of trying to keep up. Daily inspections, as they were euphemistically called, were merely visual look-sees; a millwright would glance at an escalator, and if there was no glaring problem, it would pass the daily "inspection." In his deposition, Bill Kinkle, one of the millwrights who had tried to help Shareif, said: "We would look for areas where feet would be caught. Look for tripping hazards, comb-plates, comb-plate teeth missing, handrail problems, if the handrail was working or not." The daily inspections weren't very thorough; nor were they daily. Kinkle said in his deposition that the daily inspections were a thing of the past.

> Q: *And you believe it was perhaps at least a year before this incident [Shareif's accident] that the daily inspections routine stopped?*

A: *I think so.*

Q: *Once that daily inspection routine stopped, what, if any, in-spection routine did you have after that?*

A: *If we were assigned to work on an escalator, that's about the time we would see it, or if we just happened to be in the area we would look at it.*

Q: *Was there any pattern under which you were assigned to go inspect an escalator, in other words?*

A: *No.*

Q: *. . . Once that . . . daily inspection routine stopped, can you give me a sense of how often the millwrights inspected the escalators?*

A: *No I can't.*

Q: *Do you know whether the escalators . . . were inspected at least once a year?*

A: *We've worked on some. I can't say that we inspected them.*

In other words, the millwrights responded to problems. If it wasn't known to be broken, they didn't fix it. Ray Mosley, another millwright, confirmed Kinkle's testimony. Mosley, a strapping man who lived across the river in New Jersey, choked up on several occasions during his deposition, his eyes filling with tears at the memory of that little boy being so badly hurt. After the incident he had demanded that SEPTA take him off escalator duty, which it did. Kinkle also felt ill effects from witnessing such a grisly mishap and testified that he had been to visit SEPTA's staff psychiatrist several times.

Both millwrights, who acknowledged never having been trained to repair escalators, said SEPTA's monthly preventive maintenance inspections—PMs, as SEPTA called them—were also behind schedule. These inspections were not just visual. They involved actually riding the escalator, removing and randomly spot-checking six of the steps, lubricating the chains, tightening loose parts, and replacing anything that appeared worn. Yet the inspections were conducted anything but monthly. The last one done at Cecil B. Moore was dated September 30, 1996, almost two months before Shareif's accident. A more recent inspection might have caught the problem.

Then there were the so-called annual inspections. These were the most rigorous and comprehensive that SEPTA conducted. They included removing all the steps and cleaning the inside of the machine, changing the gearbox oil and checking overall condition. But again, the annual inspections were not done once a year. "At some point they stopped doing that," Kinkle said. A mechanics' group created to perform the annual inspections had been dissolved. He had no idea when the last "annual" inspection had been performed at Cecil B. Moore, just that it had been more than a year before the accident. This was also noted by the millwright's foreman, Dan Duffy, who filed a memo on November 8, only 19 days before the accident, that described a problem with the escalator. The memo stated:

> Machine requires replacement of the step chain . . . . The chain is stretched and must be replaced in the near future or the escalator will not be safe to operate. The annual safety inspection and teardown for major repairs and preventive maintenance has not been performed.

Mosley said in his deposition that a stretched step chain could have a negative and potentially hazardous result. "The gap between the steps opens wider," he said. Yet the chain was never replaced.

Institutional knowledge of escalator maintenance at SEPTA seemed to dissipate the higher up one went in the SEPTA hierarchy. Duffy's superior, Stephen Krenzel, assistant director of maintenance and construction on SEPTA's Broad Street Line, acknowledged that the monthly reports were generally late, though, he swore, "never more than 60 days" apart. Asked at his deposition how often they were conducted, he replied, "I'm not sure."

"The annuals," he admitted, though, "have not been done for quite some time." Asked why not, he replied: "Manpower requirements. There were not enough people to do all of the work required." A memo by another SEPTA official stated that all the escalator inspections at SEPTA would require a total of 18,292 worker hours to complete in the course of a year. All of SEPTA's millwrights, who were responsible for other machinery and not just escalators, worked a total of 11,040 hours per year, or only about 60 percent of what was needed.

This shortage made the daily inspections all the more important. A problem, perhaps a space detected between two steps or a step and comb-plate, could not be fixed right away if nobody noticed it. Krenzel, in his deposition, insisted the daily inspections were performed each and every day. He just couldn't prove it.

> Q: *In connection with the daily inspections that you understood to still be in place in November of '96, was a daily inspection report still prepared by the millwrights in November of '96?*
>
> A: *Yes.*
>
> Q: *And has SEPTA maintained those reports?*
>
> A: *I don't think they could be located . . . . I have been told that the records for the Market-Frankford line have been lost and they're unable to locate them, and the records for the Broad Street line are sporadic.*

Krenzel was evidently unaware of the testimony given earlier on the same day by Kinkle and Mosley that they in fact no longer did daily inspections. As his own deposition wound down, Krenzel continued to answer questions about the inspections despite hints from his lawyer, Leon W. Tucker, that he shouldn't say another word.

> Q: *If the daily inspections were to stop, would that compromise the safety of the people who use the escalators?*
>
> A: *You're asking me to speculate and form an opinion on a hypothetical situation.*
>
> Q: *I'm asking you to give me your opinion. Don't speculate. If you know, you can tell me. If you don't, just tell me you don't know.*

> TUCKER: *If you don't know, say you don't know. Don't spec-*
> *ulate at all.*
> A: *You said if the daily inspections were stopped, that's a big "if."*
> Q: *Correct, that's a big "if."*
> TUCKER: *If you don't know, you don't know.*
> Q: *But if you do, you can tell me.*
> A: *If, in fact, the daily inspections stopped, yes, they would cre-*
> *ate a problem.*
> Q: *By create a problem, it would compromise the safety of the*
> *users of the escalators?*
> A: *It could possibly compromise the safety.*

In the course of the depositions, Dan Duffy, the millwrights' foreman, had said something striking: that the one SEPTA escalator equipped with an automatic shutoff device, the escalator at Margaret and Orthodox streets, had proven successful. One incident Duffy remembered involved a newspaper that was left on a step. The newspaper rode to the top of the escalator and was pulled under the comb-plate, much the way the sole of Shareif's shoe must have been.

"And that caused the machine to shut off?" Duffy was asked.

"Yes, sir."

DUFFY ALSO PROVIDED the biggest surprise of the deposition process. It came as he was being asked about Shareif's shoe and other items found by Bill Kinkle, who had climbed down into the pit area in the moments following the accident. What Duffy produced next would end up proving what Deneen Hall always knew to be the truth.

> Q: *As I understand it, when Mr. Kinkle retrieved those items*
> *from the pit, he then gave those items to you. Is that correct?*
> A: *Yes.*
> Q: *What did you do with them?*

A: *I took them and stored them at Glenwood [another SEPTA headquarters].*

Q: *Where did you put them at Glenwood, a locker or something?*

A: *They were in a bag in my desk.*

With that, Duffy motioned toward a brown paper bag. He'd brought it with him to the deposition.

Q: *Have there been any alterations in any way to any of those items...?*

A: *No, sir.*

Leon Tucker, SEPTA's lead attorney, opened the brown paper bag. It was one of those small bags that stores used for penny candy. With a pencil Tucker reached into the bag and withdrew a torn piece of black leather a few inches long. Duffy described the items. "Well," he began, "this is a piece of tongue from a sneaker, black, it looks like it's from a Fila." He pointed to a red marking that was part of the Fila logo. Duffy noted that the shoelace was attached to the part of the shoe that went with its tongue. The shoelace, like the shoe itself, was black, apparently the original lace. And the lace was still tied in a knot. Asked if the lace was in this same condition when he was handed the severed part of the shoe at the scene of the accident, Duffy didn't hesitate with an answer. "I imagine," he said.

It seemed to prove that Shareif's shoes had been tied. It shot down SEPTA's theory that a loose lace had caught in the escalator and pulled the child's foot into the machine, a theory that could have shown either Shareif or his mother to be at fault for the tragic incident. It was proof of innocence on the plaintiff's part and apparent proof that someone at SEPTA had done something very intentional and with very bad intent in taking that photo of Shareif's black Fila shoe with an untied white shoelace. Someone had taken a white shoelace—no one knew where it had come from—and had positioned and then photographed it to make it look as if it had been part of Shareif's shoe. Someone had fabricated evidence.

Duffy also produced other items he had received. There was a piece of a blood-stained sock, a piece of a white shoelace, a comb-plate with two teeth missing, two screws, a small chip of comb-plate. He was asked if he had any idea where the white shoelace had come from.

"No, sir," Duffy answered.

Now, AS TO SEPTA, only experts needed to weigh in. Hired by plaintiffs was Michael C. Fagan, a "vertical transportation engineer." Translation: He was an elevator/escalator guy. Fagan had more than 30 years of experience installing, modernizing, repairing, planning, and testing escalators. Now working as a consultant, Fagan, who had studied electrical engineering and computer science at Stanford University, was an expert in "failure analysis" of escalators. He and two of his fellow engineers examined the still-dormant escalator at Cecil B. Moore nearly two years after the accident, and found "several dangerous conditions and practices." Fagan, in a report he wrote for the plaintiffs' case, determined that what caused the accident was a defective step roller, the part upon which the step rested—that enabled it to move up and down in the escalator. Fagan said so unequivocally. Lending support to his theory was physical evidence showing that the steps must have been unlevel at some times. The evidence was the following:

1. Several broken pieces of step rollers found in the pit area beneath the escalator.

2. Two different types of rollers found in use on the escalators, meaning that some older rollers had broken, then been replaced.

3. Flattened areas on the underside of the metal comb teeth, damage resulting from step treads repeatedly striking the bottom of the comb teeth because of unlevel steps.

Shareif in hospital bed after the accident
(HALL CASE EXHIBIT PHOTO)

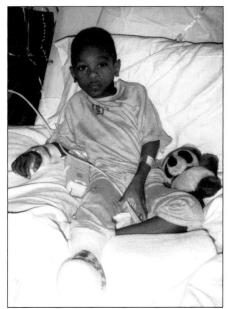

Deneen and Shareif Hall outside court in City Hall (COURTESY OF THE PHILADELPHIA DAILY NEWS)

Broad Street Line, showing top of escalator (PHOTOGRAPH BY THE AUTHOR)

The escalator after the accident (HALL CASE EXHIBIT PHOTO)

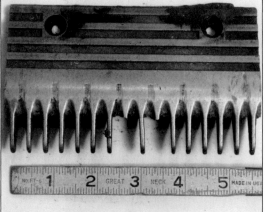

The escalator comb plate, with broken teeth shown (HALL CASE EXHIBIT PHOTO)

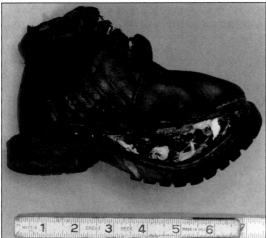

Shareif's torn black Fila shoe
(HALL CASE EXHIBIT PHOTO)

Black shoelace, from Fila shoe, still tied (HALL CASE EXHIBIT PHOTO)

Daily News front page after the contempt ruling (COURTESY OF THE PHILADELPHIA DAILY NEWS)

Tom Kline carries a pile of documents from court (PHOTOGRAPH COURTESY OF WTXF/FOX 29 NEWS)

Tom Kline surrounded by reporters (PHOTOGRAPH COURTESY O F NBC 10 NEWS)

Judge Frederica Massiah–Jackson (COURTESY JUDGE MASSIAH-JACKSON)

Fagan's overall conclusion:

> The Shareif Hall accident was caused by the step roller collapsing or delaminating thus causing the step to drop below the level of comb engagement in the step tread that Shareif was standing upon. Because the comb teeth were not properly engaged in the tread of the step, the comb was not able to slide Shareif Hall's foot up, and off the step tread, on to the comb-plate landing as it is designed to do.

Fagan noted the lack of a device that would have sensed the pitch in the step and automatically shut down the escalator, a device, incidentally, that Schindler Elevator made, and made available to customers like SEPTA. Also, the "excessive accumulation of trash, dirt, and debris" in the pit areas told him that SEPTA had let its inspections and preventive maintenance slip. He found that SEPTA had failed to test its escalators often enough, properly train its mechanics, make necessary repairs, or upgrade and install safety devices.

He noted, too, that the American Society of Mechanical Engineers (ASME) established industry codes requiring the safety upgrades in 1992. That was four years before Shareif's accident. This included step level devices. Though the ASME-recommended changes were not required under Pennsylvania law, Fagan said SEPTA should have made them anyway. "The code," he noted, "is intended to be a minimum standard for safety...."

Fagan blamed SEPTA, but he did not absolve Schindler. The manufacturer, he said in his report, has a "duty to warn their customers" of possible defects as well as to advise its customers about new devices to improve safety.

ANOTHER EXPERT, THIS one with 40 years of experience in the business, offered equally harsh criticism. Carl J. White, a consultant from Colorado Springs and a past president of the National Association of Elevator Contractors who held several patents for escalator safety devices, filed a detailed report saying that it was "virtually impossible" for a shoe to get caught underneath the comb-plate if the plate was properly adjusted and the step rollers were in good shape. If, on the other hand, any of the polyurethane wheels become delaminated (broken or chipped), the step, "like a chair with one short leg, would drop down under the weight of a passenger as it approaches and enters the points of the comb-plate teeth." Even during his inspection of the escalator years later and after it had been put back into service, White noticed a "good number" of delaminated rollers in use.

He pointed out that safety devices had been around for some time. Specifically, he cited one invented by Schindler for which the company was granted U.S. Patent No. 4,863,006 on September 5, 1989, eight years before Shareif Hall's accident. The device shut off an escalator if it noted, among other things, a lowered step. The patent also noted the reason for the device. It read: "For reasons of safety . . . ."

White, like Fagan, also quoted current ASME industry standards that called for the use of step-level devices. He went a bit further, saying that the devices would have been cheap to buy and put on SEPTA's escalators. He said he himself had seen these devices being installed on Schindler escalators, including one in 1992 at Washington National Airport. White named one device compatible with the Cecil B. Moore escalator that could detect a step drop of a mere 1/8 inch and automatically shut off an escalator. Its cost: $700.

Devices to detect jammed objects in a comb-plate were similarly inexpensive. White noted that Schindler had installed plenty of these safety devices at train stations in other cities, including New York and Jersey City, New Jersey. But not for SEPTA in Philadelphia. That, he concluded, was partly Schindler's fault, because the company had "superior knowledge" about the safety devices; yet the company "failed to use reasonable care by not advising or warning SEPTA of the need to install" them. Among White's conclusions: "Prior to Shareif Hall's accident, Schindler knew and/or should have known that without the step level device and comb-plate stop device, the subject escalator was a danger to users of the escalator, including Shareif Hall."

Now the plaintiffs had the needed ammunition. But Kline had no idea of what was to come. The information he had unearthed about SEPTA's escalators and, indeed, SEPTA itself, was merely the first few parts of the puzzle.

SEPTA, for its part, was fashioning its defense. But what defense could there be? Unlike in many medical malpractice cases in which a doctor or hospital claimed, for instance, that a patient injury resulting after a surgery was simply part of what had to be expected, part of the acknowledged and unavoidable risk, SEPTA could not claim that a certain percentage of subway riders had to expect to have their feet torn off. Not everyone makes it through surgery, of course, but people should be able to expect to make it safely to the top of an escalator. This case was not one of acceptable risk. It was, or at least it seemed to Kline, a mishap that was indefensible. So instead, SEPTA went on the offensive. It filed a counterclaim against Deneen Hall. SEPTA claimed it was her negligence, not its own, that was responsible for Shareif's injury. Shareif's own mother was to blame.

Deneen Hall "failed to supervise plaintiff, Shareif Hall, her minor son," SEPTA's complaint alleged. It went on to suggest that Shareif had been running around on the escalator and that his mother failed to "restrict [his] ambulation," that she failed to "assist" him, meaning she hadn't been holding his hand, that she failed to "keep a proper lookout," failed to prevent his injuries, and that she had failed to provide "proper treatment" after the accident. She had also not made sure that his "footwear was in proper order." The last count of the claim stated: "Plaintiff, Deneen Hall's aforesaid negligence was the sole, direct and proximate cause of the alleged injuries sustained by plaintiff."

Kline read the words. He figured it was boilerplate language, an allegation perfunctorily pleaded by defendants but rarely proven at trial. And SEPTA had no proof whatsoever that Shareif had been running around on the escalator, nor that Deneen hadn't been watching him or holding his hand, or that his shoelace had been untied. There were no witnesses to that effect, at least not any that Kline was aware of. How could SEPTA blame anything other than its own escalator for the horrible incident that left Shareif without an appendage? To Kline, SEPTA's strategy of blaming the child's mother seemed both silly and evil.

But not uncommon. Kline would discover later that SEPTA routinely filed countersuits, whether or not it believed someone else was at fault. He'd seen such a strategy—intended to present a defense as well as to try to scare off a plaintiff—used in plenty of other cases.

No one at SEPTA was saying Deneen Hall was a criminal. Just a bad mother. Yet Kline knew of no evidence that backed up the claim that Deneen was somehow at fault. There hadn't been any witnesses to the actual incident, just its aftermath.

SEPTA's lawyers called Deneen Hall in for pretrial questioning. The deposition took place in a conference room in the law offices of Leon Tucker, whom SEPTA had hired to head the defense. Tucker practiced by himself in a firm he had opened in 1979. But he was no neophyte. Tucker had tried all kinds of cases, from criminal to civil actions. He had been a prosecutor, working his first three years after graduating from Kentucky College of Law as an assistant Philadelphia district attorney. He was a short man, African American, and a sharp dresser. Philadelphia lawyers were known to have "their own style," and Tucker was no exception. With eyes set wide apart, he had a full head of hair and a trim moustache. He walked into court this particular day wearing a midnight blue suit with a faint pinstripe, cufflinks showing from a white shirt that bore thin black and gold stripes. Tucker removed his black fedora at the door.

Leon Tucker was also politically connected. He was among a small group of minority lawyers and businessmen in the small inner circle of Mayor John Street, Philadelphia's second black mayor. His law firm, which at one time had three lawyers, had a place among some of the city's biggest law firms when it came to getting legal work on bond deals and as outside counsel for SEPTA.

Deneen arrived for her deposition looking calm and collected, wearing slacks and a plain shirt. She was not nearly as nervous as might have been expected for someone not used to being in lawyers' offices or dealing with lawyers. Tucker's job, of course, was to press her hard on a number of specific points.

Generally, though, he treated Deneen gently, almost as though he didn't like what he was doing. He started by asking how Shareif was doing. Not well, she replied. The deposition was odd, the whole feel of it, with Deneen speaking from her heart, recounting the accident and talking about her youngest child, while Tucker probed for details, for something SEPTA could hang a defense on. Their exchanges were not hostile, just peculiar.

Tucker asked Deneen about Shareif's behavior after the amputation.

> TUCKER: *When you say he was banging . . . his head, what do you mean? What would he do?*
>
> HALL: *Just, I guess, from my point of view it looked like from being frustrated. Shareif was in an immobile state for a long time. He couldn't move. He started getting all these gadgets, wheelchairs. I don't know why he did it, but he was banging his head on the wall, on the floor.*
>
> Q: *When you say banging his head . . . I'm just trying to get you to describe what he would do when he was banging his head.*
>
> A: *Hitting his head on the wall, banging, beating his hand on his leg that he had the amputation done to.*
>
> Q: *When you say beating on his leg with his arm, with his hand, with an object or what?*
>
> A: *Yeah. Sometimes both, his hands and objects.*
>
> Q: *Do you recall when he started this?*
>
> A: *I don't know. I guess when we started paying so much attention to his leg. I can't really recall exactly when.*
>
> Q: *Does he still do it now?*

A: *It's getting better. He's going into another stage of, you know, like he's having nightmares and stuff now. But sometimes if he gets frustrated [he'll] get mad at his leg.*

Toward the end of the deposition, Tucker asked a question that seemed reminiscent of the old gag line, Why did the chicken cross the road? And just as silly. "Why did you get on the escalator?" he asked. To which Deneen responded, ". . . To get from the subway to the street."

Deneen recounted the disastrous event as best she could. It had all happened so fast that some of the details were fuzzy in her mind. And yet, some of it had all seemed as though it occurred in slow motion—tugging at Shareif's hand to try to free him from that giant machine, waiting for the ambulance to arrive, the wrenching feeling she had gotten in her gut seeing his fragile body laid out on the brick pavement, and then the faintness, the nauseating weakness she felt.

She testified about the SEPTA worker who ran up the escalator to help. Throughout her deposition, some of Tucker's questions seemed odd, even irrelevant, as he probed for any tidbit that could help SEPTA's case. About this SEPTA worker he asked: Any idea how tall he was? Any facial hair? Did he have a mustache, beard, goatee? Any glasses? Did he have an earring? Deneen tried to recall as much as she could about Ray Mosley, the hulking figure who had gently but sternly convinced her to let go of Shareif so his injury could be attended to. But it had been almost a year now since the accident. She finally told Tucker: "I didn't want to stay focused on him too long. My son is laying over on the ground with his foot severed from his body . . . ."

Some things Deneen could not remember at all, like details about a woman who also appeared on the scene. "I was standing . . . a girl walked up to me and put her arm around me and told me it would be OK."

Even after all this time, Deneen wept as she retold the story. There was no more screaming, no more shouts to God, just an uncontrollable flow of tears. She sat at the conference table holding a wad of wet tissues. The deposition had to be stopped several times so she could calm herself. Even Tucker could see this was no act. The woman had suffered, was still suffering. Tucker could not have felt good about how Deneen Hall would play before a jury.

KLINE HAD NOT been present for the questioning. Depositions were wide-ranging sessions intended mainly to extract information and establish a record. Even if an opposing attorney voiced an objection during a deposition, the objection was merely noted and the witness proceeded to answer. (In discovery depositions, the only time a witness was permitted not to answer was when there was an issue of attorney–client privilege.) Ross presented Deneen at her deposition. He reported back to Kline that Deneen was cooperative and presentable and was likely to be a solid witness at trial. He also reported that Tucker expressed interest in settling the case, probably for $250,000. Kline, however, wanted the $250,000 allowed under the law for both Shareif and Deneen, or $500,000. Nothing less.

Tucker, in his discussion with Ross about a possible settlement, had also tipped his hand—no doubt intentionally—about the defense's strategy. Tucker implied that SEPTA would actually be able to prove not only that Deneen hadn't been holding her son's hand but also that Shareif had been running around on the escalator. Now that SEPTA had taken Deneen Hall's deposition, had her word on the official record, it would contradict her sworn testimony. It would cast doubt on her veracity, making her out to be a liar.

SEPTA had been informed that someone had seen the whole thing, the child running about, the mishap at the top of the moving stairway. In fact, its defense team had hired an investigator to try to find this mystery witness. SEPTA even took out advertisements in local newspapers to try to find the person who might refute Deneen Hall's account.

The origin of this other account was a neighborhood store, specifically the Peralta Grocery at the corner of 28th Street and Cecil B. Moore Avenue some 14 blocks from the train station—a narrow store jam-packed with chips, candy, Tastykakes, and canned goods, and crackling with the staticky strains of merengue coming from a portable radio. Thomas Brown, a SEPTA station supervisor on the Broad Street Line, said he had gone there to buy some food for his cat a day or two after the incident, when an unidentified woman approached him. Brown had been scheduled to work a late shift that night and had his SEPTA uniform on. He wanted to give the old lady a smart-ass answer when she asked him an obvious question: "You work for SEPTA?" But he resisted, simply telling her that, yes, he did. Then, Brown said in his deposition:

> And she said, "Did you hear about the child that got its foot cut off on the escalator?" And I said no. She said, "Don't you have signs that people are supposed to hold their kids' hands?" And I said, "Yes, they're all over." And she said, "Well, you know people don't watch their kids because that child was screaming and the mother had to run back to the child. She wasn't nowhere near the child." And I said, "Oh?" And I thought no more about it. I went on down the street and went in the house and went to work that night.

Later that night, when Brown got to work, he started hearing about the boy whose foot had been severed in the escalator. Maybe the lady in the grocery store wasn't nuts. Several of the millwrights were very upset about what had happened, Brown knew. He told his supervisor, a man named Tom Dolan, what the lady had told him. (Later on, when Dolan was deposed, he said he too had "heard" that Deneen had not been holding her son's hand, but that he couldn't remember who had told him.) Dolan passed on to his superiors what Brown had told him, and the higher-ups at SEPTA treated this new "information" with great importance. They had Brown contacted on his two-way radio and ordered him to get over to the main station office ASAP. He was asked to restate what the old lady had said to him. A member of SEPTA's investigation unit wrote down every word.

About three months later, an investigator working for SEPTA called Brown. He wanted to meet with him and walk around the neighborhood, over to the Peralta Grocery, and see if they could spot the old lady. She must live in the area. Brown didn't remember the investigator's name, just that he was an older, well-dressed black man. The two men met at a local restaurant and began their canvass. But with the trail cold, there was no sign of the mystery witness anywhere. Not only that, Brown could not remember ever having seen her before she spoke to him at the Peralta Grocery, or ever seeing her afterward. Nor did he remember exactly what she looked like, just that she was African American, about 5-foot-1, and around 65 or 70 years old. He remembered her wearing a blue coat, a "car coat" with a zipper and a hood, but it was a warm day when the investigator showed up and Brown doubted she'd still be wearing it. He and the private eye walked around for some time before giving up the search. He never saw or heard from the investigator again—or the mystery woman, for that matter.

A year later at his deposition, Brown's memory was, as one might expect, a bit sketchy. His recollection also did not match the statement written for him by SEPTA when it came to certain details.

> Q: *Did she tell you whether or not she had been riding on the escalator?*
> A: *No.*
> Q: *Did she tell you how close she was to the mother?*
> A: *No.*
> Q: *Did she tell you how close she was in p.oximity to the child when the child was injured?*
> A: *No.*
> Q: *Did she tell you whether or not she was even in the subway at the time?*
> A: *No.*

Q: *Did she tell you whether there were other people around at the time?*

A: *She did mention . . . let me see . . . I really can't recall.*

Q: *Did she tell you whether or not she saw the kid at the time he was injured, that she herself saw him at the time he was injured?*

A: *No.*

Q: *Part of your description of what she told you had to do with her saying something about the mom had to run back to the child?*

A: *Yes.*

Q: *Did she tell you whether or not she saw that herself?*

A: *She didn't say, "I saw them." She did not say, "I saw the mother run back." The words were—"the mother had to run back," no prefix on that.*

Further questioning of Brown by the defense made the witness's account seem even shakier. Paul Brady, one of Schindler's defense lawyers, pressed Brown to try to confirm that the old lady had in fact been at the scene to witness the tragic accident. His questions boomeranged. Brady asked: "She told you she was there. By that she did not mean she was outside or somewhere. She told you she was there, correct?" Brown hesitated slightly, all but scratching his head. "No, she didn't say, 'I was there.'" But Brady wouldn't let it drop. He referred to Brown's earlier testimony that the old lady "said she was there at the time of the incident." Had the woman indeed said such a thing? Yes or no. Finally, Brown looked at the lawyer and said, "I don't recall those exact words. All right?"

So there was doubt, a lot of doubt, about whether the mystery witness had actually even seen the accident with her own eyes. Her account was hearsay, at best.

When the reports assessing potential damages came in from the plaintiff's expert witnesses, they made it clear that a large award or settlement would be necessary to compensate Shareif. Just to maintain continued medical care for him and to make up what he'd lose in wages over a lifetime would cost roughly $1 million. That did not include a single cent for his pain and suffering—from the real and "phantom" pains in his leg to the pain of verbal abuse from classmates in school—which he had endured and would continue to suffer for the rest of his life. It included nothing for what the lawyers termed the "loss of life's pleasures," for every soccer game Shareif would not be able to play in, every dance he would not attend, every job he would not be able to hold.

One expert who examined Shareif determined that he would probably never be able to fully develop the skills to hold down a good job. Shareif was from a poor background, and he had some learning deficiencies, which the accident might have worsened. Surely, he had severe disciplinary difficulty in a regular school environment, even in kindergarten. And his physical impairment would not allow Shareif to do heavy, better-paying manual jobs such as construction or roofing or carpentry. He would be relegated to unskilled and semiskilled work—a cashier, a news vendor, a kitchen worker, maybe a cook. One expert calculated that the best Shareif could expect to earn at current wage rates was $7.90 per hour. That was, if he could work at all.

Jasen M. Walker, director of services with the American Board of Vocation Experts, concluded in a report for the plaintiffs: "Unfortunately, a weight-bearing extremity amputation has substantially more significant consequences for Shareif Hall than it might for other children who have greater intellectual capacity and behavior controls. If he continues to falter socially and emotionally, he may not finish school and would, therefore, run a greater risk of chronic unemployment."

Almost a year had passed after Deneen Hall gave her deposition to the SEPTA lawyers, and almost two since Shareif's injury. Kline now had ammunition he could use against Schindler. Not that he had any intention of letting SEPTA off the hook—or out of a trial. Nor would he permit the public agency to get away with a meager settlement. He would seek to hold SEPTA publicly accountable. But Schindler was the big fish. Though SEPTA had its $250,000 liability cap, Schindler had no such cap. Kline filed a second suit, this one against the company that had made and installed the escalator that claimed Shareif Hall's foot. Kline knew that if he could get a large jury verdict, it would be Schindler that would be forced to pay the bulk of the money.

So did Schindler, and it was ready to do battle. Now it was Schindler's turn to take a crack at Deneen Hall in a deposition.

Schindler Elevator Corporation, which operated out of Morristown, New Jersey, with its holding company based in Switzerland, had hired the Philadelphia defense firm of Marshall, Dennehey, Warner, Coleman & Goggin. The firm had been cited as the fastest-growing firm in the Philadelphia region during the 1990s and had about 350 lawyers in 17 offices mostly in Pennsylvania, New Jersey, Delaware, and Ohio. The firm boasted "a good rapport with and knowledge of local judges and opposing attorneys." For the Hall case, Marshall Dennehey assigned two of its veteran attorneys: Paul Brady, a partner in his mid-40s, who had been with the firm almost two decades and had handled elevator and escalator cases, as well as other product liability cases; and Eric Weiss, a little older, also a firm partner and a chairman of its product liability section, who had handled roughly 80 trials in state and federal courts and had won verdicts for the defense in most. Weiss would lead Schindler's defense at trial. Brady would depose Deneen Hall.

Brady kept the questioning short and, for the most part, sweet. A trim man with wavy brown hair and soft features, he spent much of the time asking how Shareif was feeling these days. Perhaps he was hoping for good news. Maybe by now the boy had learned to live with his injury, to cope. Brady began innocently enough, asking Deneen how Shareif was doing in kindergarten. He was probably sorry he had.

> BRADY: *So this would be his first year in school?*
> DENEEN: *Yes.*
> Q: *And did he get a report card yet?*
> A: *No.*

Q: *Coming up pretty soon at the end of the quarter?*
A: *If he makes it that far.*
Q: *How is he doing? Tell us in your own words.*
A: *Not good.*
Q: *How come?*
A: *He's emotionally very unstable. His self-esteem is really low because of his foot. Not doing well at all.*

Deneen told Brady about the teasing her son had endured and that Shareif, in turn, had been troublesome at school. Brady was curious. "What's he doing? Is he disrupting class?" The attorney picked a bad day to ask the question. Replied Deneen: "Yes. He just, he really had a bad...[incident] yesterday. He had a really bad fit. He picked up a yardstick. He wouldn't listen to the teacher because someone was teasing him....He just kicked, fought, bit the security guard...." Deneen told Brady how Shareif had run about the classroom and continued to fight and scream until he was finally subdued.

She also told the defense lawyer about her own stress, how she had gone from work to welfare since the accident. "I been back to work since the accident. But due to Shareif's emotional instability, I had to stop working." She recounted the accident itself, how she had been holding Shareif's hand when the escalator grabbed him by the foot. Brady kept his questions to a minimum.

Q: *OK, so when the escalator shut off, his foot came—he came out?*
A: *Well, yeah. I didn't see any foot, no boot, no nothing. I just had my son.*

Deneen told Brady she had ridden that same escalator all the time, though it was frequently out of service. That escalator had had problems before, plenty of them. "If it was off," she said, "I just went up the steps."

Almost two years since the accident and Shareif was still doing poorly, struggling with his prosthesis, struggling at public school, struggling with his emotions. Deneen told about herself and her son and how drastically their lives had changed since the day his foot was caught in the escalator, a Schindler escalator.

Still, the company wouldn't offer a reasonable settlement. Schindler had settled previous suits, but the amounts had always been kept confidential. In the Hall case, the company hinted at an offer in the neighborhood of $700,000 to $800,000. Kline didn't like the neighborhood. The offer was not enough for what Shareif and his mother had suffered and would continue to endure for many years to come.

The answer was no.

CHAPTER 14

FIDDLERS ON THE ROOF

UNCOVERING WHAT DAISY HAD known about its guns—their power, their youthful market, their apparent defect—made the generally unflappable Specter mad. Not only was he determined to make Daisy pay financially, he also decided to go to the government. He wanted to force Daisy to recall the guns. And he wanted some Daisy executives to pay an even steeper price—time served behind bars. Specter knew the government almost never brought criminal charges against corporate executives for defective products, only occasionally for fraud or embezzlement. Even in later years, with the scandals at WorldCom and Rite Aide and Enron, punishing people who ran companies remained a rarity.

Specter knew of only one case, from years back and across the country, in which a prosecutor forced a criminal trial against a company because of a dangerous product. It happened when a county prosecutor in Indiana got a grand jury to return criminal indictments of reckless homicide against the Ford Motor Company, whose Pintos had become notorious for a fuel-system design problem that caused gas tanks to burst into flames on impact. Ford had announced in June 1978 that it would issue a recall for 1.5 million Pintos but did not actually start sending notices to car owners until August 22. That was 12 days after a van plowed into one of those

Pintos along a northern Indiana highway, splitting its gas tank open and causing the car to burst into flames. The collision also forced the doors of the car to slam shut, trapping and incinerating three teenage girls inside the vehicle.

Michael Cosentino, the Elkhart County prosecutor who took the case to a criminal trial, had seen a memo distributed among Ford executives calculating the cost of paying for deaths and injuries that might result from the faulty cars and comparing it against the cost for fixing the gas tanks, which was $11 per car. When multiplied against the millions of Pintos produced, Ford decided that fixing the cars was prohibitive. It chose dollars over people.

The criminal case caused Ford negative national publicity. But in 1980, the company, with a battalion of top-shelf lawyers, won acquittal after the trial judge refused to allow the damaging Ford memo to be introduced as evidence; nor would he permit Cosentino to call any one of 30 top Ford executives, including Henry Ford II, as witnesses. The prosecutor was unable to meet the heavier burden of proof—"beyond a reasonable doubt"—required in criminal cases. In civil trials jurors decided on a "preponderance of the evidence," or which side tipped the scale more, even if just slightly more, in its favor.

The auto companies had been successful over the years in blocking federal legislation to hold corporate executives criminally liable when products they knew to be defective resulted in injuries or death. New bills kept getting introduced, including one in the U.S. Senate in November 2000 by Sen. Arlen Specter, whose own father had been injured in a defective truck. And the bills kept failing, as was the case with Specter's legislation, which never got a vote and died with the end of the 2000–2001 session. Even when laws did not prohibit criminal charges, such as in the Indiana county court, the cases were, as Cosentino had found out, costly, time-consuming, and tough to win.

Nevertheless, Shanin Specter was determined to take the unusual step of seeking criminal charges against Daisy. The company made a toy that was nearly as dangerous as a real gun and continued to leave it out in public and on store shelves knowing it contained a serious defect. This, he felt, was criminal. (Specter at one point had suggested to a Daisy lawyer that, short of recalling the guns, Daisy at least run an ad in *USA Today* to warn owners that the guns were flawed and dangerous. The suggestion was rejected.)

Specter's opportunity to press the criminal angle came up early in the Mahoney case, shortly after the Bucks County district attorney's office had completed its investigation and hearings on whether Ty Weatherby had acted delinquently in the shooting incident. The conclusion, Specter was happy to see, was no. Ty had done nothing that lent credence to the contention he had known the gun was loaded when he aimed it at Tucker and pulled the trigger. It made a case against Daisy a little stronger because, Specter felt, it raised a simple question: If Ty Weatherby was not found to be delinquent in connection with Tucker's injury, who was? And for him, there was only one answer.

One chore Specter had as he arrived at the district attorney's office was to retrieve the gun used in the accident. He wanted it for his civil case. As an assistant was handing him the rifle, District Attorney Alan Rubenstein strode into the office. The two men were no strangers, Specter having traveled (and contributed financially) in Republican circles. Rubenstein smiled when he saw Specter.

"Shanin."

"Hello, Alan. You know why I'm here." Right to the point.

"I do."

"I'm here on the Ty Weatherby hearing. I'm involved in a suit for the family on the civil side."

"I know," said Rubenstein, who also knew that Specter was all business all the time. Specter wanted something, and Rubenstein would have to stand there and hear him out. He knew.

"What I think you don't know is exactly what the problem is with this gun," said Specter.

"Sure, I know that . . . ."

"No, you don't," said Specter, polite but firm. "These guns have this defect where the BBs lodge inside . . . ."

The explanation took less than a minute. Specter had it down pat by now. He concluded by asserting his belief that the facts in the case established the elements of a crime, a clear-cut case of reckless endangerment.

"They know it's a danger and they still let it stay on the market and in people's hands, and that activity is at least reckless, if not worse."

Rubenstein was known as a good and aggressive district attorney. He took on difficult cases. But Specter doubted he would take on Daisy because of the drain on money and manpower, and the odds against prevailing.

Rubenstein listened intently. As anticipated, Specter's pitch was futile. The district attorney gave him a look that said such an undertaking was quixotic. Specter knew the answer, but he tried to avoid hearing it right away.

"We need to get justice for this boy," Specter said.

"I agree," Rubenstein responded. "That's why the family hired you."

In prepping for trial, Specter hired Dave Townsend, the former Michigan state trooper and ballistics expert who had demonstrated the lodging defect for 20/20. At one point Townsend came to Kline & Specter's Philadelphia offices to demonstrate. For the test, a new gun of the same model was purchased from the Kmart in Doylestown, where Jay Mahoney had bought Tucker's rifle.

Townsend, Youman, Specter, and Kline rode the elevator to the rooftop just above their 19th floor offices. It was an overcast October day with a slight chill in the air, the lawyers' white shirts and ties flapping in the rooftop wind. Youman took a minute to walk over to the concrete wall that ran along the roof's perimeter, peering over the ledge as Locust Street began to swell with people heading for lunch. None of the lawyers had ever been on the roof before. Nor had they much experience with guns. Quipped Kline, "This is like a Jackie Mason joke: Three Jewish guys...." They all laughed.

But the mood turned serious when Townsend handed them the air rifle. They passed it along, hand to hand. They were taken aback by the gun's look and feel. Its unexpected heaviness coupled with the all-black body and scope gave it a sinister appearance. To Specter, at least, the gun looked very real. His first thought was of another, strangely similar, gun, the Mannlicher-Carcano 6.5 mm, a rifle Specter had seen many times before in photographs. It was the gun fired from a library window in Dallas on November 22, 1963. Specter was familiar with the weapon Lee Harvey Oswald had bought for $12.78 from a Chicago mail-order outfit. The Italian-made rifle had been pictured in history books and in the Congressional record. It had been part of a national tragedy, one that eventually thrust his father, a Philadelphia prosecutor at the time, into the national limelight. It was the older Specter who had developed the much-debated "single bullet theory," concluding that Oswald had fired a shot from his perch in the Texas School Book Depository, which hit President Kennedy in the upper back, traveled through his neck and then out of his body, and hit Texas Gov. John Connally, who was seated in front of him. Conspiracy theorists scoffed at the theory that a single "magic" bullet, as they derisively called it, struck both men. Instead, they said another bullet must have been fired from a second gun by a second gunman, most likely from the area of the grassy knoll near Kennedy's motorcade. But Sen. Specter never wavered from his belief that one man had shot at Kennedy using one gun, the Mannlicher-Carcano that became such a familiar sight to Shanin, who was just five years old when Kennedy died. The memory of that gun popped into Specter's mind now, many years later, as he stood on the rooftop with Townsend and Daisy's PowerLine 856.

Townsend took the rifle back from the three lawyers and began to load it, pouring in some BBs and closing the loading port. Then he held the gun barrel down and gave it several hard shakes with his wrist, returned the rifle upright and unloaded the BBs, pouring them into his palm. When he shook the gun again, there was no sound, no rattling of BBs. The gun was empty. Or was it? Townsend then put his hand on the pump and gave that part of the gun a slight twist; unlike a real rifle made of wood and heavy-grade metal, the Daisy's plastic parts provided some "give" to the gun. Now there was a rattling sound. Townsend pumped the gun several times and handed it to Specter. Now Specter's thoughts went back to his youth, to Jonathan Miller, a boyhood friend who had owned a Daisy Red Ryder, and how they shot at targets and screwed around with the gun. He remembered shooting Jonathan in the butt, or Jonathan shooting him. No one ever really got hurt with a Red Ryder.

But this was no toy. It had the heft and feel of a real gun. Specter hoisted the black gun stock up to his cheek, squinted through the sight and pulled the trigger. The pull of the trigger had a real feel to it as well. So did the noise of the gun firing, which was louder than Specter had anticipated, a cracking sound that pierced the strange solitude that existed 20 floors above the hubbub of the city streets. As the BB hit a piece of cardboard, there was no discernable delay from gun barrel to target. It seemed instantaneous, like a .22.

Townsend ran several tests to determine the power of the rifle. With just one pump, it fired a BB through the top and bottom of the cardboard box or through both sides of an aluminum soda can. With 10 pumps, the gun imbedded a BB into a solid piece of wood or 300 pages deep into a city phone book. A chill ran up under Specter's shirtsleeves. This was a weapon which, according to the reports, had shot out an eye, pierced a child's breastbone, punctured a heart. And had penetrated the skull of a 16-year-old boy in Solebury Township.

And to think, as Townsend had demonstrated, Specter could have been holding the gun, believing it was unloaded. This was not a trick, not some sleight of hand. It was not, as Daisy's president, Marvin Griffin, had put it in his 20/20 interview, a case in which an "expert has learned how to manipulate our gun."

Andy Youman was no gun expert, yet he was soon able to demonstrate the same defect. Not once, or twice, but virtually every time he tried. He'd drop five BBs into the chamber, close it, then hold the rifle barrel down and give it several shakes from his wrist. Then he'd tip the gun up again, open the loading port and pour out the BBs— four BBs, with one remaining lodged and hidden somewhere in the gun. He could do it with any number of BBs. Even just one, which would, after several shakes of the gun, appear to become none. With a few more shakes and twists, the missing BB would come unstuck and find its way to the magnetic bolt tip, ready to be fired. Townsend pumped the gun several times and pointed it at the cardboard box lying against the wall of the roof. He pulled the trigger. A sharp *poof!* sounded from the barrel, and a new hole appeared on the box. The four men looked at each other.

"Jesus," said Specter.

CHAPTER 15

MYSTERY WITNESS

BEFORE THE CURTAIN COULD go up on *Hall v. SEPTA*, Judge Frederica Massiah-Jackson had to consider pretrial motions, which would prove critical to the case. The plaintiffs wanted one major concession: that mention of SEPTA's mystery witness—who never did materialize—disappear permanently. Tom Kline wanted other witnesses to be barred from even mentioning her and what she might or might not have seen. Schindler wanted one thing, too—to make the brunt of the plaintiff's case disappear.

On the question of the mystery witness, the judge was told that to let Tom Brown, the SEPTA worker approached by the old woman at the Peralta Grocery, testify about the encounter would be to allow "double hearsay" as evidence. And even as hearsay, there was no testimony that the woman saw what had happened or was even in the subway station at the time of the accident. Plus, the plaintiffs' side argued, she was "unidentified and unavailable."

Tucker argued that what the woman had said was "extremely germane" to the case and that her statement transcended hearsay rules because it was an "excited utterance." He noted that such utterances are allowed because when someone relates a startling event they are generally under stress and thus "you're not predisposed to say something that's not true."

The plaintiffs rebutted Tucker's argument. How could the woman's "utterance"—supposing she had made such a statement and that she even existed—have been an "excited" one, since it occurred not immediately after the incident but, according to Brown's own testimony, a day or two later? And Brown certainly hadn't taken it as such an important statement at the time. He never took down the woman's name or address, but instead he purchased his cat food, walked home, and fed his cat.

Schindler wanted a number of things that would delay or derail the Halls' case. First, its lawyers asked the judge for time to depose Carl White, one of Kline's escalator experts, who, it turned out, had years ago helped install another safety device on the very same escalator at the Cecil B. Moore Station to prevent objects from getting stuck in the side of the machine. White could actually serve as a first-hand witness in this case about installing other safety devices, including step-level and comb-plate automatic shutoff devices. Schindler, it came out during the pretrial motions, had itself tried to hire White to testify for its side, but the plaintiffs had reached him first. Now Schindler wanted a delay to question White. Plaintiffs argued that the company's lawyers should have done that a year and a half ago.

More important, Schindler wanted to preclude Kline from arguing that the company had a responsibility after selling the escalator to SEPTA to upgrade it in future years or to advise SEPTA about available safety upgrades. If the jury found the original escalator not to be defective, then Schindler should be off the hook, argued Eric Weiss, the company's lead trial lawyer.

Kline didn't disagree with the premise that certain manufacturers who sold products deemed safe at the time of sale couldn't be held responsible for making safety upgrades later—but not if it was an escalator. The rule applied to other products, like, say, lawnmowers, which were passed on to neighbors and sold at garage sales. Such products entered the "stream of commerce," courts had ruled, and manufacturers found them impossible to track down. But to make that argument about an escalator was, in Kline's mind, folly.

Schindler made other pretrial arguments to try to get out from under the lawsuit. Some seemed a little desperate, such as claiming it never sold SEPTA the escalator. Technically, it sold the escalator to the City of Philadelphia, Schindler noted, which then leased it to SEPTA.

Schindler made another claim that wasn't so desperate, a claim that actually made sense, at least to a layman—which was what a jury would be composed of. The company said it shouldn't be held liable because it was SEPTA's duty to keep the escalator in good shape. "By 1984, 1985, we have had no contact with this product. We cannot control our own destiny. It's in the hands of the third party, and if they did what they were told to do, i.e., examine the rollers, examine the step chains, make sure the combs are tight, this accident never happens. It is virtually impossible to happen," argued Paul Brady.

In yet another motion, Schindler and SEPTA sought to prohibit testimony about New York City law regarding escalators, specifically that New York required safety devices. It seemed like a minor concession, but Kline was insistent in fighting the motion. The plaintiff's position was simple: These other laws demonstrated that Schindler was aware of the need for safety devices. In New York City, for instance, such a device was mandated after a woman was killed in an escalator accident.

It came out during the pretrial motions that Schindler might try to claim poverty in the event it lost in court. The company was privately held and had not disclosed its net worth. Eric Weiss, Schindler's lead lawyer, said he would get that information for Kline if he promised not to make it public. But the plaintiffs would be disappointed with what they saw, he said.

"I am going to tell you that the financial statement, I am told, has a negative net worth, so you know that," said Eric Weiss.

Kline scrunched his eyes as if to say, "Gimme a break!" Instead, he said, "It is wholly inconceivable to me that the second largest elevator company in the world, in the world, headquartered in Switzerland, has a negative net worth."

"That's a different company, though," Weiss insisted. He had been referring to the net worth of Schindler Elevator, not its Swiss-based mother company, Schindler Holding.

"Well then," retorted Kline, "maybe what you are asking for then is yet another trial on another day by a child who's a minor. I don't know if we are going to play those games."

Weiss hesitated a minute, then addressed both Kline and Massiah-Jackson. "Judge," he said, "I brought that to your attention and Tom's attention, because I have just found it out and I want to be up front with you. I am really trying to be up front with you, Tom, and let you know in advance what I learned. It is not a publicly traded corporation. It does show, I am told, a negative worth. I have seen a preliminary balance sheet from 1998. OK, so it is owned by another corporation....All right. And the corporation in Switzerland is an entirely different corporation. OK, so, you know, don't get angry. Don't get mad...."

"I am not getting angry or mad. I am disappointed for the citizenry," retorted Kline. "That was the only expression I had on my face."

Massiah-Jackson took a recess to decide the issues. The case was important for the judge as well as for the parties involved. The plight of Shareif Hall would ultimately be followed by the city's daily newspapers, particularly the *Philadelphia Daily News,* which less than two years earlier had printed large headlines about Massiah-Jackson herself. The judge had been embroiled in a political controversy that had made it to Washington and onto C-Span. President Clinton had honored her with a nomination to the federal bench, but a barrage of criticism ensued from the Pennsylvania District Attorneys Association and the Philadelphia district attorney, Lynne Abraham, suggesting that Massiah-Jackson was soft on crime.

Massiah-Jackson, who would have been the first African-American woman (and the first Philadelphia judge in 30 years) to serve on the U.S. District Court for the Eastern District of Pennsylvania, protested that the prosecutors were distorting her record. But the damage had been done. Despite the strong backing of Sen. Specter, a Philadelphia Republican, it became evident that Massiah-Jackson would not be able to get a majority of the GOP-run Senate to confirm her nomination. With a shaky voice and appearing near tears, she had asked the president to withdraw her nomination. (In later years, Massiah-Jackson would be elected by her peers to be president judge of the Philadelphia Court of Common Pleas, and her portrait would be displayed in the Philadelphia Ceremonial Courtroom.) Now the judge would be in the headlines again, big, bold headlines. People would be watching this case.

MASSIAH-JACKSON EVENTUALLY decided virtually all the pretrial motions in favor of the plaintiffs. For one, she would not allow any delay in starting the trial to allow the defense to depose Carl White. Also, testimony about escalator requirements in New York City and elsewhere would be allowed. Massiah-Jackson saw no reason why this information should be kept from the jury.

And any and all testimony about SEPTA's mystery witness was out. Regardless of whether it was hearsay or not, the judge felt simply that whatever the mystery witness might have seen—even if she had seen a child running up and down the escalator—was irrelevant. People ran on elevators all the time. Did that mean it served them right if they lost a limb? Massiah-Jackson was horrified by what had happened to little Shareif Hall. The judge could relate to the incident. As a girl, she herself had walked every weekday morning from her home in North Philadelphia, descended the steps at Cecil B. Moore Station, and hopped a train for Girls High School. Enrolled in an accelerated program, she had graduated at 16, then attended Chestnut Hill College, and graduated from the University of Pennsylvania Law School by age 23. She was not poor like Shareif; her mother was a French teacher and her father, Frederick, was a well-known civil engineer who owned his own firm and would later be enshrined in The African American Museum in Philadelphia as one of the nation's first successful black contracting engineers. Her two brothers also excelled; Allen earned a master's degree in mathematics, and the other, Louis, attended Cornell and

MIT and became an award-winning filmmaker and winner of a MacArthur Foundation "genius" grant. (In later years, both Louis Massiah and Frederica Massiah-Jackson would be named among the 76 Smartest Philadelphians by *Philadelphia* magazine.) Despite her success, and her family's, Massiah-Jackson was a product of North Philadelphia and no stranger to the potential perils—crowding, crime, poverty—of living in a large American city. But riding an escalator, she felt, should not have been one of them.

As the trial was to begin, Kline pressed one final item, to which Weiss objected. Kline planned to show an 11 x 14-inch photo of Shareif during his opening arguments. Kline didn't believe in parading a victim before a jury every day. It was hard on the victim, especially a little boy. Plus, it accustomed jurors to seeing a plaintiff, and Kline didn't want them becoming immune to Shareif's plight.

The decision on whether to allow the photo was, of course, up to the judge. It was a seemingly small, subtle issue—whether or not to allow the photo to be used in opening arguments before it was actually introduced as evidence in the case—but a disputed issue nonetheless. The judge felt bad for Shareif Hall, but she wouldn't let emotion enter into her decision making. Massiah-Jackson had two children of her own. Truth be known, they were the reason she had left a prestigious law firm to run for election for judge. Although the pay was less, judges worked better, more regular hours, and largely the hours they chose. Her daughter and son were attending the Friends Select School around the corner from City Hall. A judgeship allowed for more time with the kids. So, in 1981, she had run for judge (Pennsylvania elected municipal and state judges, whereas many other states appointed them). She lost her first race but came back and won a seat on Common Pleas Court in 1983, the same year W. Wilson Goode won election as Philadelphia's first black mayor. She easily won a 10-year retention election in 1993. Massiah-Jackson had a reputation for being fair but fearless, of doing what she felt was right regardless of public opinion. Regarding this motion, she knew the enlarged photo was a "prop" Kline wanted to use to set up the drama that would unfold in her courtroom. She knew it would draw sympathy from the jury, which was supposed to decide the case on the facts, not emotion. But Massiah-Jackson saw no good reason to bar the photo. She told Kline he could use it.

Everything was in place now for opening arguments. But first, Weiss asked the judge for a lunch break. Massiah-Jackson agreed. Weiss would go eat. Kline would work. More than three years after Shareif Hall lost his foot in a subway escalator, the trial was about to get underway.

CHAPTER 16

PROFIT MOTIVE

S HANIN SPECTER WAS NO STRANGER to a fight. He was only in
his second year at Penn Law when he took on the university
administration. What happened was that Specter and his
roommate felt, as only Specter might put it, "that we ought to min-
imize the boredom of the last year of law school by going somewhere else." England looked like fun. They researched the
appropriate reference material, the Penn student manual, and found
an obscure provision that said they indeed could study for a year at
another university and earn credit toward their Penn degrees.

They chose Cambridge. They applied. They were accepted.

When they informed an assistant dean at Penn law school, she
was not amused, or happy. She told them that despite their acceptance at Cambridge they would not be going abroad. It was intoler-
able. They couldn't simply go study elsewhere and redeem their
credits at her Ivy League institution as though it were Blooming-
dale's. Such a thing had never been done before; there was no
precedent for it.

"After we explained to her the irrelevancy of that," Specter recalled years later, saying he hadn't cared if he would be the first or
101st to earn his Penn credits abroad, the dean tried another tack:
The university could not afford to lose two tuitions, couldn't allow

two students to pay elsewhere and earn Penn sheepskins. This explanation, the young Specter felt, was closer to the truth. Still, he had a ready rebuttal. "Oh c'mon," he said, "there are plenty of students who want to come to Penn for a year." Which was true. However, the dean did not relent. Nor did Specter. She said he could not go; he said he was going. The matter bubbled up until a meeting of the entire law school faculty was convened. Since students were not permitted at such meetings, one of Specter's professors, Ralph Smith, agreed to argue his case before the faculty. The teachers voted, and although the verdict was not unanimous, it was final: Bon voyage. Specter had won his first case.

The new student excelled at Cambridge. In his year there, Specter was invited twice to debate at the Cambridge Union, an uncommon honor. British university debates were often attentively watched (or read about later on) far from their schools. Specter's record in these debates would end up at 1-1. Defeat would come over the question of whether Ronald Reagan should get a second term as president. The question was posed in 1984 as Pershing II and cruise missiles were being positioned by the United States at two sites in England (some were actually trucked through Cambridge), sparking massive protests. Specter, the American, was assigned to debate in favor of Reagan. The result, as he would recall, "wasn't even close."

The other debate posed a less-lopsided proposition: "The United States poses a greater threat to world peace than the Soviet Union." Again, Specter got the side of the United States. And again, it was a difficult side to take, with the U.S. having recently invaded Grenada. Specter's opponents for this debate were especially formidable, a fellow student with excellent debating skills, who was partnered with a member of Parliament. But Specter had an ace to play—he got some help from a bloke who also had a little experience with debating and who was willing to make the trip from Washington, D.C., to defend his country. When he learned from his son that the debate would be scored, Sen. Arlen Specter, a most competitive type, decided to do his homework. He went about talking to Cambridge students, interviewing them, really, about their world views. He got to know his audience ahead of time.

During the debate, the older Specter calmly articulated the long-understood truth about the nonthreatening nature of a peace-loving democracy, in this case the United States. Sometimes an act of war was necessary to maintain the peace, a point that was underscored when a Cambridge student posed a question during the debate about Cuban "construction workers" who had been spotted in Grenada doing their jobs while toting submachine guns. When the debate was over, those in attendance voted by filing out of the hall through the "aye" or "nay" doors, depending on who they thought had won. This time, many more left through the exit behind the debate team of Specter and Specter.

A FEW DECADES later, Shanin Specter would find himself back at Penn, teaching a law course at his alma mater, teaching what he had learned from his own independent, almost irreverent, path in the law.

"Lubet says to avoid having written questions in court," Specter told his class one evening as he discussed the writings of Steven Lubet, the Northwestern University author of the class text, *Modern Trial Advocacy.* "Wrong."

He went on to explain that sometimes it was better for a lawyer to write down some questions while cross-examining a witness. That will not make him or her seem uncertain in the eyes of the jury, but precise. A precise question will yield a more precise answer, "and you have to have their precise answer to impeach it."

Details were crucial, always the details.

"Anyone notice anything different about my appearance today?" Specter asked at one point.

The students eyeballed him. Specter was wearing navy pants, his suit jacket resting over the back of a chair, and a white shirt. His red tie bore a conservative geometric pattern. Nothing new there. His hair, wavy and black but beginning to gray, was close-cropped and parted on the right side, as usual. Black shoes sparkled. Of course. The students looked at one another, a few shared whispers. No one volunteered an answer, so Specter supplied it.

"I'm not wearing cuff links," he said, adding that he had just come from trying a case. "Does anyone know why?"

"Because you want to look like the average guy," offered one student.

"Do I look average?"

The class laughed, and Specter explained.

"Look, appearance matters in court. So I always wear a dark suit. I always wear a white shirt and usually a red tie. But I don't wear cufflinks to court, not outside Philadelphia. I don't want the jurors to say to themselves, 'Here comes that fancy Philadelphia lawyer with his dark suit and white shirt and red tie and cufflinks.' Now, they'll say, 'Here comes that fancy Philadelphia lawyer with his dark suit and his white shirt and red tie...,' just without the cufflinks."

More laughter. But Specter had an important message to convey. With a jury from a more rural setting he was better off dispensing with the jewelry.

"What about pant suits?" asked one female student.

"No," said Specter. "No pant suits."

"But pant suits for women are considered acceptable these days and they're very fashionable. They can be very dressy...," she said, going on for a while about women's attire in the modern world. Specter listened patiently as she spoke, then responded.

"No pant suits."

As he addressed the class, Specter was awaiting a verdict from a jury trial he had completed only hours earlier in Allentown. In the case, he represented a member of the Pennsylvania House of Representatives, Rep. Jane Baker, who was badly injured when struck by a car driven by a friend. The two had gone to a restaurant, drunk too much, and had an argument. Baker left on foot, while the friend, Judith Fulmer, followed by car. She accidentally struck Baker with her car, then left the scene. The defense had offered $1.5

million to settle the case, and Specter advised Rep. Baker to reject it. Just before the jury went out to deliberate, the offer climbed to $2.5 million. Again, Specter told the lawmaker to turn it down, that the odds were she would get more from the jury.

"We should get the verdict soon," Specter related to his class. "We're all about to find out if I screwed up."

Specter went on to talk about some details of the case, about his cross-examination of the driver, Judith Fulmer. "You've got to be able to think on your feet," he told his students, then explained. During his questioning of Fulmer, Specter asked why, when she realized Baker was too drunk to drive, she didn't call for help. Fulmer responded that she in fact tried to do just that, that she grabbed Baker's cell phone, but "when I went to use it I didn't have my reading glasses on and I couldn't see . . . ." Specter explained that this response made him suspect it wasn't true, that the real reason Fulmer didn't dial her cell phone was not that she was missing her glasses but rather because she herself was drunk. He went on to something else for few minutes before returning to Fulmer's statement, though she didn't know what Specter was onto right away.

> SPECTER: *Now, did you often go to this restaurant, LeDue?*
> FULMER: *No.*
> Q: *You didn't really know what was on the menu, did you?*
> A: *No.*
> Q: *You ordered off the menu?*
> A: *Yes.*

The questions were simple, seemingly innocuous. But that was hardly the case. Specter looked around the classroom and told his Penn pupils: "Now I've got her."

> Q: *You were able to read the menu without your reading glasses?*
> A: *No, I had my reading glasses in the restaurant.*
> Q: *Well, what happened to your reading glasses between the restaurant and getting out in the parking lot?"*

A: *They were in my coat pocket.*

Q: *Well, where was your coat?*

A: *I had it on.*

Q: *Well, I thought you told me a minute ago that you couldn't work the cell phone because you didn't have your reading glasses.*

A: *When I reached for the cell phone and tried to dial I didn't have my reading glasses on.*

Q: *So, that means you would have [had to have] reached for your coat pocket to pull your reading glasses out to use the cell phone. Correct?*

A: *Correct.*

Q: *But you didn't do that, did you?*

A: *No.*

Later, he asked Fulmer about borrowing another phone, this one from the bartender, which she had also had trouble operating. Specter asked why she wasn't able to work the bartender's phone, either. The answer this time was not about reading glasses.

Q: *That's because you were too drunk to make a phone call. Correct?*

A: *Tonight I know that I was—or today I know that I was impaired that evening, yes.*

Q: *. . . Well, did it occur to you that if you couldn't use Mrs. Baker's cell phone and you couldn't use Mr. Bedics' cell phone, that you were impaired and shouldn't be driving a 4,000-pound Jeep Grand Cherokee.*

A: *I didn't think that then, no.*

Specter looked from the transcript to his class. "She answers 'no' but the answer doesn't really matter. The point has been made. So why did I even ask the last question? Because I want to rip her head off. I want to show she's lying." His point: Lawyers aren't always nice. They can't be.

About an hour into the class Specter's cell phone rang inside his jacket pocket. The jury had found for the plaintiff, Rep. Jane Baker. It's award: $2.94 million. Specter's gamble had paid off.

Class resumed with a discussion on cross-examining witnesses, about preparation—having all the necessary documents and information before starting the questioning—and about precision. It was about questioning witnesses, about not giving up on a line of questioning until you have elicited the answers you want and not letting a witness go until he or she has been squeezed dry. Then Specter flipped on a VCR and played a videotape, the "best of" his April 2000 deposition of Ronald Joyce, the Daisy PowerLine project engineer. At the time, he explained to the class, the deposition was seen as critical in the Mahoney case because Specter might not have been able to force the retired Joyce to make the trip from Arkansas to a trial in Philadelphia. Such a decision could wind up before a federal judge in Arkansas, where Specter—a cufflink-wearing big city Northern attorney—didn't love his chances. The deposition, Specter knew, would likely be his first and last crack at Joyce and his only testimony from a key witness. In a sense, the Daisy trial was about to begin.

The deposition lasted 10 hours over two days, during which Specter questioned Joyce the way a chef might bone a chicken, with orderly and unrelenting thoroughness. Specter didn't care if he seemed repetitive or mean. Nor was he out to badger or embarrass Joyce. There was no jury watching this proceeding. Depositions are merely a search for information, for facts and statements to be used for trial, or to elicit surrender in the form of a settlement before a trial gets underway.

Specter kept Joyce, a reluctant and experienced witness who had done dozens of depositions, on point and in retreat. It took more than 1,000 questions, some of which were questions about questions. Such as when Specter asked Joyce about his examination of the guns following another shooting accident in which a child was injured. Joyce, 65, an amiable Southerner with a slack-jawed, hound-dog face and a deep, mellow voice, tried to be cagey. But he would only go so far to try to protect Daisy. Ronald Joyce would not tell a lie under oath. And both men knew it.

SPECTER: *Now, what's a person to think when they shake the BB gun and they don't hear the sound of anything inside the gun?*

JOYCE: *What are they to think?*

Q: *Yeah.*

A: *Normally they think it's not loaded.*

Q: *Right.*

A: *And no BBs in the magazine.*

Q: *Right. Does that seem a valid assumption to you?*

A: *Sure.*

Q: *Is it still a valid assumption?*

A: *Still is.*

Q: *How about for those BB guns that are out there in the hands of kids and adults all across America today that are 856s and 990s that were manufactured before the baffle was reversed [a change made to prevent the lodging of BBs] in 1999, is that still a valid assumption?*

A: *I think that a BB in the magazine that's trapped does not create a dangerous condition.*

Q: *Was that my question?*

A: *Probably not.*

Q: *Right. You're a very, very experienced man at the business of answering questions from lawyers, right?*

A: *I've answered a few.*

Q: *OK. And you're here to say today as many times as possible that a BB in the magazine is not dangerous, right?*

A: *That's correct.*

Q: *. . . For this question and for all the others that I'm going to ask you, I'm not going to ask the question again about whether a BB in the magazine by itself is dangerous or not*

*dangerous unless I specifically tell you in the question this
is one of those questions. Just so you know that. OK?"*
A: *OK.*

A small smile crept onto Joyce's rumpled face. The ground rules
had been set. Not that Joyce wouldn't try again to roam off the point,
to repeat once more the mantra that he thought the guns were not
dangerous. But now Specter had a leash he could use to tug his witness back to the trail if need be. He again asked Joyce about the safety
of the air rifles, namely those manufactured and sold before the safety
fix had been made to prevent BBs from getting stuck in the gun.

> Q: *You told me that it was a valid assumption to assume that
> there's no BB in the gun if you shake it and you don't hear
> the sound of a BB. But do you really mean that for the guns,
> the 856s and the 990s, that were manufactured before the
> baffle was reversed?*
> A: *I don't believe that those guns constitute a danger to the
> public.*
> Q: *I'm not asking about danger to the public. You know that,
> don't you?*
> A: *Yes. I know that.*
> Q: *Right. So you've got to answer the question I ask you. The ques-
> tion I'm asking you now is: Is it a valid assumption for these
> boys, Tucker and Ty. You know that these boys were using one
> of the guns that didn't have the baffle reversed, correct?*
> A: *Yes.*
> Q: *. . . Is it valid for a user to assume that one of the guns made
> before 1999 is empty of BBs if when they shake it they hear
> no sound?*
> A: *I don't think you should ever assume there's not a BB if they
> don't hear a sound.*
> Q: *Well, you told me a minute ago that it was a valid as-
> sumption for a person to assume that when they shake the
> gun and don't hear a BB there's no BB in there.*

A: *[Joyce grimaces] Did I really say that?*

Q: *You really did.*

A: *Well, maybe I didn't intend to say that.*

Q: *Well, isn't that what you know everybody out there in this country does assume? They assume that when they shake the gun [and don't hear anything] there's no BB in there?*

A: *They don't know that until they look at the bolt tip.*

Q: *They don't even know it if they look at the bolt tip, do they? There could still be BBs in the magazine.*

A: *I still say it's not dangerous.*

Q: *Did I ask you that?*

A: *No.*

Q: *Right. I didn't ask you about it being a danger or not being a danger. I asked you about what a person would assume . . . .*

A: *Most people would assume there was no BB in there.*

Q: *If what?*

A: *If it didn't rattle.*

Q: *But that's not a valid assumption, is it?*

A: *I don't . . . .*

Q: *You used to think it was a valid assumption—now let's get real specific—until you had the unfortunate experience of seeing a BB lodge in the magazine in the Wild case and until you went to the shop and pulled guns and did your own experiments and found you could get a BB lodged there yourself . . . .*

A: *If I manipulated it I could, yes.*

Q: *So beforehand, whereas you thought that it was a valid assumption there was no BB in the magazine anywhere, stuck or otherwise, if when you shook the gun there was no sound, now you believed that was no longer a valid assumption. Correct?*

A: *I couldn't guarantee there wouldn't be one BB in there.*

Q: *Is the answer to my question yes?*

A: *Yes.*

Years later, Specter told his class: "It's like pulling teeth, but you have to do it.... The lesson here is that you have to push and push and push until you get your answer." It was crucial to establishing a record, a record from which there would be no retreat, not later at trial, not ever. Very often cases were won and lost in the taking of depositions.

WITH JOYCE, MANY questions had to be asked again and again. Many were refined during the deposition. Specter often had to rein Joyce in to keep him on point and occasionally refer him to what he had said in prior depositions from prior cases. The process was grueling. Specter was relentless yet never rude. In fact, he genuinely liked Joyce, a high school graduate who had taken only a few college courses but had risen to become a chief engineer at a recognized American company. Still, Specter never allowed Joyce the luxury of sloughing off an answer; he always returned to extract another molar. Joyce eventually seemed to weary of the routine, on several occasions providing answers even as his own lawyer was voicing an objection. Once, when he gave an obviously wrong answer and Specter asked him why he had, Joyce responded that he was "just hurrying up the deposition, I guess." He occasionally smiled at his own evasiveness, even joking once when Specter asked about minors using the PowerLine guns. "Coal miners?" Joyce asked. But the levity didn't last long. Joyce knew Specter wouldn't let it go, wouldn't let anything go, and after a while Joyce seemed resigned to just giving the answers the Mahoneys' lawyer was after. The truth, in unadulterated form. At the conclusion of the deposition, Joyce could only smile at how he'd been picked clean, relieved that it was over.

Specter felt satisfied that what he had wrung from Joyce would be enough to impress a jury. For one, Joyce admitted there had been "pressure" to meet the deadlines posed by Sears, especially to construct a prototype by October 21, 1971. Joyce even acknow-

ledged to Specter that at the time he noticed the deadline, he said
to himself: "I think this is a marketing pipe dream." Yet the deadline was met. "We worked a lot of hours and we were under some
pressure, yes," Joyce said.

He also conceded that he, and presumably all Daisy higher-ups,
knew that the guns presented some danger and that many of its
users were younger than 16.

> Q: *Isn't it correct that once Daisy decided to manufacture BB
> guns that could fire over 350 feet per second, Daisy knew pre-
> dictably that there was going to be misuse of these guns and
> that people were going to get killed and seriously injured?*
> A: *I never thought of it that way, but that seems to be the way
> it turned out.*

And later there was a similar exchange when Specter sought to
debunk some of Daisy's promotional literature that made the powerful air rifles out to be harmless toys.

> Q: *Now this says . . . "a thrown baseball is far more danger-
> ous." Do you see that?*
> A: *Yes, I see it.*
> Q: *Is that true?*
> A: *Well, depends on whether I'm throwing it or Nolan Ryan is
> throwing it, I think.*

Specter went so far as to get Joyce to come close—but not quite—
to acknowledge that even the engineer himself had once had a
false sense of security when he didn't hear a BB rattling in the gun.

> Q: *A gun should never be pointed at a person even if you be-
> lieve the gun is empty?*
> A: *Yes.*
> Q: *OK. But you've done exactly that, haven't you?*
> A: *I have?*

Q: *Yes, you have.*
A: *Really?*
Q: *Right.*
A: *When did I do that?*
Q: *You pointed a gun at yourself.*

Joyce suddenly realized what Specter was talking about. It was a time years ago in another case when Joyce had been examining a gun for possible stuck BBs.

JOYCE: *Oh, come on now.*
SPECTER: *Didn't you?*
A: *Now come on, come on, come on . . . .*
Q: *I am coming on.*

It had occurred during the Wild case when Joyce had looked down the barrel of the gun while examining it. The witness protested over the question, saying he had taken other precautions, such as putting on the safety and checking that the firing bolt was open so the gun couldn't fire. Still, the fact that Joyce thought there was no BB in the gun had given him added confidence to point the gun at his own head—just as Ty Weatherby had done to Tucker Mahoney.

"Without a BB in there," Joyce retorted, "it can't hurt me." But Specter reminded Joyce that when he had inspected the gun for the Wild case, he had, in fact, found a BB lodged inside.

SPECTER: *You were shocked to see that, weren't you?*
JOYCE: *Disturbed, yes.*
Q: *Right. Surprised?*
A: *Surprised.*
Q: *Very bad?*
A: *No, I don't think it was very bad. I just said, "There's a BB in there."*
Q: *OK, well "disturbed" was your word.*
A: *It disturbed me.*

Later, when Andy Youman demonstrated how easily a BB could get stuck in the gun, Joyce again appeared nonplused. In his own tests, BBs had gotten jammed only after smacking the gun fairly hard. Youman merely shook it up a bit to dislodge a stuck BB, then handed the rifle to Joyce. Specter resumed his questioning:

Q: *Now is there a BB in there?*
A: *It's in there, yes.*
Q: *Anything surprise you there?*
A: *Yeah, I'm a little surprised you didn't have to hit it harder than that . . . .*

The gun had not been "manipulated," as Daisy's president, Marvin Griffin, had suggested in his interview with ABC's *20/20* a few years earlier.

Specter's questioning now turned to the Daisy PowerLine manual, which Joyce had helped to author. The manual cited the three major causes of gun-related accidents in the United States: (1) careless handling of the gun, (2) believing the gun to be empty when it is not, and (3) shooting at improper targets. No. 2 had occurred, Specter pointed out, to Joyce himself as he examined the gun in the Wild case.

Q: *. . . You believed the Wild gun to be empty when it was not?*
A: *Let me say this, I was surprised when there was a BB in the magazine.*
Q: *You believed the gun to be empty when it was not, correct?*
A: *Well, I could have, yes.*
Q: *Well, since you believed the gun to be empty when it was not, then anybody could believe the gun to be empty when it is not if there is a BB stuck in the gun, in the magazine. Correct?*
A: *They could.*
Q: *OK. Now, since believing the gun to be empty when it is not, according to you, is one of the three top causes of air-*

gun–related accidents occurring in this country, then
doesn't Daisy have an obligation to design that feature out
of the gun?
A: *We have designed the feature out of the gun.*
Q: *As of when?*
A: *Last year.*

Too late for all the boys who had already purchased a gun, or
those who would buy one of those still on store shelves or in existing Daisy inventory.

Specter concluded the deposition by asking Joyce if he would return to testify at the trial. "If my counsel says for me to come, I'll
probably come," he replied. Translation: Not on your life. Specter
had seen the last of Ronald Joyce.

CONSIDERING ALL THE lawsuits against Daisy, one might have expected Marvin Griffin, its president and now chairman, to have
had his turns in the witness chair already. But that had not occurred. Many of the suits had been settled early and quietly; in the
others, Griffin had been shielded by his corporate lawyers. The
only time he had ever talked for the record about PowerLine guns
and hurt kids was his appearance on 20/20 in 1996.

Specter's deposition of Griffin was, remarkably, the chairman's
first. It wasn't easy getting him in front of a stenographer. Specter
had to go to court to compel Griffin's testimony. In general, the
courts frowned on lawyers subpoenaing top corporate executives. If
a company president was forced into court every time somebody
sued, it could tie him up indefinitely and harm the company. Griffin's lawyers argued that his subordinates could answer any and all
questions Specter might have. But Specter argued that in Griffin's
case, Daisy had volunteered the chief executive to speak for the
company and to be questioned on national television for 20/20. So
why not now? The court agreed and ordered Griffin to appear for
the Mahoney case.

Yet despite mandating that he testify, the judge did not require that Griffin travel to Philadelphia to do so. Specter would have to go to Arkansas. But Griffin didn't want the plaintiff's attorney to come to his place of business, so the deposition was set up for an airport conference room. Specter didn't like this little power play on Griffin's part. But he decided to use the trip to his advantage, to make a statement of his own. To put on a show of force.

Specter brought an entire crew to Arkansas, including Youman, a legal assistant, his own stenographer, and a videographer, complete with cameras, recording devices, and other equipment. He could have hired local help, but Specter hadn't wanted to. And rather than take a commercial flight, he hired a private Learjet. Little Rock International was a small airport with just 12 gates, a limited food court, a bar and grill, and a shoeshine stand. There was little of interest to do there while waiting except to look out the large windows at the incoming and outgoing planes. Specter suspected Griffin would be watching as his Learjet touched down and he disembarked with his small entourage.

Built in 1917, Little Rock International was one of the country's oldest airports, originally erected as a World War I Army airport depot, then renovated during the Great Depression. "From Jennies to Jets" was the airport's unofficial slogan, a reference to the biwinged, 90-hp Curtiss airplane made famous during the barnstorming era. Through these reminders of the past, Specter walked while talking on his cell phone as the videographer's cart click-clacked across the worn, buff-colored brick floor in the ticketing area, then fell silent as it reached the carpeting that led to an escalator and the airport's second-floor administrative offices. Specter continued down a corridor lined with framed, sepia-toned photographs of World War II vintage airplanes. Near the end of a hallway, in an unadorned conference room, Griffin and his attorney sat in silence.

The Daisy president's deposition went much differently from that of Ronald Joyce. Unlike the project engineer, who had proudly showed detailed knowledge of the PowerLine guns, Griffin seemed to revel in his ignorance of Daisy products, an ignorance that was incredible for someone who had headed the company since 1988. "I owned a Red Ryder as a kid. That's the only gun I've ever owned.... I'm not a shooter," he said near the outset of his deposition, conducted in front of a pull-down gray background, another item brought by Specter's crew to give the deposition a professional look.

Griffin was a large, stocky man with a pumped-up appearance, his large head boasting puffy cheeks, his white shirt tight around his girth. Griffin, seemingly uneasy even on his own Arkansas turf, said he didn't know a number of things even though he was the head of the company (and owner of 10 percent of Daisy Manufacturing). He had never read an assortment of familiar Daisy documents, not even one read by perhaps millions of people, the celebrated "A Boy Is a Boy." There was so much he didn't know, in fact, that someone might have wondered whether Griffin had spent much time at Daisy at all. Indeed, over the past year the 61-year-old Griffin said he'd spent most of his time out west at another Daisy-affiliated company, Pasta Montana, where he was chief executive officer. Griffin seemed to know more about macaroni than BB guns.

Griffin claimed to have only "minimal" knowledge of all things PowerLine. He claimed he had not read the owner's manuals for the guns except on two occasions: while preparing for his interview four years ago on 20/20 and when he "scanned" them the day before this deposition with Specter. He claimed no prior knowledge of the engineering changes made to the guns in 1998 and 1999. Griffin acknowledged that it was company policy for the president to be informed of any "safety" changes made to the guns, but said that he had been elevated to chairman of the board in July or August of 1998, and thus he must no longer have been president at the time. The first design change memo was dated August 11, 1998.

> SPECTER: *Are you aware that there was an engineering change to the 856 a year or so ago?*
> GRIFFIN: *Not until yesterday [when informed by Daisy's lawyers].*
> Q: *Nobody told you that?*

A: *No. It was done after my tenure as president.*

Q: *... You were told there was a change made to the gun. That's all you were told?*

A: *Right.*

Q: *So since you didn't know about it until yesterday, that means your board doesn't know about it, correct?*

A: *That's correct.*

Q: *... So if the engineering change notice says that the change was made for reasons of safety, that would surprise you?*

A: *Yes.*

Then Specter showed Griffin the internal company change notices that were checked for "safety" reasons. Griffin reiterated that he had never even seen a change notice, any change notice.

Q: *OK. Is this the first time you've ever seen one?*

A: *Probably. I don't remember ever seeing one.*

Q: *OK.*

A: *This is handled not by the president.*

Q: *OK.*

A: *It would be handled by engineering, quality and legal.*

Q: *OK.*

A: *So I really don't know what this is all about.*

Q: *It's written in English, correct?*

A: *Yes.*

Q: *And you can read it, correct?*

A: *True.*

Q: *And you can see that the change was made for safety, correct? Do you need some help with that?*

A: *Yeah, I don't ....*

Q: *Look down at the bottom in the lower left.*

A: *Yes, the [safety] block is checked.*

Q: *Are you surprised to see it checked?*

A: *Yes, I am.*

There were many things Griffin hadn't seen or known. Or so he said. He had no idea how many people had complained about erroneously believing that a Daisy rifle had been empty, even though Daisy had logged numerous complaints.

He didn't know what kind of feed mechanism the gun used. He had no knowledge of how old the users of PowerLine guns were. He didn't know about marketing surveys done for Daisy years earlier. "I've never seen one of those," said Griffin. Specter found this unbelievable, especially for a former executive with Coca-Cola, a marketing-intensive company whose sales depended more on sales pitches than people's thirst. And Griffin said he didn't know that Daisy studies showed a large number of shooters were younger than the recommended age minimum.

> SPECTER: *Let me ask you this. If I were to tell you that market studies that were done before you were president that showed children under 16 were users of your guns in the PowerLine line, would that ring a bell with you as something that you learned while you were with the company?*
>
> GRIFFIN: *I don't remember that.*
>
> Q: *Nobody ever told you that.*
>
> A: *Not to my knowledge. Those studies were very old and I didn't read them because I don't consider any kind of study done in those early days to be relevant to today's world.*
>
> Q: *OK. So you were aware of studies, you just didn't read them. Correct?*
>
> A: *There's all kinds of studies done and I just . . . I don't know what all they were. I just didn't read them.*
>
> Q: *But you are aware they existed?*
>
> A: *Yes.*

Asked why Daisy didn't do more updated surveys, Griffin said, "It just didn't occur to me to do that." He added later that there was "nothing to gain" by doing such user surveys.

Griffin also claimed to be unaware that Daisy engineers Ronald Joyce and Theresa Wrazel had gone back to the plant after the Wild case and experimented with the gun, finding that, yes, they could replicate the jamming of BBs in the magazine. "I didn't know that until yesterday," Griffin said once again. Not until his lawyers prepped him for his deposition.

Why didn't he know so many things, Specter wanted to know. Hadn't Griffin taken time before his interview with 20/20 back in 1996 to find out just what was going on with his products? When Specter asked him that, Griffin said that he had spent about a day getting ready for his television interview. When pressed, he conceded that only a small part of that day, perhaps an hour, was used to study Daisy documents. "Maybe 10 pages" worth, Griffin estimated. The rest was spent with a New York public relations firm called Strategy 21 prepping Griffin on how to come across well on TV. How to look good and how to sound good. "... I had never been in front of a camera like that and had a media person grilling me," he said. Griffin cared more about makeup and sound bites than a possible deadly defect in a Daisy product.

Like Joyce, Griffin repeated time and again—and whether he was asked or not—that a BB lodged in the magazine did not pose a danger. He insisted the PowerLine guns had been safe so long as shooters followed the rules, which included never pointing a gun at another person. Didn't he know that sometimes people misused guns and that such warnings were not in and of themselves enough protection for younger shooters? Didn't he know that four people in his own factory had been shot with Daisy guns? No, said Griffin again, he didn't know any of that.

The head of Daisy went so far as to deny an apparently damaging comment he had made on 20/20, a comment heard across the country. He had been asked: "Isn't it true that BBs can get stuck inside here in the nooks and crannies of this gun?" And his response: "That's possible, but it doesn't happen often in our opinion or we would correct that." Griffin told Specter now that his comments on the show had been taken out of context. He said that such a jamming of BBs was not possible, that he was referring only to "allega-tions" he had heard that jamming had occurred. By not occurring "often," Griffin said that he meant never—it had never occurred to his direct knowledge.

Griffin said he would not have hesitated to order the recall of a product if it had proven defective, if he thought it was unsafe. Daisy had actually recalled a gun once, a semiautomatic .22 caliber weapon that turned out to be fully automatic. But Daisy had not sold nearly as many of those guns as PowerLine BB guns.

Perhaps the most damaging bit of information Specter was able to yank from Griffin came at the end of the deposition, almost as an afterthought. Specter had actually concluded his initial ques-tions, then, during a series of queries from an attorney for Ty Weatherby, decided to ask a few more. He wanted to know about the potential cost of a recall. Griffin tried to avoid giving an answer but in the final analysis had to acknowledge that the price was high, maybe more than Daisy could afford to pay.

> Q: *What would it cost to recall the PowerLine line of guns?*
> A: *All of them?*
> Q: *All of them that were made before the baffle was reversed.*
> A: *Oh, you mean that particular model?*
> Q: *Well, no. That would be the 856 and the 990.*
> A: *I'd have to get that. I have no idea.*
> Q: *Well, you've made hundreds of thousands of these, millions actually, haven't you?*
> A: *I'm sure there's millions . . . .*

Griffin agreed that such a recall would involve costs for alerting consumers about a defect, including advertising in publications and perhaps radio and television.

> Q: *OK. And then after you recalled them you'd have to either give people their money back or give them a non-defective gun or fix the gun, correct, one of those three things?*

A: *If we did a recall, yes.*
Q: *And that would be expensive for every single one of these guns, correct?*
A: *Yes.*
Q: *It would be a matter of at least $10 or $12 per gun, correct?*
A: *Probably.*
Q: *And if you're talking about millions of guns, you're talking about something well into eight figures to recall all of these guns?*
A: *That is correct.*
Q: *Is that correct?*
A: *Sure.*
Q: *Does Daisy have the capital to do that?*
A: *No.*

So it was profit motive. Although Daisy was a privately held company with its sales and revenue closely guarded, it was no secret that the company had seen better days. Despite hefty insurance coverage, the spate of lawsuits over its airguns and the threats of more to come didn't help. Griffin's admission that the cost of a massive recall could push Daisy over a financial precipice was important. It had shown money as motive at work once again, just as in Daisy's rush to market the PowerLine guns in Sears stores nearly three decades earlier. It was an especially tasty morsel to have educed from the head of a company whose goal going into the deposition was to provide Specter with no additional ammunition. It explained why the company was fighting so hard to deny—or keep quiet—that there was a problem with its air rifles. If forced to admit such a problem and recall millions of guns, Daisy could be finished financially. It was a matter of survival.

SPECTER FELT MORE confident in his case after getting Joyce and Griffin on the record. Yet their depositions had yielded information that posed a bit of a dilemma for him. There was no question in his mind now that there were millions of defective and dangerous guns in homes across the country and that Daisy would never act voluntarily to address the risk. Specter felt compelled to act. As a lawyer, his sole obligation was to his clients, the Mahoneys. But he also felt a responsibility to try to prevent another child from being harmed. In some ways, the two objectives were incompatible.

Specter's first instinct was to go to the Consumer Product Safety Commission, even though he knew the consumer product panel had "cleared" Daisy of making a defective product in 1995. He knew now that that decision was in error, and he wanted the commission to know it as well. Not only Specter had seen the gun jam with BBs, but also Ronald Joyce, who had been "surprised" and "disturbed" to see it. There was a clear defect in the guns. Daisy, by making safety changes in 1998 and 1999 to the gun, had admitted as much—without notifying the CPSC as required. Specter wanted the CPSC to have the same information he had unearthed. But informing the commission could hurt Specter's case for the Mahoneys. It was possible, for instance, that the CPSC could reopen its investigation of the PowerLine guns and again find them not to be defective. Such evidence introduced into *Mahoney v. Daisy* would not be helpful in court. Or what if the CPSC acted against Daisy, and the publicity spurred a rash of other lawsuits against the company? That might cut into any award the Mahoneys could expect to obtain. Specter was well aware there was a ceiling to Daisy's insurance coverage, roughly $20 million all told. Whatever another plaintiff won could mean less for the Mahoneys.

Specter weighed these negatives against what he called "guilty knowledge"—knowledge of a dangerous defect not shared with the general public.

He had possessed such "guilty knowledge" once before. The case was *Bobb v. Ford,* and it involved a faulty emergency brake in a Ford pickup truck. Derick Bobb, an infant, had been run over and seriously injured after a parking brake "popped" loose and the truck rolled away, crushing his head. Specter negotiated a sizeable settlement in the case, a settlement that included a confidentiality agreement. Specter could not alert the media or the public of the case. His hands had been tied. Still, Ford had promised to issue a recall to fix the problem—and it eventually did—though the company was slow in doing so. Specter asked an engineer for Ford what was taking so long, but he didn't make any further effort to push Ford into action. Six weeks later, a three-year-old boy named Walter White, of Elko, Nevada, was killed in a rollaway accident involving a Ford pickup and the same brake defect. Specter would wind up trying and winning the White case, but the memory of not having done more after the Bobb settlement haunted him.

"I spent three weeks in Reno trying that case, and all the while I'm out there I'm thinking to myself this boy should have never died," Specter recalled. "Ford should have acted. And I couldn't stomach the idea that I hadn't interceded in the regulatory process myself."

Specter weighed all this and asked himself a simple question: "How could you live with yourself if someone else got hurt or killed and you could have done something about it?"

Still, the decision was not Specter's alone to make. The Mahoneys had to be consulted. He laid it out to them. They didn't hesitate one second. "I just wish someone had done this years ago," said Jay Mahoney.

Notifying the CPSC was not a maneuver to pressure Daisy into a settlement. Specter never told the company of his plans. On May 23, 2000, he sent an eight-page letter to Marc Schoem, director of the commission's Division of Corrective Actions.

> Dear Mr. Schoem:
>
> We write at the request of the parents of Tucker Mahoney, a 16-year-old boy who is in a near vegetative state as a result of being accidentally shot in the head by his best friend with a BB fired from a Daisy PowerLine model 856 airgun. The gun which was used in the shooting was thought to be empty by the boys after it had fired numerous times, producing only air (dry-fired) and after it had been shaken, with no BB audible.

We have discovered startling information, which Daisy
has kept from the CPSC, about a defect in this gun and the
millions like it which are in the hands of children across
the country, which makes the gun appear empty when it is
not. It is well known and stated by Daisy in its owner's
manual that a chief cause of gun accidents is believing a
gun to be empty when it is not.

The letter went on to note Daisy's knowledge of the gun's defect, that it had made "safety" changes in 1998 and 1999, yet continued to sell unfixed guns and use up old inventory. Tucker's
gun, which did not include the design change, was bought two and
a half months after the second change had been made. Specter
cited the numerous lawsuits filed against Daisy since the commission's 1995 decision, lawsuits involving plaintiffs who had been
badly injured or killed by Daisy guns. He mentioned the *Wild v.
Daisy* case, during which Daisy's own experts made an inspection
of a gun and a BB was found lodged between the inner and outer
barrels. It included mention of how Andy Youman had demonstrated the jamming effect. And it noted that most users of the BB
guns were kids, a fact that "Daisy simply closed its corporate eyes
and ears to."

Specter's letter called it "shocking and outrageous" that Daisy
did not bring the matter to the commission's attention. It concluded:

These guns pose a serious hazard to the millions of adult
and child users and anyone within range of the guns. We
urge you to take immediate action in this matter to spare
others from the horrible tragedy visited upon Tucker Mahoney and the Mahoney family. We are happy to provide
any additional information you seek.

With the letter, Specter sent a tape of the 20/20 report aired in
1996 and an offer of his own videotaped depositions, all documents
retrieved in discovery, information about other cases and com-

plaints against Daisy, and, perhaps his most convincing exhibit against Daisy—Andy Youman himself.

The CPSC asked for it all. Youman went to the commission's offices in Bethesda and talked to several staff members. Jimmie Williams, a leading CPSC attorney, later spent a day in Philadelphia rummaging through the files at Kline & Specter. On September 26, Youman returned to D.C., where he appeared before a half dozen commission staff members and demonstrated the product's defect. He loaded some BBs into a Daisy 856, pointed it nose down and gave it several vigorous shakes. Then he unloaded the BBs— one fewer than he had put in. As usual, one BB had become stuck in the gun. Youman shook it again, not very hard, and the BB, almost magically, returned in the gun. The staff members were impressed, and inquisitive. They wanted to learn more about the guns. And though the commission did not disclose information about its cases, it seemed clear to Youman that its investigation into Daisy BB guns had been reopened.

Specter still felt an uneasy tug in his stomach. It could take a long time for the CPSC to investigate and then act against Daisy, and there was no guarantee it would. In the interim, how many kids would dump a load of BBs into their PowerLine guns? How many parents would buy new ones for Christmas? How many of their children would be injured? How many would die? There was something else Specter could do. He could warn people.

In late September, he fired off a long and detailed letter to Dave Rummel, senior producer at ABC News. "We have discovered startling information," Specter wrote, and then reminded the producer of the network's prior investigation of PowerLine guns. It had been four years since 20/20, still in a prime-time slot on ABC, had aired that show. Brian Ross, 20/20's chief investigative correspondent, had suspected at the time that BBs got stuck in the guns but couldn't prove it. Specter now had that proof.

He not only knew precisely what the defect in the guns was, but he could also demonstrate it. He had depositions in which Daisy's chief engineer, Ronald Joyce, acknowledged the problem. He had documents showing the "safety" changes Daisy had made. And that Daisy never told anyone about the problem with its guns, not the CPSC, not retailers, not the general public. Finally, Specter had physical evidence, the heart-rending sort that TV loves, of the havoc wrought by the powerful guns. He had Tucker Mahoney. ABC, Specter was certain, would be interested.

CHAPTER 17

TRIAL

T HE "SEPTA JURY" ENTERED Courtroom 654 in Philadelphia
City Hall, a colossal edifice with granite and limestone walls
and a 37-foot statue of William Penn at its apex. The building was the country's largest city hall and, at 548 feet, the tallest
structure ever built without a steel skeleton. Its construction took
30 years and 88 million bricks to complete. Inside it had nearly 700
rooms, some lined with granite and sheets of Massachusetts marble, and the exterior was adorned with some 250 statues.

But the building had aged over a century, and not so gracefully. It
appeared blemished and weary on the outside and exhausted on the
inside, its hallways lined with grimy granite walls and floors of white
linoleum, many of the squares warped and faded a sickly yellow. The
place was a workhorse, teeming with lawyers and judges, politicians
and civil servants. The mayor's office was on the second floor.

The courtroom for *Hall v. SEPTA* was on the sixth floor, a cav-
ernous room with 30-foot ceilings that created an acoustical night-
mare. It was an unattractive mishmash of colors—walls that were
white and beige with yellow columns, granite in shades of maroon
and gray and a dingy, pinkish brown. Gilded trim adorned the room
like too much makeup on an old woman's face. Two paintings of former judges peered down from behind the judge's bench, a high-

arching fortress made of marble. The room had a rich, historic feel. Until one noticed the hanging fluorescent lights, the large speakers standing atop steel poles and beastly air-conditioning units that filled the windows, their wiring draped across the walls.

The jurors filed in, taking seats marked with stick-on gold plates numbered 1 through 12. Kline liked the jury that had been picked—two men and ten women, seven of whom were African-American and had children of their own.

Kline had been shocked that one of them, an alternate, had made it to the jury, unchallenged by either SEPTA or Schindler. After a briefing about the case by the lawyers, the woman, wearing a head wrap and apparently Muslim, had indicated quite strongly that she was less than objective. "There ain't a wheelbarrow big enough for the money I would give these people," she had said about the Halls. Leon Tucker immediately wanted the woman stricken from consideration, but Weiss said that Schindler did not object to her being on the jury. Then he began asking her questions that seemed aimed at rehabilitating the woman as a juror. "But you could be objective about the case, couldn't you? You could vote fairly, couldn't you?" "Well," the woman replied, "Sure. Sure I could." Kline was praying that she would be placed on the jury, but he didn't say a word. If he supported her, Kline knew, Tucker would demand her removal. So Kline let Weiss make the case for the woman, and Tucker did not object to her being seated.

Opening arguments went about as well as could be expected for a plaintiff. Kline found he had ready allies in the fight to assess blame for the accident that occurred on November 27, 1996: Kline blamed both SEPTA and Schindler, but SEPTA and Schindler blamed each other.

Kline laid out his case, the experts he would call to testify, and the harm that was done to his clients. His case was simple and to the point. Yet he could not have anticipated the way the trial would play out.

What he did know at this point, though, was that he had a wonderful client, a sympathetic client. He jumped quite soon in his opening speech to the part about the jury awarding damages, as though that were already a fait accompli. Kline, quoting loosely from Bob Dylan, told the jury: "I'll tell you what the evidence will show. The evidence will show he never did nothing wrong to nobody." It was just a matter of who—SEPTA or Schindler or both—was liable and how much each should pay. Added Kline:

> This case is about three things. It's about compensating this little boy every penny that he deserves from the people who were at fault. Second, it's about compensating Deneen for the horror of watching her little boy, in a day when we have anesthesia to take a pimple off, have his leg ripped off, shoe and all.... And there's damages in this case, not only to compensate this boy, but you're going to have a larger voice. You are going to be able to answer a question that has to do with whether the company [Schindler] should be punished, made an example of, and it's called punitive damages.

He talked about SEPTA's aborted maintenance schedule and the November 8 memo about the stretched step chain that said the escalator was "an accident waiting to happen." He mentioned Schindler's automatic safety shutoff devices that SEPTA claimed it was never informed about. "That's a device," Kline told the jury, "that if a little boy's foot, like this little boy, got caught in it, you know what happens to the escalator? Shuts down." He noted that Schindler had installed plenty of the devices on other escalators for other businesses.

"This is Shareif's blood," Kline said, showing the jury pictures from the accident scene. "He bled for their mistake, that's what the evidence will show." Kline told the jury what was to come, that they would get to see Shareif, to see his injury and the Fila shoes that his mother "bought her little boy on her painter and laborer's salary."

He drew a picture of Deneen Hall as a helpless victim and of SEPTA as just the opposite, conniving and cold-blooded. Kline described the scene at the train station.

And as Deneen stood there screaming in horror, in shock, not knowing what she could do to help her little boy, and what she will tell you is [it is] the most helpless feeling that you could have, that any of us could have who has a little boy, a little girl.... This thing [escalator] kept running and running and running and running some more.

Kline added: "And one last thing, one last claim. For her troubles, Miss Hall was sued by SEPTA. And you will have to hear what they have to say about trying to blame her. But they actually sued her. That was her reward."

Kline urged the jury to make an example of SEPTA with its verdict. And especially of Schindler, which could be made to pay not only compensatory damage to the Halls but also punitive damages. He would ask the jury not only to find negligence on the part of the large company but then also to punish it, sternly. "The case is about Shareif standing up to this company. On one leg, yes, but standing up."

Tucker and Weiss opened their cases by also trying to portray their clients as somehow sympathetic, as more than simply faceless corporate entities. Tucker talked about the working men and women that were SEPTA. Weiss said Schindler was a company comprised of hard-working, flesh-and-blood employees. Kline felt that neither argument stood terribly tall next to his own opening, delivered with the large color photo of Shareif Hall peering down at the courtroom.

The defense lawyers each claimed his client was not responsible. SEPTA's escalators were maintained properly even though inspections were missed, asserted Tucker. Schindler's escalators were safe even without being retrofitted with the safety devices the company knew had existed for years, insisted Weiss.

Tucker spoke of how November 27, 1996, was a "terrible day for SEPTA," a claim that must have rung hollow to the jury after it heard how Shareif had spent that day.

So, too, Tucker's claim that "SEPTA did everything that it should to prevent this from happening, and nonetheless it happened." He likened the event to an unpreventable act of nature or God. Just something that happened. Tucker added, "Nothing was wrong with that escalator that they can determine."

He did not say what proof SEPTA had in filing its cross-claim against Deneen Hall; he only alluded to Shareif's running on the escalator. The millwrights who were beneath the machine, the lawyer said, "heard feet running down the escalator and then running back up the escalator, and then screams . . . ." Repeated Tucker, "It was a terrible day for everyone."

He said SEPTA was unaware of the automatic shutoff devices, that "had SEPTA been informed of a comb-plate shutoff device, in all probability it would have been installed." SEPTA, he asserted, had not known about such a device, and that ignorance was Schindler's fault. "And SEPTA didn't know about the step-drop device, the step-leveling device, I believe it's referred to. So, [it] comes down to notice. Now, SEPTA did everything that they should have done in this instance. It's unfortunate that it happened."

ERIC WEISS WAS an experienced lawyer. A former football player who had played "monster back" on the Villanova University freshman team, Weiss had been practicing law for 25 years. He had been successful in defending corporate clients and headed Marshall Dennehey's product liability section. Not as tall as Kline but broader, he had a strong if scratchy voice, and he commanded attention in the courtroom.

Weiss started his opening remarks by flattering the jury. Over and over he thanked the panel for its time, for putting "aside your busy lives to take that oath, to live up to that oath." As though they had volunteered for jury duty. He talked about the "fancy woodwork" in the courtroom and how it signified "that justice is the most important part of our society, our culture, and our government." He talked about the jury's "awesome responsibility" and urged the jurors to "keep an open mind." He urged the jurors, begged them, really, to decide the case "without sympathy for any side."

When he did address the actual case, Weiss said, "This accident should never have happened. Let me repeat that. This accident should never have happened."

Then he aimed his arrows at SEPTA. "An escalator that is properly maintained and adjusted, this accident can't happen," Weiss said. "From approximately 1987 to 1996, SEPTA and SEPTA alone maintained this escalator." He agreed with Kline that SEPTA did not devote the manpower to keeping the escalators in tip-top shape. "We learned in 1994, as Tom Kline just told you, SEPTA's escalators had gotten in such bad condition as to be called, in a document offered by SEPTA, critical. They were in critical condition." It seemed as if Kline had helped Weiss write his opening speech. Weiss even quoted the opposition: "Well, on the day of this accident, the accident that was waiting to happen, as Mr. Kline said, happened."

Weiss concluded by saying that the installation of safety shutoff devices might not have prevented the accident. In fact, he said, sometimes they could even be hazardous because they could stop an escalator too abruptly, causing people to fall. "If you stop them too suddenly, then any person who is not holding on—a child, an older person, me, as clumsy as I am—is going to get thrown down or up that escalator, and that is the most common cause of injury . . . from people falling on escalators."

The accident was SEPTA's fault, Schindler was insisting. It didn't maintain the escalator. And if SEPTA had wanted safety upgrades, all it had to do was ask.

Weiss told the jury: "You will learn that it's up to the owner to decide whether or not he wants upgrades or he wants retrofits or whatever he wants on his escalator. Schindler will sell you whatever you want. Schindler is in the business of making profit off of selling parts for escalators." He also mentioned one other thing that appeared to punch a gaping hole in SEPTA's argument that it hadn't known about the availability of the safety devices, and that, had it known, it might have installed them at Cecil B. Moore Station. "That escalator," said Weiss, "is running today, it's in service, and SEPTA has not put those devices on that escalator. Right now, it's running."

THERE WAS A third defendant in the case, the City of Philadelphia, sued by Schindler, not Kline. Just as SEPTA had tried to deflect blame to Deneen Hall, so, too, Schindler wanted to involve the city as a defendant. Philadelphia's attorney, Edward Jefferson, noted that it was merely a technicality that the city had purchased the escalator in 1984, that it had leased the entire subway station, escalator included, to SEPTA. He compared the city to a car dealer who leases an automobile. "Before they give the key over to the person that's leasing the car they say, 'Take care of that. Get it fixed, keep it maintained, do whatever it takes....'"

"Schindler brought the City of Philadelphia into this case," Jefferson told the jury. "And what did we do? The City of Philadelphia bought their escalator."

COULD IT WORK? Could the scatter-shot of blame—with SEPTA blaming Schindler and Schindler blaming SEPTA—sway a jury into finding one or the other was not at fault? Or maybe that neither was at fault? Tom Kline doubted that SEPTA could convince the jury to blame Deneen Hall for the tragedy. And yet someone or something had to be at fault, had to be held liable. But maybe the defense arguments would leave the jury unconvinced to hold Schindler responsible along with SEPTA. Kline doubted the possibility, but he did not discount it. He had seen stranger things—and unpredictable jury verdicts. Anything was possible.

KLINE WANTED TO start the trial with drama, with something graphic, something the jury would remember. He asked Michael Fagan, one of his two escalator experts to take the stand. Fagan brought with him a piece of evidence that would demonstrate, perhaps better than any words, the violent nature of what had happened on that pre-Thanksgiving Day at the Cecil B. Moore Station.

> KLINE: *Let me start by marking plaintiff's exhibit No. 1. What to your understanding, sir, is plaintiff's exhibit No. 1? It's a little boy's boot. Is that correct?*
>
> FAGAN: *Yes. This is the shoe that Shareif was wearing at the time he was injured.*

As Fagan answered, Kline held up the torn and twisted child's size 9½ hiking boot. Its sole had been half torn off. The top section containing the tongue and laces was missing. The leather side of the shoe was marred by a series of deep indentations, parallel scars made by the steel teeth of the escalator comb-plate.

Next came Shareif's gray jeans, which gave the jury a vivid idea of just how forceful the incident had been. The small pair of pants was ripped into large shreds, some of the damage caused by the escalator and some by emergency personnel as they tried to administer first aid. The bottoms of the pants were spotted with brown drops, Shareif's blood. The section of comb-plate that had ripped off his foot and then fell into the pit was entered into evidence as were the two screws that had once held it in place on the top escalator landing. There was a photo of the pit area. Then another part of the hiking boot, the tongue. Then a piece of the boy's gray sock, just a piece. Then the shoelace. It was a black shoelace that had been torn from the shoe but remained intact, still in a double knot.

> KLINE: *And for the record, are they still, to this day, tied?*
>
> FAGAN: *Yes. They are. Clearly, they're tied.*

Kline reviewed Fagan's impressive resume for the jury, from his Stanford bona fides and years of experience that included work on the original escalators at Philadelphia's Veterans Stadium to his time as project manager for a modernization program for the World Trade Center's 43 escalators. Fagan acknowledged this was his 10th time testifying as an escalator expert and that he charged a hefty sum for his work—$240 per hour. But he described his mission—studying the escalator in question as well as depositions and other information in the case—as "my search for truth."

> KLINE: *Now, sir, based on the information that you have, and you have them documented in your report, did you reach an opinion with reasonable professional certainty as to whether the maintenance and repair of the escalator at Broad and Cecil B. Moore, which this little boy, Shareif Hall, was injured on, on November 27th, 1996, was negligently maintained?*
>
> FAGAN: *Yes. It was absolutely negligently maintained.*
>
> Q: *And was the negligence of SEPTA, sir, one of the factors, a substantial contributing factor in causing the child's injuries?*
>
> A: *Absolutely. It was one of the substantial contributing factors that led to this accident.*
>
> Q: *[after a few minutes] Did the conduct of SEPTA fall below the conduct of a reasonable and prudent operator of an escalator . . . ?*
>
> A: *So far below, it was unacceptable.*

When asked about the city's role, with Kline trying to discredit Schindler's joining the city into the case, Fagan gave an answer that provided the jury with its first chuckle, though it would be far from its last or best laugh. "Did you know of anything that the City of Philadelphia did wrong in terms of the maintenance or repair of this escalator?" Kline asked. Fagan answered quickly. "They hired SEPTA," he said.

Fagan concluded that Shareif's injury was caused by a step roller breaking or chipping, causing a space between the step and the top comb-plate, a space large enough to catch Shareif's shoe and pull his foot in. Fagan's report blamed SEPTA for not making the safety changes but also said that Schindler should have alerted SEPTA to the updated devices. Fagan said the new safety mechanisms would have prevented the accident.

———————

ON CROSS-EXAMINATION, Tucker mentioned that Fagan had not inspected the escalator until nearly two years after the accident. So, SEPTA's attorney wanted to know, how could Fagan know when step rollers had been broken or that they might have caused the accident? The expert witness responded that there was ample evidence the escalator had been poorly maintained for some time. "In my 34 years of...experience," he said. "I have never seen an escalator with so many broken rollers in such poor shape as this particular escalator that I saw at the time of my site inspection."

Weiss crossed Fagan next, and he sought to contradict Fagan's theory of the accident and his assertion that it could have been prevented. In fact, asked Schindler's lawyer, wasn't it true that SEPTA "has admitted that they found no problems with the rollers" after the accident? Fagan agreed that was SEPTA's conclusion but said he didn't believe it for an instant. SEPTA's maintenance was so poor and its staff so inadequately trained, Fagan said, that they would not have known what to look for. "So, in other words," Weiss asked, "it's your opinion, based upon everything that you have seen, that SEPTA would not even know how to examine a roller?" Fagan's reply: "That is my opinion."

On redirect, Kline summarized and simplified. He wanted to leave the jury with a fresh, succinct understanding of Michael Fagan's expert testimony.

> KLINE: *First question, sir, having answered questions from Mr. Weiss for the better part of two hours—Is there any way this accident could have happened without that step dropping down?*
>
> FAGAN: *No.*
>
> Q: *Was this little boy's foot caught underneath that comb-plate?*
>
> A: *Yes.*
>
> Q: *Do the SEPTA documents say that these two missing [comb-plate] teeth were fresh cut, freshly cut off?*
>
> A: *Yes.*

> Q: . . . And that would mean it happened when?
> A: It happened at the time of Shareif's foot being amputated.

Kline asked about Schindler's claim, which he expected later from the company's own expert, that the comb-plate was already missing when the accident occurred, causing Shareif's foot to get lodged in the escalator. Fagan had already said he believed the comb-plate had torn off the child's foot. Now he showed the evidence. For the jury to see, he held the steel teeth of the plate against the marks in the child's boot. "And when you line these up," he said, "they match just perfectly on the shoe."

> Q: And, sir, is there any evidence that you reviewed, any evidence that prior to the incident, somebody unscrewed the plate, put it underneath in the pit, coincidentally ending up right where the little boy's shoe was, next to the plate?
> A: Absolutely not.
> Q: Would that be too much to believe, sir?
> A: That's too much for me to believe.

With that, Kline asked the judge's permission to pass Shareif's scarred boot and the comb-plate to the jury. Permission was granted.

DAY Two OF testimony brought another Kline expert, one with even more experience, one whom, the plaintiffs made certain to point out, SEPTA itself had tried to hire. Carl White was an expert's expert. He held several patents on escalator safety devices, one of which protected objects from getting stuck in the side of escalators. White's company had actually retrofitted such a device on the escalator at the Cecil B. Moore Station in 1991, five years before Shareif's accident. SEPTA could have installed additional safety devices on the escalator for relatively little cost, White testified. But it never did. Why did SEPTA buy White's side-safety device and not the step-level and comb-plate shutoffs sold by

Schindler? Because, White surmised, he had gone to SEPTA hawking his product. Schindler had not.

White, a squat man of 68 who didn't mind talking in front of a crowd, demonstrated to the jury that he was quite an expert, perhaps *the* expert when it came to escalators. Besides his patents, he had served on a number of industry boards and had worked on all kinds of escalators all over the country. He knew the history of escalators, back to the inventor, a man White spoke of with great reverence— "Jesse Reno, rest his soul, who got the patents in 1892." (Reno operated the first escalator, more of a moving ramp with wooden slats for steps, as an amusement ride in Coney Island, New York, in 1896, a century before the injury to Shareif Hall.) White had been published in *Elevator World* magazine. He'd appeared on several TV shows, including NBC's *Dateline,* to talk about escalator safety, or the lack thereof. He'd done work, including consulting, for 17 different manufacturers and had visited, at Schindler's invitation, that company's world headquarters in Lucerne, Switzerland. Twice.

White's conclusion was the same as Fagan's, that a dropped step caused Shareif's foot to get caught under the comb-plate, and that the addition of safety shutoff devices could have prevented the mishap.

He further concluded that Schindler had never notified SEPTA of the availability of the devices. White's side-safety device had cost SEPTA $5,400 to install. Schindler's mechanisms were far less expensive. Other companies for years had made the step-level and comb-plate shutoff devices standard equipment on their escalators, including Illinois-based Montgomery Elevator Company, which began including its version of the automatic safety equipment back in 1958, said White. Haughton Elevator Company had made a comb-plate shutoff mechanism a standard feature for many years, going back to before 1973. Haughton, White further noted, was purchased—along with this technology—in 1979 by a company that then should also have been well aware of the safety mechanisms. It was bought by Schindler Elevator Corporation.

The safety devices went back even further. Westinghouse Elevator Company was well aware of safety devices as far back as 1938, when it patented a type of comb-plate shutoff device, then invented another form of the device in 1978. Westinghouse (and thus its safety devices) was, like Haughton, also later bought by another company. Again, by Schindler Elevator.

Not only was Schindler well aware and in possession of the safety devices, but it had also retrofitted them onto existing escalators in other cities, including New York and Orlando. New York upgraded about 2,000 escalators citywide. Schindler did much of the work and completed it by New York's deadline of December 31, 1993. That, White pointed out under questioning by Kline, was almost three years before an escalator without an automatic comb-plate shutoff tore off Shareif Hall's foot. Similar retrofits were completed on escalators in Jersey City, New Jersey, and at Orlando Airport.

"Would little Shareif have his foot today if he was riding an escalator in Jersey City or Orlando, Florida, if it was a Schindler escalator?" Kline, standing near the jury box, asked his expert. Weiss objected. The judge overruled him, but Kline then withdrew the question. The answer was no longer necessary. Instead, he went on to a broader line of questioning.

> KLINE: *Sir, was the escalator at Broad and Columbia [Cecil B. Moore] defective and unsafe as manufactured and sold in 1984?*
>
> WHITE: *In my opinion, yes. Absolutely, it was.*
>
> Q: *. . . Was the escalator, sir, the escalator in question, defective and unsafe without a retrofit of the comb-plate shutoff device or the step-leveling shutoff device between 1984 and 1996?*
>
> A: *Yes, sir.*
>
> Q: *. . . Was Schindler negligent, sir? Did Schindler fall below the standard of a reasonable, prudent escalator company in failing to equip the escalator with the comb-plate shutoff device or the step-leveling device in 1984?*
>
> A: *In my opinion, they were.*
>
> Q: *. . . Were the Westinghouse and Schindler companies negligent in failing to take steps to retrofit and make available*

> the comb-plate shutoff device and the step-leveling device in
> the period from 1984 through 1996?
> A: Yes. Yes, sir. In my opinion, they were.
> Q: And, sir, was the conduct, was the conduct of Westinghouse
> and Schindler in reckless disregard of the safety of passen-
> gers on that escalator, including Shareif Hall?
> A: [after objections by Weiss] Yes, sir. I sincerely and honestly
> believe that it was reckless disregard. And, in addition, I
> think it was unconscionable with the superior knowledge that
> they had, far more than mine, for all of the years beforehand,
> not to have included it as standard as other companies within
> the industry, they did, and that they knew they did.

Now Kline asked a crucial question, one that he hoped would lead
the jury to a huge award. He wanted to know if Schindler's conduct was
so bad as to meet the criterion for a jury to award punitive damages.

> Q: Does the conduct rise to the level of outrageousness?
> A: Yes, sir, it is outrageous.

White, who, it seemed, had finished his answer, then launched
into a speech of sorts. The escalator expert was, as Kline would describe it, on "autopilot."

> WHITE: I don't mean to be a bleeding heart, or a Ralph Nader
> up here, but if you know that this kind of thing happens,
> and you know other companies have it [safety devices], and
> it's not that much more expensive on an expensive piece of
> machinery like this, and I have testified to this many times
> in almost every case where safety devices or lack of safety de-
> vices . . . I think it was outrageous. I think it was . . . reck-
> less disregard. Period.

Kline concluded by asking the witness his opinion of how the
accident happened. As if on cue, White requested to see Shareif's

torn shoe. He wanted it in his hand while he gave his answer. The twelve members of the jury had their eyes fixed on that little shoe as it rested in White's large hands.

> A: *The only way it could have happened, and the proof is in the shoe, is that it entered when the step was below the points of the comb-plate teeth, it can't be any other way. And those comb-plate teeth, as Mr. Fagan yesterday showed you, line up perfectly on this, right inside . . . part of the shoe, and these marks on the other side show the step continuing to go through.*

Weiss did little on cross-examination to unsettle White's expert opinion. He did ask whether SEPTA ever installed the additional safety devices, knowing full well the answer was no. Again, the goal was to blame SEPTA. Tucker immediately objected. Massiah-Jackson overruled, allowing the question but only after she herself poked a damaging hole in Weiss's premise.

> WEISS: *[to the judge] The relevance is—the suggestion has been made that SEPTA would have bought these upgrades if Schindler had made them available. My point is, the escalator has been running since they have known about them and they still haven't put them on.*
> MASSIAH-JACKSON: *Well, you know, in opening statements, SEPTA said they had no idea that such a thing would happen because such a thing had never happened before. If SEPTA had been informed of the comb-plate safety device, in all probability it would have been installed. Such as the side safety device, when they found out about it, they did put those in.*

Weiss continued the line of questioning, but Massiah-Jackson had taken the steam out of his argument. Although juries may doubt what lawyers tell them, they put unwavering stock in what judges say. Weiss wrapped up his questioning of Carl White a minute later, and Massiah-Jackson sent the jury home for the day.

Kline didn't go home. He went to his office to keep working on the case. It was a good thing he did.

WITH EXPERTS DONE, the rest of the case figured to be rudimentary. Not boring, just basic. The defendants had already agreed in advance—"stipulated" was the legal term—to allow Kline to enter testimony from reports given by other experts about Shareif's health care and medical costs. It had been agreed that rather than call the millwrights and their boss, Steve Krenzel, to the stand, Kline would be permitted to read key segments from their depositions. This would speed the trial along.

But first, Kline wanted to call one SEPTA employee as a witness. It might not amount to much, but he wanted Russell Figueira, SEPTA's director of Safety and Risk Management, on the stand. He would call Figueira as a hostile witness. Figueira had reviewed and signed off on SEPTA's investigative report filed on November 29, 1996, two days after the accident. There was something about that report that bothered Kline, and he wanted to get to the bottom of it. The report had described two screws that held in place the broken comb-plate at the top of the escalator as having been "sheared off." This meant the screws had been damaged as a result of the accident—a counterpoint to any suggestion Schindler might make that the comb-plate had been missing at the time of the accident. The screws' being "sheared off" demonstrated the force of the accident, a force so great—one expert estimated it at 1,600 pounds—that after it caught Shareif's foot, it had sliced through the two metal screws.

There was only one problem: The two screws that SEPTA had later produced for evidence, the two screws that Bill Kinkle had supposedly retrieved from the escalator pit, showed no sign of damage. They had not been sheared off or stripped of their threads or damaged in any way. They looked, to Kline's layman eyes, like two ordinary, undamaged screws. They even looked newer and shinier than the metal comb-plate. It looked as if maybe these two screws might not be the same two screws that had held the comb-plate in place on the day of the accident. Had new screws been substituted for the originals that SEPTA had said earlier were damaged in the accident? There was a conflict in the evidence. Something smelled fishy. If nothing else, this would show the jury that someone at SEPTA appeared to be lying.

Also, SEPTA's investigative report of the mishap seemed skimpy to Kline. Something was missing. SEPTA had tampered with evidence before, he was well aware. This had occurred only five months earlier in a case his firm had handled against the transit agency. That lawsuit involved an elderly woman who had tripped in a pothole formed next to a SEPTA trolley track in Center City and broke her hip. When the case finally made it to trial 20 months later, one of Kline's associates drove by the accident scene and noticed that the pothole still had not been fixed. He asked the judge to bring the jury there to see the hole for itself. The judge agreed and set a date for the following Monday. But when the jury went to the scene, it found no pothole. SEPTA had repaired it the night before.

Kline didn't know where his questioning of Figueira would lead. But he forsook the old adage that lawyers should never ask questions to which they didn't know the answers. Wherever his grilling of Figueira went, Kline wanted to explore this little mystery about the screws, wanted to ask about the report in open court first thing tomorrow morning.

It didn't take even that long.

KLINE WAS BACK in an office conference room, near-empty Chinese food containers and Diet Pepsi cans littering the long gray and white marble table, when, at 7:28 p.m., he walked down the corridor leading to his office and noticed the fax machine buzzing. The fax was from Leon Tucker. Kline skimmed the words as he walked back to the conference room; then he stopped in the hallway and read them more carefully. He could scarcely believe his eyes. What he held in front of him was a final accident report from the Hall case dated May 15, 1997. It contained some incredible information.

For one thing, it had information on those two screws that contradicted the original report. The screws had not been sheared off at all, SEPTA was now saying.

As Kline kept reading, something else grabbed his attention even more. It was a reference to another document, a memo dated May 4, 1996—six months before Shareif's accident—reviewing the condition of SEPTA's 27 escalators. It wasn't so much a report as an admission of guilt. It was the transit agency's own report, stating that the condition of its escalators was "poor and getting worse at an ever-increasing rate." Kline read the passage again. This was proof that SEPTA had known just how deplorable things had gotten systemwide.

Perhaps worse was that SEPTA had never shared this with the plaintiffs' counsel. That 1996 memo had shown up nowhere in the 44 pages of documents that SEPTA had handed over as part of discovery. The more he read, the more Kline's temperature rose.

WHEN THE TRIAL resumed the next morning, but before the jury was brought into the courtroom, Kline pounced. "Your Honor," he said, "this case has been in litigation about three years. We issued a request for production of documents, interrogatories, took depositions, during the course of discovery. Last night on the telefax at 7:28 p.m., approximately two hours after both of plaintiffs' liability expert witnesses testified, I received an accident investigation report on this very case—from SEPTA, prepared by the safety officer, signed off on by the director of System Safety, the director of Safety and Risk Management and the assistant general manager of SEPTA. . . . The conduct of SEPTA, Your Honor, I can tell you as a lawyer who's been at this bar practicing in this courthouse for over 20 years, and I regret to say it this way, is deplorable, unconscionable, and must be dealt with by this court. Plaintiffs are seeking contempt and a fine of $1 million."

At the mention of such an enormous fine, Kline heard snickering coming from the defense table. Surely, the lawyers' expressions said, this was Tom Kline grandstanding. But Kline meant it. For SEPTA to withhold important information from—not so much from him but from a little boy missing his foot—was a travesty. He looked over at the defense table. He didn't say a word, but he had a thought. *Just wait and see....*

Weiss was also upset that Schindler had received this information so late in the game. He demanded that the judge declare a mistrial. How could he conduct an adequate defense without the necessary information? He hadn't had the latest SEPTA documents in time to question Kline's expert witnesses, who by now had flown their separate ways, Fagan back to California and White to Colorado. Kline argued against a mistrial, and the judge eventually agreed the case would go on.

Tucker, for his part, pleaded ignorance. He told the judge he hadn't received the memo himself until that same night from Figueira. "As an officer of the court, I felt it incumbent upon me to produce it, not withhold it," he said. And he had, albeit after the trial was well underway.

What about the screws? Well, said Tucker, they never were sheared. The original report was simply wrong. "It was," insisted Tucker, "a matter of understanding, or misunderstanding." He said that to the SEPTA employee who had filed the report the term "sheared off" meant undamaged, that the screws had been pulled cleanly from the plate without damage. And Figueira hadn't known the difference (or the significance), either. "Mr. Figueira is not a mechanical person," said Tucker.

Maybe it was a misunderstanding, a matter of semantics. Maybe not. Kline had seen it all in his legal career, particularly in medical malpractice cases, where you would have thought health-care professionals were above cheating. But he'd seen sections of medical records altered with whiteout by doctors concealing mistakes, records missing important information, records missing altogether, even follow-up reports (Kline called them cover-your-ass reports) written by doctors and nurses—after things had gone wrong—that contradicted the official records. He'd seen plenty of cover-ups.

As for SEPTA's handing over its information late, Tucker told the judge that, too, was simply a mistake. "There was nothing willful about this. There was nothing malicious, underhanded. . . . Perhaps there was some negligence on the part of the client, but there was nothing sinister. There was nothing contemptuous. There was nothing done here to derail justice, or to hide anything." Massiah-Jackson seemed none too happy. Her tone bore a tinge of mockery.

"Have you sent any letters [or] faxes right away [to SEPTA] to put it on the record that you, as outside counsel, are outraged and concerned that you misrepresented to the court and to colleagues that you have produced all documents and, gee, would you look at what I have done?"

"I have spoken to them and let them know that I am indeed outraged," Tucker said about his client, SEPTA. "I am terribly upset, because it's a reflection on me."

Replied the judge: "It certainly is."

Kline continued to insist that SEPTA be cited with contempt for withholding important documents. "They have an attitude at SEPTA that they are immune from the courts of this commonwealth, that they don't have to comply with the rules of the game." It was not a sentiment reserved only for the Halls, but a sort of institutional indifference that was also well known by other people who had dealt with SEPTA, an ambivalence felt by victims of the government-related gargantuan. Massiah-Jackson responded that she would consider a contempt citation, but later. "Let's go. Let's go," she commanded the lawyers and signaled for the jury to be brought into the courtroom.

KLINE BEGAN DAY Three testimony by reading into the record SEPTA's cross-claim against Deneen Hall, a claim for which the transit agency had little or no evidence. Massiah-Jackson had barred any testimony about SEPTA's mystery witness, the unknown and unfound old lady.

Figueira took the witness stand. Kline asked for his job title at SEPTA—director of Safety and Risk Management—and ascertained that his duties had included investigating the accident involving Shareif. Then Kline threw a roundhouse, the blow direct and unexpected.

> Q: *What did Miss Hall do wrong, sir?*
> A: *Pardon me, sir?*
> Q: *What did Miss Hall do wrong that SEPTA sued her?*
> A: *I have no idea, sir.*
> Q: *Then why did they sue her?*
> A: *I have no idea, sir.*

Kline didn't let up. Instead, he now asked one of his favorite questions—maybe his very favorite. It was reserved for special occasions, when he had a witness cornered.

> Q: *Aren't you embarrassed as the director of risk safety that inspections weren't done on these escalators? Embarrassed?*
> A: *I personally feel terrible that they weren't done.*
> Q: *Yes, but I am asking you if you were embarrassed for SEPTA.*
> A: *I feel personally terrible that they weren't done.*
> Q: *Well, your personal feelings, sir, since you're here in a professional capacity, OK, do you feel professionally embarrassed, professionally embarrassed? Yes or no?*
> A: *If you are asking me whether I would have conducted inspections . . . .*
> Q: *No. No, I'm asking you if you are professionally embarrassed?*
> A: *I am embarrassed.*

Kline pummeled Figueira about the documents that had not been turned over, asking which SEPTA employees might have even more files pertinent to the case, and where one could find them. Exactly where.

> Q: *If you were a fellow about six-foot-three and in a black suit most days who was trying, on behalf of a little boy, to get the*

backup information, how would you go about it? Where
would I go? What, first of all, what address, so I know where
to go, what address?
A: *I would go to the legal department at 1234 Market Street.*
Q: *1234 Market Street. And what floor?*
A: *. . . the sixth floor.*
Q: *And now I want to find out where. 1234 Market, 6th floor,*
make a right or left?
A: *Depends on what door you go in, sir. You just ask.*
Q: *Tell me. Give me directions.*

Once he got the directions, Kline made an unusual request of
the judge. He wanted her to order Figueira to follow them, to walk
to SEPTA's offices during the lunch break and get any additional
documents pertaining to the accident. "Everything," Kline said. "In
other words, we want him to bring back the original file to the
courtroom." The judge told Figueira to take a walk.

And, she warned Tucker, "I can tell you this, if he comes back
here at two [o'clock] and says he didn't find it, it will be . . . it's not
going to be good." She then called Figueira to the bench and told
him to fetch "the entire investigative file that relates to this incident . . . all drafts, all memos, all photographs, any comments, anything." Massiah-Jackson had a generally pleasant way about her, her
soft features often forming a smile so large it forced her eyes into a
squint. But not now. She wasn't smiling now.

The judge added one other instruction to Figueira: "But don't
talk to Mr. Tucker about it. You just go back and riffle through
everybody's files that you have to riffle through." Even if it included the files of Jack Leary, SEPTA's general manager, Massiah-
Jackson said she didn't care. "Anybody!" she said, "You just get
those files. Tell them the judge said you have to."

In the interim, the jury heard from Dr. John Gregg, the orthopedic surgeon who treated Shareif after the accident at Children's Hospital of Philadelphia. He recalled for the jury seeing Shareif come
into the hospital, seeing the torn skin and broken bones and the

shredded tendons. He remembered seeing part of the boy's foot resting on ice, though he knew immediately the tissue was too torn apart, the remnants too small, to be usable. He described in some detail the operations Shareif had to undergo, from cleaning dirt from the wound to amputating his foot to removing the sutures. He told the jury of the "phantom pain" Shareif had felt in a foot that no longer existed. "They feel like they have pain in a part that's not there. And in adults it's a big problem. But in children, after a while, it goes away." He described how the muscle above Shareif's ankle, the calf muscle, shrank from lack of use. "He doesn't have a foot, so it atrophies."

THERE WAS A break in the trial as Figueira was out retrieving documents from SEPTA's main offices. Kline waited patiently in the courtroom, which had become taught and tense, very different from the trial's earlier days, which had allowed for occasional moments of levity. One such moment had occurred previously on a slow morning as the judge and both sides waited for a tardy witness. Massiah-Jackson had noticed Kline stretching in the back of the courtroom, an area known as the robing room, and motioned for him to approach the bench.

"Gee, you must have been working all night. You look tired," she said, smiling.

"No, not tired at all," Kline responded. He was used to getting by without much sleep during trial.

"And you have the same suit on."

"What do you mean?"

"Same suit you had on yesterday."

This really woke Kline up. A concerned expression crossed his face. He considered himself something of a clotheshorse, in the latest style, the best wools and silks.

"No, this is a different suit," he protested.

Massiah-Jackson was having fun at Kline's expense. She chuckled lightly, then confided to Kline that several of the jurors, in the pri-

vacy of the jury room, had mentioned to her bailiff that they
thought Kline wore the same black suit to court every day. "I guess
they think you only *own* one suit," she said. Though Kline was
hardly flashy, always wearing black suits and ties bereft of color,
the judge imagined that he spent a good buck on his clothes. But
here the jury thought he wore the same suit every day.

"The jury is really starting to feel sorry for you." The judge was
on a roll.

"Your Honor, my suits are very different, different fabrics . . . ."

"I'm not saying it's a bad thing. The jury maybe thinks that
you're very engrossed in the case, very committed, so committed
that you slept in your clothes."

"Your Honor."

"Maybe you ought to go home for lunch and put on a blue suit,"
she said, unable to hold back a hearty chuckle. "You do own a blue
suit, don't you?"

Kline smiled himself. "Yes, Your Honor," he said.

The judge could see Kline wasn't completely amused. He knew,
as did she, that juries, especially Philadelphia juries, watched everything very closely, especially the lawyers. And what they wore.
"Philly has a style," she would say. Though suburban juries might
not like the "sharp look"—lawyers wearing expensive suits or
flashy cufflinks—Philly juries expected it. A crisp suit, a flamboyant
tie, a piece of jewelry (even a Rolex or a gold bracelet for a man)
were not considered over the top in a city courtroom.

Kline was always impeccably dressed and not much for jewelry
or showy ties. He believed in simplicity in message and attire. But
when he returned to the courtroom, he was wearing a navy suit, albeit a very dark navy.

FIGUEIRA FINALLY RETURNED from 1234 Market Street, the 20-floor
steel-and-glass skyscraper that was SEPTA headquarters. It was an imposing place, with a massive lobby lined with polished travertine and
an atrium that contained a 50-foot steel sculpture. Figueira entered

this modern fortress—except for its size, the very antithesis of City Hall—and rode one of the 13 elevators to the sixth floor, walked down a carpeted corridor to his office and reached into a metal file cabinet. When he walked the two blocks back and into the courtroom, he held a canary yellow folder stuffed with documents, a lot more than the scant pages Kline had been given during discovery. Kline resumed his examination.

> KLINE: *Mr. Figueira, good afternoon.*
> FIGUEIRA: *Mr. Kline.*
> Q: *You were sent on an errand by the judge over the lunch hour, weren't you?*
> A: *Yes, sir.*
> Q: *And you went back and got the file, didn't you?*
> A: *Yes, sir.*
> Q: *Wasn't too hard to find, was it?*
> A: *No, sir.*
> Q: *SEPTA bought these nice Wilson Jones bright yellow files, didn't they?*
> A: *Yes, sir.*
> Q: *. . . And, sir, for a little boy who's bringing a claim, there's nothing funny about not getting the information that his lawyer is entitled to, is there?*
> A: *No, sir.*

This additional documentation—and the way it came to light—made an obvious impression on the jurors, a few of whom now leaned forward in their seats. It could not have worked out better for Kline had he received it all during discovery. SEPTA had not played fair, its duplicity evident in the file Figueira held in his hand. It wasn't just a claim by a lawyer; it was a fact that had surfaced right before the jury's eyes.

> Q: *You're aware of the fact, sir, that a substantial amount of*

this information was never produced. You know that now,
don't you?
A: *I'm getting that sense.*

The file contained typed reports and handwritten notations. One yellow Post-It note read: "Loose shoes and sneakers?" Figueira didn't know who had written the note or what it referred to. Kline pointed to various names that appeared on documents, names of other SEPTA officials who, presumably, knew of the documents' existence. Throughout the questioning, Figueira, though acknowledging poor maintenance, refused to concede that the accident was SEPTA's fault. Kline changed his approach, instead challenging SEPTA's claim that Deneen Hall had somehow brought this misery on herself and her son. Kline's voice had an edge to it now, though he knew he had to be careful lest he become the bad guy. But it was hard to be restrained.

Q: *You say SEPTA wasn't at fault? Here's the next question: Do*
you have any information that little Shareif deserved this?
A: *I don't think anybody could say he deserved this. I certainly*
could not say that.
Q: *Nobody deserves this?*
A: *Absolutely not. No.*
Q: *It's one of the most horrible things that could happen to a*
mom, to watch her little boy have his leg ripped off and
ground by an escalator. Correct?
A: *I certainly would not want it to happen to my child.*
Q: *I didn't ask you if you want it to happen to your child, but*
I thank you for telling us that. I asked if it was one of the
most horrible things that you could imagine.
A: *Yes, one of the most horrible things.*

The initial accident report filed by SEPTA two days after the mishap had mentioned sheared-off screws. Those screws were still on Kline's mind.

> Q: . . . *Where are the sheared-off screws? Let's have them. Did you bring them?*
> A: *No, sir. I don't have sheared-off screws. And in the final report, sheared-off screws were not mentioned.*
> Q: *Oh, in the final report, there's no sheared-off screws described?*
> A: *Uh-huh.*
> Q: *Let's take a look. Wait, the sheared-off screws, the cat ate them?*
> A: *No sir, it was an honest mistake.*
> Q: *The dog kicked them?*
> A: *No, sir.*

Kline ordinarily did not use sarcasm. It could backfire with juries. But he knew instinctively that he was in what he referred to as the "safe zone." He could sense the jury's ire. It was open season on SEPTA—though the transit agency executives seemed to take it all in stride, presumably because of the $250,000 cap on damages. This testimony might be discomforting, but so what?

Kline gave Figueira a chance to explain the mistake about the screws. James Bahn, the investigator on the case, Figueira testified, had thought that "sheared off" meant the screws were not damaged, that they had been "pulled out" cleanly from their sockets. But how could Figueira know what Bahn had thought? Kline sensed that the witnessed had been prepped, so he asked if that had been the case. "We discussed that this morning," Figueira responded.

Kline noticed that the final SEPTA accident report, which he had just seen for the first time, included a notation that one "probable cause" of the accident was a shoelace, that "the laces of the sneaker became entrapped between the steps allowing the child's foot to be drawn into the escalator." Figueira testified he hadn't written the report and that he had never seen the actual laces in question.

> Q: *Would you like to see the laces?*
> A: *If you would like to show them to me.*

Kline took a few steps to the evidence table and retrieved the piece of the tongue from Shareif's Fila shoe, the piece with the black lace still tied in a knot. He showed it to Figueira.

Q: *Double tied?*
A: *Yes, sir.*
Q: *Just like you expect a good mom to do, right?*

Kline then passed the tongue to the jurors. One by one they took the evidence, handling it gingerly, inspecting the tied black lace. As they passed it along, Kline had one more question for his witness.

Q: *... What evidence that the lace ends were entrapped do you see?*
A: *I don't see any, sir.*

The next day, Friday, began like most of the other days, with the lawyers making motions before Massiah-Jackson. Weiss grew more emphatic as the defense fared worse and worse. He wanted his client out of this case. This "whole debacle," as he termed the eleventh-hour discovery of more SEPTA documents, had rendered him and Schindler ill prepared.

"I have not had an opportunity to use these documents to ... conduct discovery with respect to these documents in order to prepare for trial," he told the judge before she called the jury in. "The prejudice, in my 26 years of practice, I have never seen such prejudice." The recently revealed SEPTA documents, Weiss said, showed just how badly the transit authority's escalators had been maintained; one memo from 1994 stated about escalator maintenance: "The work backlog is so large that only one-third of the required annual inspections were done in the past 12 months, and six escalators have not had an annual inspection since 1990, further eroding escalator reliability." Weiss's motion to the judge bordered on begging.

"I would never have known about these documents unless you had ordered the witness to go get the file. I have never been given an opportunity to review some of the attachments. They still have not been produced, judge. I mean, it's just, I have never been left so bare in terms of preparing for cross-examination of witnesses and preparing for trial and doing depositions and getting documents as I have in this instance. It's frightful."

One thing had to have been bothering Weiss immensely. Yes, the trial was going better for Schindler as things worsened for SEPTA, which was seeming more and more to be the "bad actor" in this drama. This would ordinarily have been good for Schindler, except for one thing: Under Pennsylvania law, if Schindler was found even 1 percent liable (and SEPTA, 99 percent), Kline could go after the escalator company for the bulk of the entire damage award, or that amount over SEPTA's $250,000 legal limit (or $500,000 if both Shareif and Deneen won verdicts). The law allowed the plaintiffs to collect from either defendant, and Kline was likely to go calling on the defendant with the most cash and no sovereign immunity. And that was Schindler. Kline's strategy had always been painfully apparent to Weiss. He knew that unless the jury found Schindler had zero liability, absolutely none, the company could get stuck holding almost the whole bag. This had to have been playing on Schindler's corporate mind as the odds of an adverse verdict and a large damage award seemed to be mounting.

Next before the judge was SEPTA's Leon Tucker. He asked the judge to bar Kline from discussing the newest documents in open court or from giving them to anyone. He apparently was worried about publicity, since he had spotted a newspaper reporter in the courtroom. Kline's response was swift: "Your Honor, as a resident and citizen of the City of Philadelphia and a rider of SEPTA"—Kline did in fact ride the 42 bus the 12 blocks to work some mornings—"I have a public obligation to make this public and I am going to. This is a public trial."

Massiah-Jackson agreed, and she ruled against Tucker.

In the days to come, Tucker would have more to concern him. The case of the little boy with the amputated foot had, like most civil cases, attracted little media attention when it started. But early on, Chris Brennan, a young reporter working the mass transit beat for the *Philadelphia Daily News,* happened onto the case and sensed that it had front-page possibilities. Soon afterward came Fox TV's Jennaphr Frederick and then Vernon Odom, a veteran reporter with ABC-affiliate Channel 6, whose nightly news shows had the city's highest viewer ratings. Odom, who had covered many of the city's biggest trials, liked the angle of David fighting Goliath that *Hall v. SEPTA* presented. He also knew that Kline had a flair for the dramatic. In later years, in fact, Kline would stage a one-man production titled *Trial as Theatre,* packing Philadelphia's 300-seat Wilma Theater to recreate portions of his most celebrated trials. As the stage lights dimmed, he recollected the workplace demise of a loving husband or reprised his closing speech about the drowning death of a mother's son—a clock ticking off the seconds while Kline assumed the role of the eight-year-old child, relating how the tragic last two-minutes of his life must have felt. Odom recalled with a chuckle the first time he had seen Kline in a courtroom, how when he had spotted the tall fellow with the thick peppery mane and the black suit, he had immediately taken him for a corporate lawyer. "When you first see him, you think he's got to be the bad guy. He looked like the railroad lawyer who tells you the train's going to come right through your backyard and you're not going to get paid for it," Odom would say years after the trial. "And then you see him go to work for the little people and start pounding the belly of the establishment and you want to start cheering for him . . . ."

A legion of TV cameras and radio and newspaper reporters were posted daily inside and outside the courtroom. Kline played to the throng, sparing no emotion in his condemnations of SEPTA. "Disgraceful! Shameful!" he exclaimed, citing the lack of maintenance of its escalators and the agency's behavior throughout the legal process. Maybe the media glare might force the agency to change its ways.

But Tucker wasn't finished. He told the judge that SEPTA had been treated unfairly. Because of the way the documents had surfaced in court and in front of the jury, he said, his client had been "portrayed in such a light as to prejudice SEPTA, and the prejudice by this jury is incurable. And we would ask for a mistrial, Your Honor."

The judge didn't ask the obvious question: If the way the documents came to be revealed prejudices the jury, whose fault is that? She denied the motion offhandedly, as a busy mother might have dismissed a complaining child.

TESTIMONY RESUMED, AND Kline began grilling Figueira for a second straight day. By this point, Kline had had a chance to sift through the contents of what he dubbed "the canary yellow file." He liked the imagery of a file so brightly colored; how could it have been missed? It contained several versions of the final report completed by SEPTA almost six months after the accident. One had been written May 7, another May 8, and the final version on May 15. These were the reports that Figueira had said a day earlier he had never seen. Yet Kline discovered that Figueira had made editing changes throughout the documents. The hot seat got hotter.

> KLINE: *And these documents have, contrary to what you told the jury yesterday about never having seen it before, your handwriting is all over these documents?*
>
> FIGUEIRA: *Sir, I didn't recall.*
>
> Q: *You edited the whole document, will you admit that to us now?*
>
> A: *I made some edits, yes.*
>
> Q: *On page two, you made one, two, three, four, five, six, seven, eight . . . eight to ten edits, correct?*
>
> A: *Yes.*
>
> Q: *On the third page . . . one, two, three, four, five, six, seven, eight, nine, ten to 12 edits on that page, correct?*
>
> A: *Yes.*
>
> Q: *You made . . . 40 or 50 edits on the document, correct?*
>
> A: *Yes.*
>
> Q: *And you came to court yesterday and told us that you didn't even know if you saw the document, because you might have been out with sciatica, correct?*

A: *Sir, I can explain. . . . I admit that I said I didn't remember*
seeing that report. I mentioned yesterday to the jury that I was
out with sciatica for a prolonged time. I was taking pain
killers and muscle relaxants. I was supposed to be home in
bed. I was in very bad shape. . . . I came back to work far
sooner than I should have come back to work and I was doing
my best, but the combinations of all kinds of things, includ-
ing the medication, probably caused me to forget. . . .
Q: *Can I ask you a question sir?*
A: *Yes.*
Q: *Were you on medication yesterday when you testified?*
A: *No.*

Figueira went on to list several other people who had knowledge or perhaps even copies of the report, including his direct supervisor, a department general manager, an assistant general manager, and the folks in SEPTA's legal department. Kline also discovered a memo asking that certain information be omitted from the report, including research the agency had done on other transit authorities and their escalators, for example, those in Washington, D.C. Such research was proof that SEPTA knew of new devices that could have been installed for safety's sake.

Kline brought up the 1994 memo that detailed the poor condition of SEPTA's escalators and asked Figueira who else would have received it. He named Judith Pierce, an assistant general manager at the time. So, Kline asked, "It was known then to one of the No. 2 people at SEPTA, correct?" Replied the witness, "Yes."

Kline dug out of the yellow file another memo, written by a consultant who stated that not only wasn't preventive maintenance being done, but SEPTA also had not assigned enough millwrights to maintain a regular inspection schedule. Figueira remembered seeing that memo. He even recalled one of his subordinates bringing him it to him and saying, "You're not going to believe this."

Q: *. . . When you saw this memo, you read it? This one you read?*

A: *Yes. Yes.*
Q: *You were shocked?*
A: *Very surprised.*
Q: *Shocked?*
A: *Uh-huh.*
Q: *Yes?*
A: *Yes.*

Figueira insisted he merely helped compile and edit the investigative reports, that he never was a part of the investigation, never personally went to inspect the scene. He said the employees from his office who compiled the report were, as he put it, like "fish out of water." That analogy brought another from Kline, which sparked a debate between Tucker and the judge that seemed comical. Except perhaps to Tucker.

KLINE: *Yes, and the fish out of water found a lot of rotten fish in the barrel, didn't you?*
TUCKER: *Objection.*
MASSIAH-JACKSON: *What's the basis of that?*
TUCKER: *To the characterization, Your Honor.*
MASSIAH-JACKSON: *Well, that was the witness's words.*
TUCKER: *No, he said rotten fish, and the witness didn't say anything about rotten fish.*
MASSIAH-JACKSON: *Talked about fish in a barrel. They got to be rotten if they're in a barrel.*
TUCKER: *Pardon me?*
MASSIAH-JACKSON: *Fish have to be rotten if they're in a barrel.*
TUCKER: *Why would that be, Your Honor?*
MASSIAH-JACKSON: *(to the witness) Just answer the question.*
KLINE: *... To use your characterization in the fish world, we are swimming there, these things you found would be like rotten fish, correct?*
FIGUEIRA: *All right. If you want to, if you want to say that, that's fine.*

When it was his turn to question Figueira, Tucker tried his best to undo the damage. He directed the witness's attention to one version of the accident report and a section in which were listed "probable causes" of the accident. Under No. 1, it stated: "The laces of the sneaker became entrapped between the steps, allowing the child's foot to be drawn into the escalator." Tucker handed him the piece of white shoelace. He then passed to Figueira a photo of the white shoelace positioned on top of Shareif's damaged black boot.

> TUCKER: *Does it appear to be comingled with the top of the boy's boot?"*
>
> FIGUEIRA: *Yes.*
>
> Q: *Would it be accurate to say that that photograph was taken within an hour after this accident?*
>
> A: *Yes.*
>
> TUCKER: *Your Honor, I would ask that the photograph be passed among the jury, please.*

The judge said she was confused. "I thought they had already seen the tied shoelaces. Yes, they saw the tied shoelaces already, the black one . . . , " she said. Tucker replied, saying he just wanted the jury to see the white lace also. "My only thought was that since it's a photograph of both of them together, that perhaps the jury would want to see that."

Massiah-Jackson still seemed puzzled, as did some jurors. Where had this photo with the untied white shoelace come from? How could the white shoelace have gotten on top of the black shoe? Kline knew damned well how it got there. Someone at SEPTA had placed it there, posed it for the photo. Yet Kline was relaxed and unruffled, and he did not object. He volunteered that it was all right with him for the jury to see the white shoelace and the photo. And the black, double-knotted shoelace as well. He wanted them to hold both, to see for themselves which lace matched the shoe leather. Jurors weren't stupid. Seeing SEPTA's "evidence" would only insult them. Or, worse for SEPTA, it would inflame them.

Tucker ended his questioning. Kline began redirect by asking Figueira about his education. He had earned a college degree, a master's degree in public administration, another master's degree in human resource management, and had begun course study for yet a third master's. Counting elementary school and high school, it all added up to about 20 years of formal education. Very impressive.

> Q: *And you're the guy who signed off on the report, correct? Four and four is eight, and 12, that's 20 years of education, correct?*
> A: *OK. Yes.*
> Q: *Now, I am going to ask you to try to figure something out for me, OK? Now, I am going to ask you a question, sir. If you have 40 years of education . . .*
> A: *Uh-huh?*
> Q: *. . . could you figure out, do you think you could figure out, that this [white] shoelace didn't come from this Fila boot that in a couple of minutes this mom is going to tell us she bought for her boy? Do you think you could figure that out, yes or no?*
> A: *I don't know. I wasn't there. I didn't see it. I only have a picture.*
> Q: *OK. Do you think if you had 60 years of education, you could figure it out?"*

Tucker bellowed an objection, that Kline was ridiculing Figueira. Normally, Massiah-Jackson might have agreed with him. But SEPTA had brought this upon itself. The piece of white shoelace was a mate to Shareif's black boot like a dog was to a cat. Even raising the notion seemed farcical.

> TUCKER: *Objection!*
> MASSIAH-JACKSON: *What's the basis?*
> TUCKER: *Asked and answered, Your Honor. He said he wasn't there.*

MASSIAH-JACKSON: *[asserting that Kline's questions were different]* *The first one was 20, then 40. So now, we are up to 60.*

KLINE: *I will withdraw it.*

MASSIAH-JACKSON: *OK.*

TUCKER: *I move for a mistrial!*

MASSIAH-JACKSON: *Based on what?*

TUCKER: *Based on the court's comments, on counsel's comments, and the accumulation of prejudice against my clients . . . . The court has influenced this jury now. My client is prejudiced and we cannot have a fair trial, Your Honor.*

MASSIAH-JACKSON: *Well, sir, you brought up the white shoelace for the first time in this trial.*

TUCKER: *I understand that.*

Tucker stood from his seat, pumped full of anger. It was one thing for Kline to appear to be ridiculing his client, quite another for the judge to join in. But there was nothing he could do about it.

MASSIAH-JACKSON: *You passed the pieces of white shoelaces with the photo. I am ruling, so you can have a seat now. You passed the piece of white shoelace with the photo asking the witness whether or not the white shoelace and the black tongue with the double tied shoelace comingled, I think those were the words you used . . . then you asked him whether or not the white shoelace came off the black boot, or something like that.*

TUCKER: *I don't recall asking him if he could [tell whether the white lace went with the black shoe], Your Honor.*

MASSIAH-JACKSON: *Maybe you didn't. That was the inference, you know . . . . Now, what Mr. Kline is doing is following up on your questions . . . .*

Massiah-Jackson paused and looked down from the dais and told Tucker: "I am not arguing. I am ruling. Your motion for mistrial is denied."

But still he refused to quit.

> TUCKER: *Your Honor . . . my basis for a mistrial is based solely on the overruling of the last objection and the comments that the court made, the snickering, and that type of thing. That's the basis of my mistrial.*
> MASSIAH-JACKSON: *I haven't snickered. The jury is falling out of their chairs, Mr. Tucker, but it wasn't me.*
> TUCKER: *Very well, Your Honor.*

Kline resumed his examination of Figueira, who now suggested the white shoelace explanation was merely cited in the report as a "possibility." Which led to another taunting question by Kline.

> Q: . . . *Would an accident investigator with a brain in his head suggest this in this report, yes or no? If they had these two pieces in their possession, would an accident investigator with a brain in his head suggest that this was the lace that caused the accident, yes or no?*

Figueira was defiant. "I will not concede," he said.

He didn't have to.

ALTHOUGH SEPTA WASN'T willing to concede anything, Schindler was. In fact, it was ready to surrender. The escalator maker must have come to realize two things: First, it was no longer the main target of the plaintiff's case and, second, it was, to use elevator parlance, going down. Now was its best opportunity to get out of the case.

Schindler's insurance agent from Zurich (the Zurich Insurance Company) arrived by way of Baltimore. He had taken the train that morning with the idea of settling the case. He had an offer to discuss. The judge's court crier, Boyd Taggart, ushered plaintiff's lawyers and Schindler's lawyers, Eric Weiss and Paul Brady, into a small conference room behind the courtroom. The room bore evidence of City Hall's former grandeur—intricately tiled walls, a fireplace lined with decorative tin and adorned with colorful mosaics. And also its decline—some tiles and parts of mosaics had fallen, leaving gaps filled with concrete. Someone had been saving these loose pieces, placing them on top of the mantel in the hope they would someday be cemented back into place. The players in *Hall v. Schindler* sat around an old, wooden table.

Schindler's insurance agent, Joe Kostkowski, made his offer. It was for a lot of money.

"Rejected," Kline said flatly, without a second's hesitation. He slumped slightly in his chair, legs crossed, looking as relaxed as if he'd been sitting at home in front of the fireplace. He peered at the insurance man. And launched into his "dress–down speech." It was something he delivered when he knew—and his opponent knew—that the fight was essentially over. That Kline had won and the opponent had lost.

"Look," Kline said, "you're on a runaway bus with no driver, and you're sitting all the way in the back and you can't stop. I'm giving you a chance to get off the bus."

"All right," said Kostkowski. "I'm listening."

"This is what you're going to have to pay to get off the bus. Here's the price." And then Kline mentioned a number. It was a large number. It was also a sum of money he felt certain Schindler's insurance company had never parted with before in an escalator case—but that it would now. The amount, Kline told the insurance agent, was fair. And, he said, there would be no more negotiating. "Take it or leave it. Pay that amount or we go continue the trial against Schindler," Kline said. Kostkowski said he would have to speak with his superiors. He left the room with Schindler's attorneys.

Ten minutes later, he was back. OK, Schindler would pay what Kline wanted. No haggling, no counteroffer. There was just one proviso: Schindler insisted that the amount of the settlement be kept confidential. Kline had refused confidentiality agreements in the past and would continue to do so in the future, most notably in a case against Motiva Enterprises, a Delaware oil refinery, where a worker was killed in a fiery explosion. Kline would settle that suit for $36.4 million, an amount believed to be a record in the United States for a single worker killed on the job. It was also an amount that Kline would insist be made public. And it was, the story carried in at least 15 television news reports and many newspaper stories.

Here, Kline was OK with keeping the settlement confidential. It wasn't as if Schindler had a hazardous workplace or was now producing a dangerous product; it was just this older model escalator. And the problem had been its upkeep and lack of upgrades, which were added to later models. He also had a duty to his client. He couldn't gamble on a verdict when Schindler was offering a fair settlement. It would ensure medical care and income for the rest of Shareif's life and also provide compensation for the pain and hardship he had suffered and would continue to suffer.

ABOUT THE SAME time, SEPTA also came forward with an offer. It was an amount Kline had asked for a long time ago—$500,000, the $250,000 cap each for Shareif and Deneen Hall.

SEPTA was offering the maximum it could, said Tucker. "Take it now, while the offer's available," he said.

"Thanks," Kline said, "but no thanks."

The jury, of course, knew none of this. As far as it was concerned, the trial simply continued, though now with just one defendant. The judge let Schindler out of the case—agreeing it had been prejudiced by the last-minute release of SEPTA documents—but Schindler also agreed to drop its counterclaim against the City of Philadelphia. Messrs. Weiss, Brady, and Jefferson, the city's attorney, went home.

Leon Tucker and his client, SEPTA, remained in court as the sole defendant.

As THE TRIAL was nearing an end, Shanin Specter telephoned his partner. He urged Kline to adopt a new strategy against the transit authority. It was a strategy he had used himself once before to get around the sovereign immunity the state had bestowed upon public agencies. It might work against SEPTA. Kline had rejected the idea, but Specter wanted him to reconsider.

Specter's own case had come a few years earlier against the Philadelphia Police Department and resulted in the city's paying $2.5 million—despite the $250,000 cap—to settle. A Philadelphia man, LeeMore Rich, and his seven-month-old son, were struck and killed by a speeding police car as Rich stood on a street corner with the baby carriage. Specter had filed his suit in federal court, not city or state courts, on the claim that the city had violated the victims' civil rights guaranteed under the U.S. Constitution. In the case of the Riches, it was their right to personal safety.

In researching his case, Specter had discovered other, smaller settlements paid off by the city to victims of similar accidents. Over roughly four years leading up to the death of his clients, he found, city police vehicles were involved in 3,800 collisions, most of them avoidable. A judge in the case, in allowing proceedings to go forward despite limited liability of the police department, had found that the city maintained "an implicit policy sanctioning reckless driving" by police.

Specter had not been satisfied with merely a financial settlement. As part of the deal, he got then–Police Commissioner John Timoney to agree to a series of reforms. Police officers no longer could drive alone until they logged at least 60 hours behind the wheel with a veteran officer. District commanders were given the power to suspend a driver "on the spot" for up to five days for reckless driving. And police drivers were no longer permitted to speed through stop signs or red lights, but had to slow to 10 mph.

In the SEPTA case, Specter felt there might be enough evidence to show that the transit agency, through its conduct—operating unsafe equipment and, now, hiding documents—also deprived Shareif Hall of his right to personal safety.

The strategy was a bit of a long shot, and not without hazards. Of greatest concern was the fact that a civil rights suit would give SEPTA the option of moving the case to federal court. That could mean starting the case over from scratch, and a delay of perhaps a year or more. Also, federal trials drew jurors from the entire court district comprising all of eastern Pennsylvania, whereas Common Pleas Court jurors came just from Philadelphia, a city considered plaintiff-friendly. A city-only jury would resemble the city itself— Democratic, liberal, poorer, and racially diverse. One that also included the outlying suburbs and farther-off places like Lancaster, would be the opposite—more Republican, conservative, affluent, and white. Less, in other words, like Shareif and Deneen Hall. Less a jury of their true peers. Less sympathetic.

To win such a civil rights claim, a plaintiff also had to show that a governmental agency had acted in "reckless disregard" of public safety. Kline had rejected the notion of a civil rights suit before because that element had been lacking. SEPTA clearly didn't intend for Shareif to get hurt, hadn't acted with malice. It had been negligent at worst. But now things had changed. SEPTA had indeed acted outrageously in trying to shirk its responsibility, cover up documents, hide the truth.

It was late on a Thursday night. Specter knew Kline would probably be home by now. He dialed his partner's number.

"Tom, it's an attempt by a state actor to seek to deny the life, liberty, or property to a citizen without due process. That's the language right from the Constitution. That's just what they did!"

"I know."

"You know, when I see a corporation hide or fabricate evidence, it makes me sick to my stomach. But when you see your own government do it...."

"It's disgusting."

"Go for it!" said Specter. "File a federal civil rights action."

"Shanin, the case is going really, really well right now. I don't want to lose momentum or lose this jury."

"Tom, I'm tellin' yuh," said Specter, drawling the word, a remnant of his father's upbringing in rural Russell, Kansas. "It's there. You've got a case for his civil rights being violated."

Kline knew from a defendant's previous attempt to remove him to federal court in a trial that he could "turn back" by withdrawing the federal claim. So there was little to lose by trying.

"Tom, you've got to go for it."

"Right," said Kline.

After Figueira's time on the stand, the rest of Kline's case seemed to go by in seconds. If you didn't listen carefully, you might miss something important. And SEPTA did.

On Friday afternoon, the last day of the trial's first week, Kline told the judge he planned to amend the lawsuit following the weekend recess. He didn't spell out his exact intention but this would be his civil rights motion. OK, Massiah-Jackson said matter-of-factly.

Rather than calling more witnesses, Kline now finished the week by reading the "best of" the depositions given months ago by three SEPTA employees. The witnesses included the two millwrights, Ray Mosley and Bill Kinkle, and their boss, Steve Krenzel. This rapid, staccato presentation of testimony had impact.

Mosley had been asked if he remembered anything about the shoe that was retrieved from the pit. He had gotten a good look at it but was hard pressed to remember details. He didn't even remember what color it was. But the little he did remember was just what Kline was looking for. It was a missing piece of the puzzle he was putting together to nail SEPTA.

Q: *Do you recall anything about the shoe as you sit here? If I were to ask you to describe the shoe, what would you tell me?*

A: *Well, the laces were tore off, that's all I know. Whatever was identifiable that was left of the shoe, that was it.*

Q: *What do you mean the laces were tore off?*

A: *Tore off. They were still tied . . . high–top shoes.*

Q: *Are you saying the laces were still tied?*
A: *Yes.*

Kinkle had testified that SEPTA ceased having the millwrights do daily inspections. "If we were assigned to do work on an escalator, that's about the time we would see it," he said. In other words, escalators were attended to when problems arose, not on any sort of regular schedule. This testimony was important because Krenzel, the assistant director of maintenance for SEPTA, had previously testified he wasn't aware that daily inspections were no longer being performed. And he had acknowledged that if that was the case, it "would create a problem." What kind of problem? "It could possibly compromise the safety," he had said. Now Kinkle had confirmed the fact.

KLINE ALSO QUIETLY entered the next testimony into the record, without witnesses or objections. It included information from Dr. S. Ross Noble, a physician specializing in rehabilitative medicine, who had examined Shareif and spoken about future complications he might suffer and additional surgeries he might have to endure; Jasen Walker, the vocational economist, who calculated the loss of Shareif's career earnings because of his amputation; Elizabeth Anne McGettigan, a nurse with U.S. Healthcare, who estimated the past and future costs for Shareif's health care and prostheses; and David Hopkins, an economic actuarial consultant, who tallied all the costs. This total did not include damages for pain and suffering nor punitive damages. It was just for actual expenses Shareif would have to bear. It came to about $1 million.

Kline's final witness was Deneen Hall. The jury had seen her sitting in the courtroom in the front row behind her lawyers' table for a week but had not heard her utter a word. They had heard her cry during some of the testimony, so uncontrollably at times that Massiah-Jackson had called a recess and asked Kline to control his client. Otherwise, Deneen merely sat and listened. She had come to court each day in casual clothes, mostly slacks and a shirt, all she had. Deneen still lived in the same cramped, second-floor apartment in the same North Philly neighborhood. She was working again, but her hours were limited and the job didn't pay much. And the trial was cutting into her hours. Each day she waited for the adjournment before boarding a SEPTA bus bound for the suburbs, where she worked an evening shift at a cash register in a Value City department store.

Kline didn't waste any time getting to the heart of the matter.

> Q: *Deneen, Miss Hall, I will call you Miss Hall during this part of the testimony. Miss Hall, did you do anything to hurt your little boy?*
> A: *No.*

Deneen relived for the jury the events of November 27, 1996. She had gone into the office with her boys for just a few hours to do the payroll. About 11 a.m. they left for home, riding the elevated train to City Hall, then transferring from the el to the Broad Street subway. When they arrived at the Cecil B. Moore Station, they got on the escalator to the street. Shaheed was on a step in front of her. Shareif was on the same step, next to her.

> Q: *And where was his left hand? Where was his left hand?*
> A: *In my hand.*
> Q: *Did you think he was secure?*
> A: *Yes.*
> Q: *And had you tied his shoes?*
> A: *Yes. I always check them, make sure their shoes are tied.*
> Q: *Before getting on an escalator?*
> A: *Before they go outside to play. Before anything.*
> Q: *That shoe that we see, that we see here, the black shoelaces . . . is that your knot that's in those laces?*
> A: *Yes. Because I usually tie it twice.*

Kline then pointed to the piece of white shoelace on the evidence table.

Q: *And if I can just step back for one minute. Is that Shareif's shoelace?*

A: *No.*

Q: *And before we continue, do you have any idea why SEPTA sued you and said that you owe your boy money?*

A: *No.*

Then Kline prompted Deneen to tell about the accident.

Q: *Tell us what happened. You're riding up the escalator....*

A: *We got to the top of the escalator, Shaheed steps off and I proceed to step off but Shareif wasn't coming off.... The escalator was still moving, so the only thing I could do was like stand there... the escalator was still moving, he's not moving, and I have no room to stand.... At first he was calm and then he started to scream.... I am grabbing him, try to see why he's not moving and, and I don't know, just seemed like forever he was stuck in this machine.... I could remember after it stopped, looking down, and my son's boot and his foot were gone. I had Shareif in my arms and all I am doing is looking up in the sky because I keep looking at his foot and it wasn't there. And all I can remember is asking God: What is going on?*

...And I seen two guys coming from the bottom of the stairway and the one guy screamed, like, "Oh shit!" Excuse me. "Oh, my God!" or something to that effect. And before I knew it, it was a guy in uniform, I believe he was police or SEPTA police, and he was saying, "You have to let him go!" And he finally took Shareif from me, he put him on the ground, he snatched the scarf... and tied it on his leg.

At the hospital, someone gave Deneen some pills to calm her down. "I couldn't stop crying," she said, her eyes damp now as well. The jurors seemed transfixed by her testimony. "They just took Shareif away from me, and when I calmed down, then they came to talk to me, and it was then that they told me what was probably going to happen." It was then they told her Shareif would lose his foot.

Deneen described the surgeries and the suffering.

> *Shareif was in a lot of pain and they couldn't give him any more medicine. They had gave him, as the nurse said, enough morphine to kill a horse. But they had to call in a special team because he wouldn't stop screaming. And these doctors came in, I don't know [from] where, they had to put him on a new medicine.*

Kline asked about the Fila shoes. They were fairly new, Deneen said, with good soles on them. She remembered how much she had paid for them, $65. When Shareif left the hospital, she could have used the shoe that was not torn in the accident. But she didn't have the heart to. She bought a new pair.

Deneen's testimony hung over the courtroom, each juror no doubt forming a mental picture of the gruesome scene at the subway station, the days of pain, the little boy in a sterile hospital, the agony, and the tears.

KLINE PAUSED TO allow the images to harden. The courtroom was still. Then Kline broke the silence with an announcement.

"We now have with us Shareif Hall."

Shareif, now seven years old, entered from a side door, walking to the front of the courtroom and straight toward the jury. Several jurors sat up. As they watched Shareif make his way to the witness stand, the faces of some showed obvious emotion. Until now, Shareif had spent most days of the trial at the offices of Kline & Specter, where the staff tried to make him comfortable and keep him entertained. The firm's legal assistants made daily trips to the nearby Dollar Store, where they bought him plastic toys. He would play with them for hours. Some days, however, he was bored and unhappy. One day he overstuffed a toilet, flooding the men's room. On another, he got hold of a clay figure of a golfer that was on an attorney's desk. When the clay golfer was found, it was missing a leg and an arm.

The jurors had never seen Shareif before, except in the pictures Kline had set up in court. Kline hadn't wanted the jury to become accustomed to seeing the child. He wanted his appearance to have an impact, and it did.

Shareif was a pretty child and shy, with an upper lip that pushed slightly forward, almost in a pout. His eyes were bright but down-cast. He seemed still stunned by the bright media lights and flash-ing cameras that had greeted him before he entered the vast courtroom. His gait was noticeably awkward. Shareif's prosthesis did not fit well. It slowly swivelled on his stump, turning out of po-sition, the shoe on the fake limb turning inward as he walked. Shareif would occasionally kick the crooked leg with his good foot to get it back in line. He did this automatically. He had become used to his deformity. That was good, yet it was sad to see.

Shareif sat on the carpeted floor in front of the jury box as Deneen, who had stepped from the witness stand, rolled up her son's pant leg, then rolled down his sock and removed the prosthesis. Jurors could see the withered brown stump of his leg. The skin at its base was a cream color, nearly white. A few of the jurors winced and turned their heads away. Shareif seemed impervious to it all. It was just their regular routine. Kline asked Deneen to describe the prosthesis.

> A: *I mean, I don't know how to explain it. I mean, this is what Shareif wears. It's his foot. That's his foot.*

As MONDAY MORNING began, the lawyers appeared before the judge. Tucker wanted either a mistrial or a judgment of "nonsuit," a dismissal. He said SEPTA had already offered Shareif Hall all it could offer—$250,000, which was still on the table. He suggested a mistrial was in order because with Schindler gone, SEPTA now sat alone at the defense table, giving the jury—unaware that a financial settlement had been made—the misimpression that Schindler hadn't done anything wrong. That, he asserted, constituted prejudice against SEPTA.

Hogwash, said Massiah-Jackson. Defendants were dropped from cases all the time. There would be no mistrial. She also refused to declare a "nonsuit." After all, Deneen Hall's claim remained undecided. And SEPTA's initial offer to pay $250,000 had come with "strings attached," namely the end of its liability for Deneen's suffering.

Kline also noted that there was a question of delay damages, interest that SEPTA could be forced to pay above and beyond the cap if the jury handed down a larger verdict. For instance, under Pennsylvania law at the time, if the jury awarded $10 million, SEPTA would pay not only the first $250,000 but also interest (at prime plus one percent) on the full $10 million, starting from one year after the defendant was served. In this case, that would come to more than $1 million. To determine delay damages in *Hall v. SEPTA*, the trial would have to go to verdict. So a "nonsuit" was out of the question, Kline said, regardless of whether SEPTA was willing to pay the $250,000. Massiah-Jackson nodded agreement, and noted that she had recently had such a case in which delay damages against SEPTA amounted to $1.5 million.

Kline wanted to take things one step further. He asked the judge to order SEPTA to start lining up witnesses for a contempt hearing. He hadn't forgotten, or forgiven, SEPTA for withholding documents. He wanted an investigation. He wanted SEPTA to tell the court "who knew what and when." He wanted SEPTA punished, and not just with a rap on the knuckles. He again demanded a $1 million fine. "There has to be some recognition by the court," he told Massiah-Jackson, "that some good may come out of telling SEPTA they have to play by the same rules that everybody plays by." The judge took the motion under advisement.

Getting back to the ongoing trial, Kline also gave notice that he wanted to question several more witnesses, rebuttal witnesses to whatever defense Tucker had planned. Kline wanted to call the past and present general managers of SEPTA, Louis Gambaccini and Jack Leary. He would subpoena them if necessary.

That wouldn't be necessary, however. Kline would not have to call any rebuttal witness because there would be nothing to rebut. Tucker made a sudden pronouncement that came as somewhat of a surprise to those in court.

"Your Honor," he said, "SEPTA is going to rest."

The transit agency would have no witnesses. It would present no defense.

And SEPTA was withdrawing its claim against Deneen Hall. It was no longer accusing her of causing her son's injury.

SEPTA evidently was hoping to simply pay its $250,000 cap and end the ordeal.

As morning turned into afternoon, the case seemed ready for closing arguments. But Specter had one more pitch to make to his partner. Kline was out in the hallway when his cell phone rang. Only a few people knew the number.

"Tom, you've got to do it," Specter implored. "File the civil rights claim! The SEPTA claims department tried to use its clout to deny a kid, a hurt kid, his day in court...."

Kline didn't answer. He just smiled to himself.

"This is intentional wrongdoing. Absolutely intentional! When they wrote the Civil Rights Act in 1864...." Specter was on his high horse now, in full gallop.

Kline was smiling broadly on the other end of the phone.

"Tom, you've gotta do it! Even if SEPTA tries to move the trial to federal court you can...."

"Shanin...."

"I'm tellin yuh, it'll work."

"We are."

"What?"

"I have it covered. We're going to do it right now. As soon as we get started. Any minute now."

A MOMENT LATER the plaintiffs made the following motion:

> *Your Honor, in light of what we did not know coming into this trial concerning SEPTA and what SEPTA knew about these escalators, and that's all related to the documents that were not produced to us prior to the trial starting. We know a number of things now from those documents, including the fact that these escalators were extremely dangerous for passenger use, and that SEPTA knew it and nonetheless kept the escalators in operation, leading to many other things, [including] the child's injury.*
>
> *In light of what we now know from those SEPTA documents, we would like to submit appropriate points for charge for the jury's consideration of whether or not SEPTA had deprived the minor plaintiff of his constitutional rights . . . whether or not he was deprived of his life and liberty, in particular, his liberty, and his right to be free from bodily injury.*

The plaintiffs were claiming a violation of the 14th Amendment, which states that no state shall deprive any person of life, liberty, or property without due process of law. An argument that Shareif's civil rights had been violated turned the notion of sovereign immunity on its head: Being a public entity afforded SEPTA some limits on liability, but it also placed on the agency's shoulders certain responsibilities.

Tucker was floored. He appealed to the judge not to allow the suit to be altered.

> TUCKER: *Obviously, I am at an extreme disadvantage. If the plaintiffs were aware that they were going to make this motion, I think out of an, as a matter of fundamentals, I should have been notified . . . .*
>
> MASSIAH-JACKSON: *. . . Except that Mr. Kline did mention it . . . . I don't remember if it was Thursday or Friday, but I know he did make reference to it.*
>
> KLINE: *And far be it from SEPTA to complain about late notice.*

Tucker pleaded for time to research the issue and consult with a constitutional expert, as Kline had done over the weekend. Kline had had an entire weekend; Tucker wanted 20 minutes. Had he known that Kline would be making such a claim, he said, he might have done things differently, might have put on a defense, might have had someone at SEPTA testify that there was no intent to deprive Shareif of his constitutional rights. Twenty minutes was all he wanted.

Kline argued that Tucker should get no time for consultations on the question. He had told the court, with Tucker present, on the previous Friday that he planned to amend the lawsuit. He just hadn't said how. Tucker could have asked; he just hadn't.

Tucker pressed: "Your Honor, we are supposedly minutes away from doing a closing statement. I just think that it would be inappropriate for the court at this juncture to allow them to amend their complaint...."

This was "the exact appropriate time," Kline argued, since the judge had not yet given her instructions to the jury. And besides, he said, it was SEPTA's own fault he could not file such a claim earlier. "SEPTA put us in this position.... Had they produced that file during discovery a year ago, when they should have produced it, we would have raised this claim a year ago."

Massiah-Jackson agreed: "And what SEPTA has done is put itself in this predicament, and I don't know how else to explain that. SEPTA has brought this upon itself."

Tucker was furious.

He could have parried—really, the mere threat would have sufficed—to switch the case to federal court. Then Kline would have had to withdraw his motion. And immediately. He stood poised to fold his cards.

But Tucker made no such motion. He let the case go on as it was. Kline let a small sigh escape his lips. *Hall v. SEPTA* had just become something more than just a "cap case," much more.

Closing arguments would be interesting. It seemed pretty obvious what Kline would say. The only question was: How deep would he plunge the knife? He felt that this jury despised SEPTA. Still, Kline wanted to be certain, and certain that the 12 jurors would have no qualms about giving Shareif a large award. He didn't think they would mind if he roughed up the transit agency one more time. Hell, they looked eager to hear it. Kline didn't disappoint them.

> *I thought about this whole thing last night again, much like I have been thinking about it for two years. But Shareif, of course, has been living this horror for two years. And I want to come to you today as a fellow citizen and tell you why it is so important to do right here in this case. This is big. And Shareif Hall never should have been injured on that escalator. He was injured because of the callous and reckless indifference of SEPTA. And you saw here with your own eyes, and I saw some laughter, but it was really laughter in disgust. And I saw some tears, and those are the tears that you can't help but have if you are a human being.*
>
> *. . . It happened because SEPTA, which we all ride, all of us, and depend on, was callous and reckless and uncaring. Then they decide in the end not to defend themselves. Oh, Mr. Tucker will give a closing speech, but I guess that's his job. But they have nothing to say.*

Kline talked about how Shareif had been "maimed, maimed and deformed by them" and how the child would have to live with pain and awkwardness, embarrassment and humiliation, for the rest of his life, projected by experts to be roughly 26,000 more days. He mentioned to the jury that SEPTA "never said they were sorry. And do you know why? You know why? Because their answer, their answer is to keep it in the file cabinet," referring to SEPTA's concealing documents. Kline accused some SEPTA officials of having lost their "moral compass." None of SEPTA's highest-ranking executives had bothered to testify. A drama had unfolded, Kline reminded the jury, before its very eyes, a drama during which SEPTA was forced to come clean about the deplorable condition of its escalators.

> *... Their secret is out. And you are the voice of the community.*
> *You're standing between them and their persistent neglect, their*
> *persistent arrogance .... Where is that white shoelace? It's on*
> *the floor, where it belongs. You're allowed to do things besides*
> *just, besides just award money. You can award the shoelace to*
> *Mr. Tucker. And you should tell him to put it in a brown enve-*
> *lope—I told you we were going to laugh, we are going to laugh*
> *and we are going to cry—put it in a brown envelope ... and*
> *send it to Mr. Leary at SEPTA. Would you do that, Mr. Tucker?*

As Kline spoke, a photograph was placed on an oversized easel.
The photo was SEPTA's photo of the white shoelace on top of
Shareif's shoe. It had been placed there in a loose loop, made to
look almost as if it had been tied there. Or untied. Kline looked at
the photo with disgust.

> *... Whatever figure you come up with, and I cannot suggest to*
> *you a figure, that's in your province, as the court says, but on*
> *the jury slip will you put $65 at the end of the number? You*
> *know why: because they haven't even offered to pay for the shoes.*

He also asked the jury to be generous with Shareif Hall.

> *I have never told a jury, but I am going to tell you, err on the*
> *side of giving him everything. Everything. No little boy could*
> *be more deserving than this plaintiff. You saw him here. What*
> *in God's name did he ever do to anybody, let alone SEPTA?*

Hitting his stride, a sort of closing cadence, Kline reminded the
jury of Shareif, who had left the courtroom after his brief appearance.

> *A more handsome little guy you will never see.*

And of how, because of the accident, he would suffer for the rest
of his life.

It is Shareif who, every night, will take that prosthesis off.

Kline delineated the claims for which the jury might award damages.

What amount of money would any person accept to have done to them what Shareif had done to him? . . . It's a horror. . . . Every time that he has phantom limb pain, every time that he goes to kick a football, every time he wants to play with the other children, every time that he wants to run down the street. . . . The school children will tease him. . . . Every time this young man, and as he grows to be an older man . . . every time that somebody looks at him, he will know what they're looking at.

Was there any question that SEPTA was negligent? But it went beyond just negligence, Kline said. SEPTA showed "deliberate indifference," enough to "shock the conscience." Both were tests of whether SEPTA violated Shareif's civil rights.

This case went beyond, as the evidence showed, way beyond, way beyond somebody just forgetting to do something. You see, that's negligence. . . . This was callous disregard. . . . A public carrier has an obligation to do things safely. They have a duty to regard the public highly, and to make sure that people don't get their legs ripped off.

Tucker was up for the defense. He began by coming clean.

When I last spoke to you [at opening arguments] a lot of things have changed since, obviously . . . I suggested to you at that time that my client had no knowledge of certain things, and you have since learned that perhaps there was knowledge of certain things. . . . What happened to Shareif is inexcusable. . . . I am not going to stand before you and tell you that there's an excuse for what happened. There isn't an excuse for what happened.

Tucker seemed perfunctory, especially compared to Kline. He tried to deflect blame to Schindler Elevator, quoting Kline's expert, Carl White, who had testified about safety devices that could have automatically shut the escalator down but which had never been brought to SEPTA's attention.

Tucker seemed almost to be conceding the verdict, turning his attention now to minimizing any damage award. "It's not about money," he told the jury. "Money will not bring his foot back." It was a statement Tucker would repeat toward the end of his closing:

> If there was a way that Shareif could get his foot back to play like kids normally play, if that could be done, I am certain it would be done. But it can't be done. And no amount of money is going to bring that back to him.

Tucker used the bulk of his speech to deny that a civil rights claim existed, summoning a bit of emotion in denying that SEPTA had been deliberately indifferent. He insisted there was proof, in fact, of the opposite: Though SEPTA's maintenance may have been shoddy, it nevertheless did make some repairs, with its millwrights trying desperately to keep up with the work despite depleted manpower. "That's not deliberate indifference," he said. And, after all, Tucker added, the memos were produced at trial, albeit late.

> It's not as though the management and people at SEPTA just turned their eyes, their head on their riders, and didn't care. They did care. If they didn't, that memo would not have been produced, the memo of May 4, 1996, I believe it was, that set forth those [poor escalator] conditions. They cared and they still care.

Figueira, he said, could have chosen to return to the courtroom after that lunch break without that canary yellow file folder.

> He could have just as easily come back to court and said, "Judge Jackson, couldn't find the files. There's nothing there." He

could have done that, but he didn't. He cared. He knew that
he had a moral obligation to do the right thing . . . It's not as
though SEPTA is some, just a big brick or block building some-
where. SEPTA is composed of people, people who care . . . .
Thank you very much. On behalf of SEPTA, I thank you.

Tucker's closing was clearly not intended to try to get SEPTA completely off the hook, but rather to keep the damages to a minimum—hopefully the $250,000 cap. He could do this if the jury found no violation of Shareif Hall's civil rights. Tucker could still win this case, at least from a monetary point of view.

Kline was not impressed with SEPTA's stated level of caring, nor did he share Tucker's view that Figueira had acted valiantly by turning over those documents, that he was some sort of hero for not committing perjury. Kline shot his opponent a look as he rose for his rebuttal. His last words, the last words either lawyer would speak in the case, poured out almost as a sonnet, a searing, scornful sonnet.

I thank you very much on behalf of SEPTA, so does Shareif. I
hope that Mr. Tucker has been well compensated for his
speech. "Septa cares." The new slogan for SEPTA.

SEPTA cares so much about Shareif Hall that they let the
escalator be in disrepair for two and a half years or more.

SEPTA cares so much for Shareif Hall that they never fixed
the escalator.

SEPTA cares so much for Shareif Hall that they never in-
spected the escalator, daily or monthly or annually.

SEPTA cares so much about you that they didn't bring in
one witness.

SEPTA cares so much for the legal process that they didn't
bring in the documents until they were forced to bring in the
documents.

Mr. Figueira is such a good man that he was afraid that he
would get thrown in the slammer by Her Honor if he didn't
bring that document back.

SEPTA cares so much about the legal process and about you and me that they hid the May 4, 1998, memo.

SEPTA cares so much about Shareif Hall that they didn't do anything, nothing about those escalators.

SEPTA cares so much about the other escalators that the City Hall South escalator has been down, or was down, for nine years and used for spare parts. Last time I looked, that was, that was the center of the city. It's where William Penn stands.

Now Kline delivered the final blow.

They don't give a damn for Shareif. The only reason that they're trying to even offer a speech is because they have nothing to say, and they're trying to say something. And then they have the gall, the gall, the unmitigated gall to suggest that no amount of money could put his foot back. Oh, there's an amount of money that could compensate him.

Wake them up. Wake them up!

CHAPTER 18

A BOMB

A FTER MORE THAN A YEAR of work, of court motions and court rulings, of research, discovery, and depositions, Shanin Specter was ready to go to trial against Daisy. A trial date was set. In about two months, the opposing parties would walk into federal court in Philadelphia and pick a jury, then call the first witness. D-Day was on the horizon.

And then Don Sonlin called. Sonlin was litigation supervisor for the Chubb Insurance Group, Daisy's principal carrier. Sonlin wanted to talk. That could mean only one thing. Daisy was willing to settle the case, or at least test the waters for a deal. This, of course, was a good sign. Specter felt he had a solid case. Daisy had to be worried. The only question was what Daisy would offer, not that it mattered. Specter knew exactly what his answer would be to Daisy's initial offer—whatever it was. The answer was no. Specter knew how much he would accept. Anything less, and he was ready to deliver his opening argument.

Settlement talks were nothing new. The vast majority of personal injury cases settled. Probably 90 percent, somewhat less for Kline & Specter, whose lawyers built strong cases they wanted to bring before a judge and jury. Still, if the goal was to get money for injured clients, a settlement was the route most traveled.

Settlement negotiations also were a strange, bittersweet time for plaintiffs' attorneys, dredging up an internal conflict that was sometimes hard to reconcile. On one hand, it was a victory in which the enemy handed over the spoils, albeit after only a partial surrender. But on the other, settlements were often a letdown, at least for Specter—after spending months, sometimes years, prepping for a case, sharpening his weapons and psyche for the ultimate battle, only to lay down his arms on the eve of engagement. Even when it meant a hefty check, Specter often disliked settling.

If the Daisy case settled, he'd make the company pay a steep price. Up until now, Daisy's settlements in other cases, Specter felt, had been inadequate, especially since many of its victims would have to pay with lifetimes of pain and suffering. And most had long lives ahead of them. They were only boys.

Daisy had settled some suits involving serious injury for as little as $300,000. Few went to trial.

In one case that did make it to trial, the results were far different. It occurred in Michigan and involved the shooting of a two year old, Joshua Rewis, the day after Christmas in 1982. Little Joshua was shot by an older boy who thought his BB gun was unloaded (and who had previously "dry fired" it nine times). Joshua was left badly brain damaged. The jury awarded $14 million. The Rewis family, seeking to avoid a prolonged appeal, later settled for about $10 million.

But the Rewis case was different from the Mahoneys' in one important aspect: There had been no claim of BBs lodging in the gun. It wasn't even known in 1982 that BBs did get jammed in the magazine. The Rewis suit instead theorized that the fault lay with the gun's gravity feed system, in which BBs basically free-fell into the firing chamber instead of being pushed in by a spring mechanism. The suit claimed the system was unreliable. But Specter had proof of a defect and proof that Daisy had known about it.

In the years since that tragedy, Daisy had not had to make another payment as large. The largest of them all—at least among those that were disclosed—was the $5 million settlement arising from the 1994 case of Tony Washburn, the eight-year-old Michigan boy who had suffered brain damage after he was shot by a gun believed to be unloaded. That $5 million was the most that Daisy had paid out in nearly two decades since Joshua Rewis was hurt. But Specter felt his case could produce more. It had a concrete foundation formed with the knowledge gleaned from prior lawsuits. His own additional discoveries completed a tall and sound edifice.

Specter had already met once with Sonlin, but it had been a typical first-round affair, with the combatants pawing about, feeling for each other's strengths and weaknesses. No haymakers were thrown, none landed. Each was testing the other's resolve, trying to learn something without exposing themselves. The meeting lived up to expectations. It was cordial and accomplished little.

But something that arose toward the end of that session struck Specter as odd. Before he left, Sonlin had asked a question about the Daisy guns that Specter hadn't heard before. It was a strange question, delivered in an offhand fashion.

"Do you think it was possible for two BBs to get lodged in that gun?" Sonlin asked.

"Why do you ask?" said Specter. The question seemed to come from left field.

"Just curious. You think it's possible?"

"Well, we haven't looked at that carefully because there was no reason to."

"But do you think it's possible?"

"I don't know."

Specter didn't give it another thought. Perhaps he should have.

Now, several weeks later, on October 24, Sonlin once again stepped off the elevator and walked straight back to Specter's corner office. The receptionist didn't have to show him the way. He'd been there before on other cases. Also, Kline and Specter had their own policies with Chubb. (Lawyers can get sued, too.)

Sonlin and Specter greeted each other with a friendly handshake, because there truly was no bad blood between them. Sonlin took a seat on the burnt–orange leather sofa, sun streaming in from the glass ceiling on the building's top floor onto Specter's double-wide partner's desk. The office was sprinkled with photos of Specter and his family, hugging his wife in one, holding a toddler in another. A pair of tickets from a St. Louis Cardinals game were encased in Lucite on a windowsill. The tickets were dated September 8, 1998, the date that Mark McGwire broke Roger Maris's 1961 record by hitting his 62nd home run of the season. The day before, when McGwire had tied the record, Specter had announced, "Tomorrow's going to be the day." He grabbed his wife and Kline and Kline's son Zac and hopped a plane the next morning for St. Louis, where he was among the 43,688 to bear witness to McGwire's fourth-inning line drive that curled just over the fence in the left–field corner.

Nothing was outwardly imposing about Specter's office. No noticeable pictures of Specter's prominent father. (Actually, there was one, but it was angled so that only he could see it.) No photos of Shanin Specter mugging it up with governors or presidents.

But a visitor should not have been fooled. There was nothing light-hearted about the man who occupied this space. Specter, though always soft-spoken and courteous, was all business. Here, he held the upper hand. He sat at his desk, illuminated by the afternoon sun.

But Sonlin had not come unarmed. He carried a potential bomb, a bit of information the folks at Daisy felt could detonate the plaintiff's entire claim, or at least convince Specter to accept a lowball settlement. It was only a question of when Sonlin would light the fuse.

"Hey, Don, how are you?"

"Good. How about yourself?" asked Sonlin, also acknowledging Andy Youman, who was sitting in on the meeting.

"Wonderful," said Specter, a sincere smile on his face. Specter felt empathy for Sonlin, whose own child, he knew, had been badly injured because of medical negligence. The Sonlins had sued and won an award that was covered, no doubt, by an insurance company. The whole story was sadly ironic. It had concluded with Sonlin—a man in the business of battling personal injury claims—forever etched in case history as a successful plaintiff in a personal injury case.

"How is your child?"

"Oh, you know. It's tough . . . . "

"It must be. You worry so much about your kids."

"I know," Sonlin said. Then he referred to the case at hand and Tucker Mahoney. "This is a tough one."

"Tell me."

"Poor kid," Sonlin said, meaning it. "And money can only do so much, only mean so much."

"It's a thoroughly insufficient method of compensation for such severe injuries," agreed Specter, who in 18 years had witnessed all sorts of catastrophic injuries, many of them to children. "Yet it's the only way that we human beings have for dealing with an injury . . . ."

"Yep."

". . . absent the uncivilized means that exist in other countries. Or in the Bible."

The small talk departed as quickly as it had arrived.

"I have an offer," said Sonlin.

"Go ahead."

"I'm going to offer you a lot of money today but before I do . . . do you remember that question I asked a while back?"

"Which?"

"Do you think two BBs could have gotten lodged in that gun?"

"This again?"

"Do you think they could?"

"Why are you asking?"

"Well," said Sonlin, his words coming slowly as he pulled a single sheet of paper from his brief case.

It was the bomb.

"There's been a big debate on our side over whether to give this thing to you," Sonlin said, still holding the paper a distance away, giving Specter time to wonder what it was. "Some of the lawyers said not to. They wanted to spring it at trial, as a surprise."

"What is it?"

"I wanted to give it to you. They didn't," Sonlin continued. He let the moment linger.

"Here," he said, finally, "I'll show it to you."

The fuse had been lit.

Specter opened his gold-rim reading glasses. What he peered down at was a half-page statement from John Kenderdine, someone Specter hadn't heard a word about for a long time. Kenderdine was the Solebury policeman who had investigated the Mahoney shooting. He had interviewed the families of Tucker and Ty, gone to the hospital and retrieved the BB that doctors had removed from Tucker's brain, and had taken the gun from Tucker's home. His statement was dated February 23, 2000. The date in itself was peculiar—nine months after the accident. It was also eight months before Specter's meeting now with Sonlin, meaning that Daisy had been hiding the statement under its sleeve all this time. Handwritten, not typed, it read:

> My name is John Kenderdine. I have been a police officer with Solebury Police Department for 28 years. On May 25, 1999, at 1:35 a.m., I took possession of the BB gun. When I picked up the gun, I heard the rattle of BBs in the gun. There were two or more BBs in the gun. I did not bang or bump the rifle before hearing it. I have read this statement. The foregoing is true and correct.

If indeed true, the statement contradicted the word of Ty Weatherby, who had told the police and testified in depositions that he heard no BBs, that he believed the gun was empty when he fired it at Tucker. If true, it meant that he had fired a gun loaded with several BBs, that Ty, the only eyewitness to the incident able to talk to the authorities, had made an awful mistake. Or that he was lying. If true, it cast doubt on whether there was a defect in the gun that resulted in Tucker's being shot. This was potentially devastating to Specter's case and could completely exonerate Daisy. If it was true.

Specter knew it wasn't. Not only had Ty told police he thought the gun was empty, but nobody else who inspected it afterward—including the district attorney's office—had found any other BBs.

The gun had not been opened until a joint inspection with Daisy, which revealed no BBs inside. Why Kenderdine would say such a thing and put it in writing for Daisy, Specter didn't know. He had his suspicions, but he didn't know for sure.

"Wow, this is something," he said after reading the statement. Now Specter let *his* comments hang in the air. He allowed Sonlin an illusory taste of triumph.

"Now, let me tell you about the offer," said Sonlin, a shaky, uncertain smile on his face. "Ten million dollars."

The sum was staggering. Rarely, if ever, was an opening offer so generous in this type of case. Daisy was no General Motors. It had only paid that amount once before, many years ago in the Rewis case, and only after losing in court. Youman got a lump in his throat when he heard the offer. He had never heard eight figures mentioned to start a negotiation. Specter's response, delivered without missing a beat, almost threw Youman out of his chair.

"You're crazy," Specter said.

"What?" said Sonlin.

"I said you're crazy. Why would you fellas be offering this kind of money, I mean $10 million, when you have this perfect defense here?" Specter held the Kenderdine statement aloft.

Sonlin's brow scrunched up a bit. "What are you...."

"This statement, from this cop, it gives you a perfect defense. If there were BBs in the gun, well...."

"Well, I don't know what was in the gun...," Sonlin started to say, but Specter didn't let him finish.

"Why would you be willing to part with $10 million if you have this?"

"I'm not sure what it is. You know, it's just what he heard...."

"I mean, you know I'm a Chubb policyholder myself and I'm thinking now that maybe I should change carriers," Specter chided Sonlin. "My rate is obviously inflated by your company settling cases that aren't meritorious. You're offering $10 million for a case that's without merit? I can't believe it."

"Well...."

"Because if this statement is true, and you must think it is, you wouldn't be offering me this $10 million because you have a perfect defense. This $10 million is ridiculously high."

Sonlin didn't say much, seeing that the Kenderdine statement had not had its desired effect. Hardly. Rather than intimidating Specter, it had brought disdain. Even worse, mockery.

"Hey, Tom. Tom!" Specter shouted through the doorway that separated his office from his partner's. "Can you come in here for a sec? You gotta see this!" Specter wore a thin smile now.

"What's up?" Kline appeared in the doorway. "Oh, hi, Don." Kline had had dealings with Sonlin in the past as well.

"Tom."

"You won't believe this," Specter said to his partner. "You can't imagine what our homeowner's carrier is doing. They're offering us all this money in the Mahoney case and they have this statement that gives them a perfect defense."

"Hmmm." Kline was reading Kenderdine's statement.

"Tom, don't you think we should get a different homeowners' carrier?"

"Damn!" said Kline, playing along. "Maybe we need to."

"I mean, look at this...."

"Oh, yeah. That's very generous of them knowing they have this...."

"Don't you think?"

"Oh, yeah."

Sonlin let the teasing continue until Kline went back to whatever he had been doing and Specter sat back down. Then Sonlin spoke, seeking an earnest response from Specter.

"What do you think?"

"I think it's bullshit," said Specter, now showing a flash of genuine anger. "I think it's bullshit and I think this is a violation of the federal rules of civil procedure."

"Oh, c'mon."

"C'mon, nothing. You've had this since last February and you spring this on us now. And some of your lawyers wanted to keep it quiet until trial? And besides, it's bullshit. No one else found any BBs in the gun. This statement isn't true, and, what's more, you know it isn't true or you wouldn't be offering this kind of money."

Specter said he wouldn't take the $10 million, wouldn't even consider it.

"What's more," he told Sonlin. "I plan to get to the bottom of this, this statement from this cop. Whether it helps me or it helps you, I don't care. I aim to get to the bottom of it. And I will."

Sonlin asked for the Kenderdine statement back. He wouldn't even let Specter make a photocopy, saying he wasn't authorized to do that. He took back the paper and then gathered up his coat and briefcase.

Two weeks went by. Sonlin arrived for another meeting.

"I have another offer," he announced.

"Uh-huh."

"Twelve million."

"Don...," said Specter, exasperation in his voice.

"It's a very good offer, Shanin."

"No, it isn't."

"What do you want?"

"I'll take something off the policy, but not much," said Specter. This was lawyers' code, meaning that Specter wanted almost the full amount for which Daisy had insurance coverage. That, he knew, added up to $20 million—the first $1 million as Daisy's deductible, $4 million from a secondary policy with the Zurich Insurance Company and $15 million from the excess policy with Chubb.

"Don, you know, because you guys at Chubb are such square shooters, I'll knock something off, say 10 percent." Again, code. That meant that Specter, without actually naming a number, would settle for Daisy's maximum coverage minus 10 percent, or $18 million.

"I don't think that's going to happen," Sonlin said.

"All right. Let's see."

"Shanin, I'm telling you...."

"Let's just see."

For a minute, a very long minute, neither man spoke. Specter was playing hardball, refusing to compromise. Was it just a ruse?

He'd take $15 million if it was offered, wouldn't he? The two men stared at each other, saying nothing and revealing less. If Sonlin was hoping for a sign of Specter wavering, some reddening in his neck or perhaps Specter averting his eyes for a split second, he didn't get it. The reason was simple. Specter wanted $18 million, not $12 million, not $15 million. Otherwise, he would put on a pair of cufflinks and head to federal court in Philadelphia.

Later, long after the case had been concluded, Specter would comment about his meeting with Sonlin: "I saw in him a guy who personally thought these guns were horrible, who knew me and knew my office and knew that we were willing to try the case in the face of an eight-figure offer." In one case that would come just a few months later, Specter and his client rejected a $22 million settlement offered during trial in a medical malpractice case. Most lawyers would have leaped at $22 million. Not Specter. He was a hardball negotiator, and he trusted himself to win in court if it came to that. Defendants sensed this, and often increased their settlement offers. In this case, Specter's medical malpractice client eventually accepted a $25 million settlement in the trial's second week.

Again, Specter knew there would be no agreement on this day with Sonlin. Only the president of Chubb could agree to go as high as $15 million, or higher. There was no sense trying to hash this out with Sonlin, who by now had his hand on his coat.

Despite his rejection of the latest offer, Specter was compelled to share it with the Mahoneys. It was, after all, a lot of money. He also mentioned the Kenderdine statement to them. Initially, it had the effect that Daisy had sought, frightening the Mahoneys into thinking their case was in trouble. Specter assured them it wasn't. When they understood someone was trying to hoodwink them, the statement had the opposite effect. The Mahoneys became infuriated, and more determined than ever to make Daisy suffer. Still, $12 million was $12 million.

"Gee, that's a big number," Becky said when Specter told her of the offer.

"We can do better," he said.

"I suppose, but we don't want to end up with nothing."

"That won't happen."

"But what if we lose?"

"That won't happen."

"OK."

"Look," said Specter, seeing Becky wasn't 100 percent convinced, "I've brought you this far . . . ."

"I know, Shanin. We trust you."

"Then trust me to bring you the rest of the way. We can do this."

IN THE MEANTIME, the Kenderdine statement had touched off a tempest. Specter went back to court and filed a 30-point motion seeking to force Daisy to hand over not only a copy of the statement but also Kenderdine himself to be deposed. A lawyer for Daisy, Nancy Winschel, indicated that the company would ask for a protective order to prevent Specter from questioning Kenderdine, claiming his signed statement was protected by lawyer–client work-product rules.

Specter knew that was a bunch of nonsense. For one thing, Kenderdine wasn't Winschel's client, so how could there be any attorney–client privilege? And for another, the statement was potential evidence for trial, evidence that Daisy had a responsibility to turn over. In making his point to the court, Specter quoted in his motion Joe Pinto, a prominent Philadelphia defense attorney, whom Daisy had hired to help in the case. Pinto had told Specter he thought it was "outrageous" that the statement had been withheld from the plaintiffs. Specter knew Pinto well, and he knew he was honest, that Pinto would not deny saying what he had said.

Specter also protested the late surprise tactic of revealing the statement during settlement talks as "unconscionable," especially since he had requested—and the court had granted—access to any documents Daisy might offer at trial. He called Daisy's actions an "unethical and improper effort to conceal" critical information in the case, in violation of the federal Rules of Civil Procedure. On top of that, Specter sought now to depose the lawyer, Winschel, who had

gotten the statement from Kenderdine. His motion also requested
that she be disqualified from the case. He didn't expect that to happen, but he wanted to send a message. *You want to play hardball? We
can play hardball.*

It didn't take the court long to rule. Judge Joyner ordered that
Kenderdine's statement be handed over to the plaintiff.

While the judge had pondered the matter, Specter had hired a private investigator named Ed Koerper to drive to Bucks County and
talk to Kenderdine. Koerper took a friend who was an ex-cop from
the area and who had known Kenderdine personally. Maybe, man
to man, they could get to the bottom of this thing, even though
Specter thought he already understood what had occurred. He suspected that Daisy's lawyers had talked to Kenderdine, and, in the
process, they had become chums. Kenderdine was a gun buff; he actually had owned a gun shop at one time. Another Daisy lawyer,
William Griffin, had represented several gun makers and knew a lot
about the industry. Griffin and Kenderdine would have had a lot to
talk about, Specter figured. The cop was being schmoozed. Kenderdine, at 48 still a patrolman working the night shift, was overweight
and generally unkempt. He struck Specter as a guy eager to make
new friends, friends who might make him feel important. He had
perhaps found them in Daisy's high-priced lawyers. As Specter put
it, "He had chosen sides."

Kenderdine was anything but friendly to Koerper and his policeman pal, who met him in his police station office. But he did
agree to talk. Griffin and Nancy Winschel had indeed called and
they had met in nearby, trendy New Hope at a Best Western Hotel.
Kenderdine spent about two hours with them, time for which they
paid him on the spot, with a check. Kenderdine didn't say how
much. He said the lawyers asked him about the gun, he told them
what he knew, and then Winschel asked if he would be willing to
sign a statement. Kenderdine said, sure, why not?

What *did* Kenderdine know about the gun? He told Koerper that
he'd heard something rattle. Maybe it was BBs, maybe it wasn't. He
didn't know for sure and he never looked inside the gun to find out.

That was a far cry from the statement he had signed: "...When I picked up the gun, I heard the rattle of BBs in the gun. There were two or more BBs in the gun...."

In the meantime, Specter had also hired a scientist, an expert at Penn in the field of material science, to determine whether or not more than one BB could get stuck in the gun. Could Kenderdine have found Tucker's rifle with BBs still in it? Campbell Laird, a wonderful witness by virtue of both knowledge and appearance (and a rich Scottish accent that made him seem even more credible), had been consulted by Specter in another major case, and he employed him again now. Laird found that, yes, more than one BB could get jammed in the rifle. So even if Kenderdine was not lying, it still did not blow Specter's case—two BBs could actually have been stuck when Ty Weatherby fired at Tucker.

But Specter felt that had not been the case, especially since no one else saw or heard any BBs in the gun. Specter had even gotten a signed statement from former District Attorney Alan Rubenstein, now a Bucks County judge, that there had been no BBs in the gun when his office got it from the police. His assistant, Gavin Laboski, also signed a statement for Specter saying that he had kept the gun in a locked location.

> I handled the gun many times during the months that it was in my possession and at no time did I ever see, hear or feel any BBs in the gun. No other person, including District Attorney Rubenstein and Officer Kenderdine, ever notified me that they had ever detected or suspected the presence of any BBs.

In his statement Laboski also said that he had spoken with Kenderdine several times about the case, and, "at no time during any of these discussions did Officer Kenderdine ever mention the possibility that there were BBs in the gun at the time Ty Weatherby fired it or at the time he retrieved it." Laboski said Kenderdine was also present at a hearing for Weatherby, that Kenderdine heard the boy's testimony about believing the gun was empty, and that "at no time during that proceeding did Officer Kenderdine mention any belief or possibility that there were BBs in the gun at the time Ty Weatherby fired it or at the time he retrieved it."

Yet many months later, Kenderdine seemed pretty certain: "When I picked up the gun, I heard the rattle of BBs in the gun. There were two or more BBs in the gun...."

Specter was convinced now more than ever that Kenderdine had done one of two things. Theory One: Eager to please Griffin and Winschel, he had conjured up—perhaps had even believed—a fanciful recollection of events. Theory Two: Kenderdine was lying.

When the police officer, accompanied by Daisy lawyer Nancy Winschel, showed up for his deposition with Specter on November 13, his disdain was obvious. Kenderdine did not wear a coat and tie, just a warm-up jacket. He was a hostile witness from the outset, stating his age and occupation for the record but then refusing to give Specter his home address. "You can always find me through the police station.... I don't think it's necessary to know my home address," he said.

"Are you angry with this office, Officer Kenderdine?" Specter asked, referring to his law firm.

"Matter of fact, I was," Kenderdine answered, saying he was upset that a subpoena server had gone out "looking for me at my ex-wife's house for four days where I hadn't lived for over eight years." This from a guy who wouldn't give his home address.

Kenderdine did agree with Specter's assessment that in 28 years as a police officer the Mahoney case was probably one of his most stressful cases, topped only perhaps by the three times he had saved lives giving CPR and the one time, he recalled matter-of-factly, "I saw a guy burn up in a car, tried to rescue him, pulled his arm off."

Specter also noted to himself early on that Kenderdine was on a first-name basis with the Daisy lawyers. It was "Will" and "Nancy," not Mr. Griffin or Ms. Winschel. Specter was "Mr. Specter," and Kenderdine at one point insisted that Specter refer to him only as "Officer Kenderdine."

Winschel interrupted repeatedly with objections, as in one exchange about Kenderdine's retrieving the gun from the Mahoneys after the incident, placing it on the floor in the rear of his Chevy Blazer, and heading home:

> SPECTER: *Did you hear any sound coming from the gun on your drive home?*
>
> KENDERDINE: *I did hear a rattling from the back area.*
>
> Q: *[a bit later] Are you able to state to a reasonable degree of certainty under oath what the rattling constituted?*
>
> A: *It sounded like one or more BBs in the gun.*
>
> Q: *Are you able to say to a reasonable degree of certainty that it was BBs?*
>
> A: *It sounded to me like BBs because I've had a lot of dealings with BB guns. I've shot them a lot of times. I've had other incidents in the township where I've handled BBs.*
>
> Q: *You said to me twice that it sounded like BBs. You didn't open the gun and see BBs?*
>
> A: *No, I didn't do anything to the gun.*
>
> Q: *. . . Do you know to a reasonable degree of certainty one way or the other whether there were BBs in the gun?*
>
> A: *I just know what I heard, believed to be BBs from my experience.*
>
> Q: *Does that enable you to say one way or the other to a reasonable degree of certainty whether there were or were not BBs in the gun?*
>
> WINSCHEL: *Objection. Asked and answered. He already answered that three times. You're badgering the witness at this point.*
>
> SPECTER: *Officer Kenderdine, there's a question pending.*
>
> A: *You want an answer? Yes, I'll say there was BBs in the gun.*

The significance of whether BBs were in the gun—information potentially paramount to the case—seemed lost on Kenderdine. If the gun still contained BBs after the incident, then Ty Weatherby could have given a false statement, whether intentionally or not. Yet there was no mention of it in Kenderdine's police report on the shooting, a report that ran five and a half pages long in single-spaced type.

Wouldn't Kenderdine have checked the gun to see if there were BBs in it? To Specter, there were only two ways to explain how Kenderdine could have missed all this: He was either a lousy cop, or he never really heard BBs rattling in the gun at all.

Specter grilled Kenderdine on this point.

> Q: *If you could hear BBs rattling around in the gun, then you had information that he [Ty Weatherby] knew or should have known himself. Correct?*
>
> A: *It didn't have any bearing. I already had the BB out of the gun that was in the kid's brain.*
>
> Q: *But that was . . . .*
>
> A: *So that showed there was a BB in the gun.*
>
> Q: *But that was the one that had been shot.*
>
> A: *Right. That's all I was concerned with.*
>
> Q: *But you're telling us now in the year 2000 that there were more BBs in the gun?*
>
> A: *And it didn't matter to me at that time because for my criminal case . . . .*
>
> Q: *Did you think it might matter to the adjudication of the case that you might be hearing a rattling of BBs in the gun?*
>
> A: *No. Because it was obvious that the kid thought the gun was empty and there was still a BB in there because it went into the kid's brain.*
>
> Q: *And you never considered the possibility that maybe the one BB that went into his brain couldn't be heard, is that right?*
>
> A: *I didn't think it had a bearing on the case. I investigated the case as I saw, as you see, and that's what happened.*

Kenderdine's deposition testimony contained a variety of minor inconsistencies. He remembered, for instance, being handed the gun by Maggie Mahoney—he was very insistent on this point, that

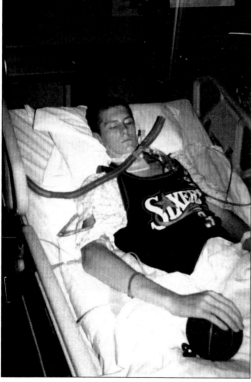

Tucker's Daisy air rifle (MAHONEY CASE EXHIBIT PHOTO)

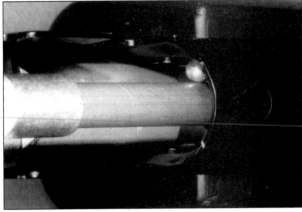

Photo showing a BB lodged against the gun's inner barrel (MAHONEY CASE EXHIBIT PHOTO)

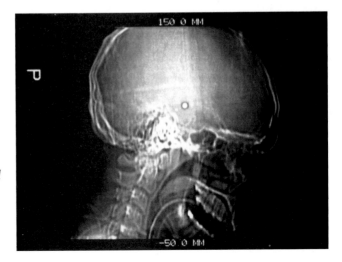

X-ray of BB lodged in Tucker's brain (MAHONEY CASE EXHIBIT PHOTO)

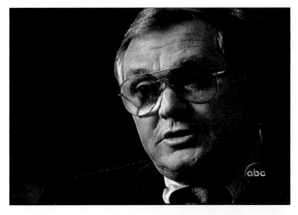

Marvin Griffin, president and chairman of Daisy, appearing on ABC's 20/20, in 1996
(PHOTOGRAPH COURTESY OF ABC NEWS)

Ronald Joyce, Daisy engineer, from his videotaped deposition testimony

Becky Mahoney and Ann Brown, CPSC chairman, after the commission voted on seeking a recall of Daisy guns
(KLINE & SPECTER FILE PHOTO)

Andy Youman examines an exemplar gun used in the Mahoney case (PHOTOGRAPH BY THE AUTHOR)

Shanin Specter on ABC's 20/20, in 2000 (PHOTOGRAPH COURTESY OF ABC NEWS)

he had not picked up the gun from the garage or in front of the house, that Maggie had handed it to him. Maggie said in her deposition that she had not handed it to the officer, that she had never touched the gun that injured her brother. Not then, not ever.

Kenderdine, who had managed to recall a rattling noise from nine months earlier, had no recollection of other, simpler details. He could not, for instance, remember a single thing about Maggie Mahoney, not what she was wearing, not her hair color, if she was short or tall, not anything.

Kenderdine remembered chatting with Griffin at the hotel—"I talked to Will at length about hunting, because we both enjoy hunting....It was just, you know, casual bullshit talk amongst the guys"—but he didn't recall who wrote out the statement for him to sign, Will or Nancy. Kenderdine didn't remember how much the Daisy lawyers compensated him for his time, and wouldn't even hazard an estimate (or ask Winschel, who was next to him, to refresh his memory).

He also said in his signed statement for Daisy, and without any seeming uncertainty, that "there were two or more BBs in the gun." Now Kenderdine was saying there was "one or more" BBs in the gun. "I don't know," he told Specter in his deposition. "There was something that sounded like BBs in the gun. It could have been one. It could have been two." He didn't waver on one point, though, that he never bothered to check.

And now, asked by Specter if it was possible that something else in the rear of his Blazer had made the sound, the officer answered, "Of course."

Sufficient holes had been poked in Kenderdine's statement, Specter felt. With this nasty business over, there was little left for him to do now. The trial judge, bogged down with several criminal cases, had delayed the start of *Mahoney v. Daisy* until early spring, some six months away. Such was the federal court system. Both Specter and the Mahoneys were now more resolute than ever to see this thing through. Specter had his mind fixed on only one of two outcomes. He wanted a very large check. Or a verdict.

WHILE HE WAS waiting, one of the seeds Specter had sown bore fruit. On November 24, 2000, Barbara Walters opened ABC's 20/20 with these words:

> Good evening, and welcome to 20/20. We hope you had a happy Thanksgiving. And if you were out fighting the crowds today, you know this is traditionally the busiest shopping day of the year. The perfect time, we thought, to warn you about a gift that might be on your child's Christmas list—a BB gun.
>
> Now you may think that your child is responsible. You may trust him, or her, to follow the rules. But what if they don't? As Brian Ross, our chief investigative correspondent demonstrates, some BB guns match the speeds of a police pistol and can turn child's play into tragedy.

The 20/20 show in 1996 told of injuries suffered by three boys, but this new edition focused on one: Tucker Mahoney.

Becky Mahoney told her story to a national audience, referring to Tucker, the Tucker she knew before the shooting, as a boy who had been "kissed by the angels." The show used video clips of Tucker before the shooting—Tucker walking, talking, laughing. Tucker happy.

The producers again got gun expert Dave Townsend to demonstrate the rifle's firepower. First he shot his .38-caliber special at a target and timed the bullet speed—762 feet per second. Then he pumped the Daisy 856 a full 20 times (without great effort) and pulled the trigger: 780 fps.

Armed with evidence by Specter, 20/20 had an X-ray showing the BB deeply imbedded in Tucker's skull. Townsend now was also able to demonstrate not only that BBs got stuck in the gun but also just how easily, and precisely where—in the baffle section between the rifle's inner and outer barrels. Videotape was shown of Daisy engineer Ronald Joyce admitting in his deposition given to Specter

that BBs got lodged in the gun. The Daisy engineering–change notices, with the "safety" box checked, were flashed on the screen.
"But," proclaimed Brian Ross, "Daisy issued no recall and proceeded to sell off its old stock."

Specter issued a warning to parents. "There are millions of defective guns that can cause someone to be seriously injured or
killed in households across this country," he told Ross.

Becky also addressed the show's national audience. "Some other
little boy is going to be hurt," she said. "It's a matter of time."

This time, Marvin Griffin did not appear on the show. Nor did
any Daisy representative.

SEVERAL MONTHS OF quiet ensued. February arrived. From the right
window in the Philadelphia federal courthouse, through the leaf-
less trees, you could see clear across Market Street and the snow-
blanketed mall to Independence Hall. The trial was set to begin in
March, and Specter, in the courthouse on another matter, imagined
himself peering out one of these windows while he waited for a verdict in *Mahoney v. Daisy.*

He wasn't at all anxious about reaching this final episode. He
thought his case was watertight. His expert witnesses would do
well, especially Townsend, a tall, handsome ex-cop with white hair
and a believable, blue-collar way about him. Tucker's story would
move the jury. How could it not? His parents and sister, Maggie,
would be pure gold on the witness stand, smart and credible and
likeable. Everything he felt Daisy wasn't.

Specter's first witness would be Ronald Joyce. The first plaintiff's
witness would be one of Daisy's own. With Joyce providing confirmation along the way, Specter would paint a historical picture of the
PowerLine guns he helped to create, from the early pressure to produce a more powerful gun for Sears to the safety changes made in
1998 and 1999. If Joyce refused to appear in person, electing to testify through a videoconference center nearer his home (which the
federal court system permitted), Specter would ask early in the

questioning why Joyce chose not to come in person. It would seem as though he was trying to avoid appearing in court. Which would be true.

Ditto for Daisy's chairman Marvin Griffin, whom Specter also planned to call as a plaintiff's witness. He would come off as cold and unsympathetic, even antagonistic and not credible. Specter would show the jury the Daisy change notices, proof the company knew about the defects and had fixed them without telling any-one—even the Consumer Product Safety Commission—or doing anything to separate unsafe guns from their owners. Owners like Tucker Mahoney.

Solid evidence and solid witnesses belonged to Specter. Daisy had a bad record, weak excuses, and indifferent corporate execu-tives. Without a doubt, Specter had a good case. Still, you never knew about juries, and in federal court, where he would need a unanimous verdict, it took just one juror to screw up the works. Just one who felt that Tucker's shooting was primarily the fault of Ty Weatherby, the shooter, not the gun manufacturer. Just one who felt the parents had not provided the proper supervision. Trials, Specter knew, were a tricky business. There was no such thing as a perfect case.

He also had to contend with the public's negative perception about lawyers. There was a festering mood sweeping the country that lawyers were bad, that they created much of society's ills. How many stories had he heard about sue-happy people blaming corpo-rations for their problems. Something bad happened and right away people looked for a way to cash in. Remember the lady who spilled hot coffee on her lap and sued McDonald's, winning mil-lions? Specter knew this antipathy could poison jury pools, or at least skew them.

In the McDonald's case, the hamburger chain had had several chances to settle before the case went to the jury. One report suggests that originally all the victim—an older woman who suffered third-degree burns and was hospitalized for eight days—wanted was $11,000 for her medical bills. Instead, she was awarded $2.9 million, including $200,000 in compensatory damages and $2.7 million in punitive damages, by a jury angry that McDonald's served its coffee dangerously hot, about 20 degrees hotter than other restaurants. And indeed, there were reports of some 700 other burning incidents. The $2.9 million jury award, though highly publicized and considered as a travesty by many, was never paid. Compensatory damages were lowered to $160,000 because the woman had been held 20 percent liable, and the judge reduced punitive damages to $480,000, or a total award of $640,000. That was roughly half of what McDonald's made on the sale of coffee in a single day.

Nevertheless, there was an overall negative perception of lawyers, and this made Specter's job harder.

JURY SELECTION WAS a few weeks away. Specter was in his office glancing over some files when his phone rang. "Can I come over?" Don Sonlin asked.

What seemed like only a few minutes later, Sonlin walked into Specter's office. He said a brief hello and, as he had with Kenderdine's statement during his previous visit, handed Specter a single sheet of paper. The letter contained only three paragraphs.

> Dear Mr. Specter:
>   Please allow this to confirm our settlement of this case.
>   As we discussed, the breakdown of the settlement is as follows....

The amount was not one that had been "discussed" as the letter mentioned, and not precisely what Specter had demanded. But it was close enough to his demand for him to accept, a staggering amount of money, particularly for a settlement. And unlike a jury verdict, there would be no appeal, no reduction by a trial judge or appellate court. No reversal.

But there was one condition—the amount was to be kept confidential. Daisy didn't want to publicize a huge settlement. Who knew how many more lawsuits would come flooding in if word got out? And this payout had Daisy approaching the edge of its insurance coverage, at least for the current year. Another successful lawsuit against the company could lead to bankruptcy. Specter didn't like the idea of keeping mum, but he had a responsibility to Tucker and his family. In the months and years to come, the news media would report that the total settlement was "nearly $18 million." Specter repeatedly refused to confirm or deny the news accounts.

THE REST OF Sonlin's letter was brief and boilerplate.

> We have agreed to annuitize your client's future medical costs, and I have enclosed illustrations for your review. Your clients are certainly welcome to annuitize more of the settlement if they desire. Please feel free to work directly with Settlement Funding Associates for any specific quotes you desire.
>
> It has been a pleasure working with you on this case. Once the settlement has been approved by the court, and the releases have been signed, I will forward our portion of the settlement monies.
>
> Sincerely,
> *Donald J. Sonlin*
> Litigation Supervisor

Specter removed his reading glasses and placed the letter down on his desk.

"Don," he said, "this is fine."

And just like that, the lawsuit was over. The case that had taken months of painstaking work and legal infighting had come to a close.

Or had it?

CHAPTER 19

VERDICT

I N LATE AFTERNOON THE CELL PHONES started ringing in suit pockets all around Philadelphia City Hall. The SEPTA jury was back with a verdict. It had taken only five hours for it to consider a complicated verdict sheet. The lawyers hustled back to the courtroom.

As did the news media. None of the reporters thought SEPTA had much of a chance because it hadn't put on a defense. They assumed that the only question was how much the jury would give the Halls.

"Five million, easy," one reporter predicted.

"Ten," another guessed.

Vernon Odom, of ABC Channel 6, who had covered a number of trials, sensed in this one something special. Shareif was a sympathetic plaintiff. SEPTA's folks had seemed so cold. The documents came to light so dramatically in open court. The judge seemed annoyed with SEPTA. And, with great emotion, Kline had presented Shareif as a victim hurt not only by SEPTA's escalator but also by its heartless management in the three years that had followed.

Sitting in the back of the courtroom, Odom, a large man with a Barry White bass voice and a penchant for bold pronouncements, had his own prediction. "Fifty million!" he declared. A few of the other reporters laughed aloud.

Kline, too, expected a big verdict. But would the jury recognize Deneen Hall's damages as well as Shareif's? Would the jurors accept the civil rights argument? Maybe they would award millions but not find that the child's civil rights had been violated, thus effectively capping the award at $250,000 plus delay damages.

You could never tell with a jury.

Judge Massiah-Jackson instructed Boyd Taggart to poll the jury.

COURT CRIER: *Ten out of 12 jurors agreed on a verdict?*

JURY FOREMAN: *Yes.*

Q: *. . . Do you find that SEPTA was negligent?*

A: *Yes.*

Q: *Was SEPTA's negligence a substantial contributing factor causing harm to Shareif Hall?*

A: *Yes.*

Q: *What amount of damages do you award Shareif Hall?*

A: *Twenty-five million dollars.*

Q: *Do you find that SEPTA and its officers and agents were deliberately indifferent to the bodily security of Shareif Hall and the deliberate indifference shocks the conscience such that his civil rights were violated?*

A: *Yes.*

Q: *Did SEPTA violate Shareif Hall's constitutional rights by subjecting him to a state-created danger?*

A: *Yes.*

Q: *What amount of damages do you award to Shareif Hall for violation of his constitutional rights?*

A: *Twenty-five million dollars.*

In the matter of Deneen Hall:

Q: *Do you find that SEPTA was negligent?*

A: *Yes.*

Q: *Was SEPTA's negligence a substantial contributing factor causing harm to Deneen Hall?*

A: *Yes.*
Q: *What amount of damages do you award to Deneen Hall?*
A: *One million, sixty-five dollars.*

Kline turned back to the gallery briefly. He noticed one reporter asking another, "Sixty-five dollars?"

His colleague explained: "The kid's shoes."

The total jury award was staggering: $51,000,065.

Deneen Hall's eyes filled with tears when she heard the verdict. Not an outwardly emotional woman, she embraced Kline. The judge asked the members of the jury not to speak with anyone as they left the courtroom. But as they exited the jury box in single file, they stopped one by one and shook Kline's hand.

What they didn't know was that although their job was completed, Kline's battle with SEPTA was not.

CHAPTER 20

SHOOTING FOR A RECALL

IT WAS THE LAST WEEK OF OCTOBER 2001, and, after seven years, Ann Brown's last week on the job as President Clinton's chairman of the U.S. Consumer Product Safety Commission. Soon she would pack up her things and walk out the door. But first, there was one thing left to do.

"I've made no secret," she told Becky Mahoney as the two were seated on a sofa in Brown's office, "this is what I intend to go out on."

Brown, a petite woman with an abundance of frenetic energy, was referring to the compulsory recall she wanted of millions of Daisy PowerLine BB guns. That would be her CPSC legacy, or at least the final chapter of her tenure. The commission, in a letter, had asked Daisy to voluntarily recall some of its guns. The company refused. While the commission had no unilateral authority to force such a recall, it could go to court and ask a federal administrative law judge to mandate a recall. It could sue.

Brown, Becky Mahoney, Specter, and Youman sat around a coffee table in the chairman's office, a large and colorful room with lots of toys, toys that looked innocent but had brought tragedy into American homes. Brown had determined that the CPSC would not be a morose place despite its mission and had adorned her office and others with brightly colored artworks, about 50 in all. On a wall near this particular meeting hung a large painting by the Washington artist Sam Gilliam, a mix of bright coral, blues, and greens. Brown had a soft smile and a penchant for cheery objects, but she was a tough little lady.

She announced to her visitors what she wanted to do. She would call for a commission vote for a Daisy recall of its defective BB guns, and she would provide the first vote to file the lawsuit. Technically, Brown was not supposed to reveal her vote (or even make up her mind) until that meeting, to be held behind closed doors. But she wanted to reassure Becky that she wanted to protect other children from Tucker's fate. She didn't give a damn about protocol.

What's more, even if the vote of the three-member commission didn't go her way, Brown promised that she would do one other thing that violated the rules—go public with her opinion that the Daisy PowerLine guns were unsafe. That might not be kosher, but it could save lives. The ends, Brown felt, would justify the means.

"I'll come out and say it's not safe even though that's against the law, even if I end up in jail," she vowed privately.

Brown hoped it wouldn't come to that. Her staff had been working on the case for nearly a year and a half. It had conducted a detailed and exhaustive study of the Daisy product. Jimmie Williams, Brown's top attorney, had become as quick as Andy Youman at demonstrating how a BB got stuck in the gun. Not that it was terribly hard to do. Williams also knew how to twist the barrel to show how—just when you thought the gun was empty—a BB dislodged and fell into the magazine and on to the magnetic bolt tip, ready for firing.

Specter had been nudging the commission all along. Every few weeks during this lengthy process Youman sent a letter or made a call to the CPSC asking about what progress had been made, offering to lend assistance if the commission needed it, to move the issue along. At one point, unhappy with the lack of progress he felt the commission was making, Specter fired off a letter to U.S. Rep. James Greenwood, a friend and fellow Republican from the Mahoneys' congressional district. Greenwood was a soft-spoken yet influential congressman who just happened to be chairman of the House Subcommittee on Oversight and Investigations, one of the most visible subcommittees in Congress that had spearheaded investigations into the Ford–Firestone dispute, wholesale prescription drug prices, and, later, the Enron debacle. The subcommittee also had oversight authority over the CPSC. Greenwood then dashed off a letter to Brown expressing his interest in her commission's probe and requesting information and documents the panel had culled about Daisy.

Now the CPSC staff felt that it had a solid case against Daisy. Many were committed to a mandatory recall. More than that, after hearing the stories of so many hurt children and seeing the 20/20 show about Tucker, the staff had developed an emotional investment in the Daisy case. "We all feel like Tucker is an adopted child around here," Ann Brown told Becky. Indeed, during a briefing on the Daisy case before the full commission and staff, Jimmie Williams got so caught up in retelling what had happened to Tucker that he had to stop in the middle of his presentation to gather himself and wipe away tears. But he did finish, presenting powerful evidence, as powerful as Daisy's BB guns.

Brown believed all the guns needed to be recalled, if only because of the sheer power of the rifles. It was an odd case for the CPSC, which had no authority over real guns but could act against a "toy." That Daisy's PowerLine BB guns were so close to real guns was evident in the mail flooding Brown's office since word had come out about the commission's impending vote to force a recall.

Over just one week, Brown's office received nearly 2,000 e-mails and letters—1,400 addressed specifically to her—from supporters of Daisy, many of them obviously from members of the National Rifle Association. It was the most mail Brown had ever received on any topic during her lengthy tenure with the commission. And the nastiest.

Many of the messages were similar, using "suggested" wording supplied on an Internet website. Many borrowed language from KeepAndBearArms.com, a grass roots progun group founded by a fellow in Flagstaff, Arizona, named Angel Shamaya, who was outraged by the commission's "obnoxious abuse of federal power." He insisted that BB guns were no more dangerous than kitchen knives, that the true danger was "stupid parents." Shamaya noted that BB guns led to the use of grown-up firearms and he stated proudly: "My Daisy 880—one of the models under attack—was my best friend for at least a year or two. (I wore it out!) Then I went up to a Sheridan .20-caliber pellet gun. Then a .22, shotguns, higher-caliber rifles, etc., etc. And now I pack heat everywhere I go . . . ."

Many claimed in e-mails and letters that the government was trying to run their lives and erode the citizenry's Second Amendment right to bear arms. Some letters were reasoned and polite. Some were not.

"Leave the airguns alone, bitch," one man wrote to Brown, signing his name only as "Charlie." Others called Brown a moron, idiot, Grinch, "a disease," arrogant, silly, inane, socialist, "fascist jerk," even anti-American. Asked one Navy sailor, "Is your name Brown or Bin Laden?" Some, related Brown, were "filthy," one even making a "sexual innuendo" about her and President Clinton.

Many of the e-mails suggested the BB guns were only dangerous because people misused them. "Big Brother cannot protect people from themselves," said one. Several others pointed to the box cutters used by terrorists to hijack the planes that crashed in the September 11 tragedies. "Why don't you start with [banning] box cutters and jet planes first?" wrote one person. Others sarcastically suggested the government also recall all forks, fishhooks, hammers, baseball bats, golf clubs, skateboards, and slippery bathtub bottoms. "What's next? Will you recall . . . envelopes because a few lunatic terrorists are using them to deliver anthrax?"

"Your brain should be recalled," said one writer. "We [the American public] are sick of worthless bastards like you. You would ruin a great American company like Daisy because you are afraid of the Bill of Rights. You suck and go to hell."

Some of the letters were a bit scary. One was a lengthy poem, whose author wrote, "I'm one of those bad things that happen to good people . . . . Don't upset me! I'm running out of places to hide the bodies." Another told Brown that he knew where she lived and that she "better watch out." That particular note was turned over to the commission's security office; its point was clear.

Brown didn't pay much attention to the hate mail, dismissing the pile on her desk with a smile and a shrug.

She was worried more about children's safety than their future freedom to shoot bullets. She was concerned about the immense power of Daisy's airguns, but for the moment decided to deal only with the narrow issue of the guns' defect. Brown didn't want to take on an entire industry merely to remove what she saw as the worst of the BB guns. Someone else, perhaps her successor, would deal with the guns' power some other day. "I'm an incrementalist," she told Becky and her lawyers. "If we get this recall in court, then the whole thing will crumble."

Specter felt certain that the CPSC would vote—that it was compelled to vote—to file suit to coerce a recall. "When the commissioners learn what Daisy paid to settle this suit, what the hell more do you have to know?" he said to Youman. He would not, of course, put it that way to the commissioners, but he did plan to let them know of Daisy's big settlement to the Mahoneys. Though he had signed an agreement not to disclose the settlement to the news media, there was no prohibition against telling the CPSC.

While driving earlier to the commission's Bethesda headquarters with Youman and Becky Mahoney, who planned to meet with the commissioners and tell her side of things, Specter had felt optimistic, but only guardedly so. Common sense did not always prevail in Washington, he knew, and politics and government sometimes acted strangely. Still, nearly two and a half years after taking the Mahoney case, he felt good that justice was on the horizon. "This is like Mrs. Smith and her lawyer go to Washington," he said during the car ride to Becky, who was a little nervous. "This is big stuff."

In Brown's office, the chairman talked to Becky about how to lobby the other commissioners, Mary Sheila Gall and Thomas Hill Moore. The two had already had been briefed on the case and were gathering comments from the interested parties, Becky among them. Brown wanted to know what Becky intended to tell her colleagues, prompting Becky to launch into the story of Tucker's shooting for the umpteenth time; yet the repetition made her no less emotional. Becky, her eyes damp, managed to get through the story, concluding by saying, "We just do not want another little boy to go through what we're going through." Jimmie Williams, who after all this time had finally met Becky face to face, again found himself fighting back tears. Specter, who had heard Tucker's terrible story almost as many times as Becky had told it, nevertheless pulled out a handkerchief and dabbed at his eyes as well.

Brown looked at Becky: "Perfect. Just perfect."

After meeting with the chairman, Specter knew he was halfway home. "You need two votes," said Brown, her hand resting on Becky's. "You've got mine."

But getting one more appeared difficult. Specter felt certain that Gall, named to the commission by President George H.W. Bush in 1991, would vote against a lawsuit to force a recall. Gall, who was quoted often by the KeepAndBearArms.com website, had reason to be unhappy in recent days. After Brown announced she was leaving the CPSC five years before her current term elapsed, the president—this time Bush's son, George W. Bush—nominated Gall to replace her as chairman. But Democrats in the Senate, citing what they felt were Gall's probusiness tendencies, fought her nomination. The Democratic-controlled Senate's Commerce Committee voted 12–11 along party lines to reject her nomination. Bush still wanted Gall to head the CPSC, but in September, barely a month before, Gall decided to call it quits and withdraw her name for chairman, a position that held much of the power at the CPSC.

When Specter and Becky arrived at Gall's office to press for a vote to recall Daisy's PowerLine guns, they were informed that she was out. Dennis B. Wilson, the commissioner's special assistant—whose manner proved as cold as his handshake—met them instead.

He went immediately on the offensive with Becky and Specter. "Didn't he read the warning?" Wilson asked about Tucker. He pointed out that Daisy guns came with a stark warning printed on the box. Becky started to answer but Wilson cut her off.

"'Danger,'" he read aloud, "'Not a Toy.' It says it right there. Doesn't it?" He stuck the box under Becky's nose. "'Not a Toy. Adult Supervision Required. Misuse or Careless Use May Cause Serious Injury or Death.'" Wilson's thin, sardonic smile seemed to ask, *What do you have to say now?*

Becky, accustomed to the sympathy of Brown and the other staffers, was taken aback. When she finally answered, she sheepishly said something about Tucker not being at fault for his injury. Specter didn't say a word.

After a few more minutes of Wilson pressing his point, Specter answered. "Warning or no warning," he said, "the guns are defective." Andy Youman rose now from a sofa in Gall's office to do his demonstration. Wilson appeared unimpressed. He interrupted Youman several times to point out that several steps had to be taken before a gun would fire; a BB stuck in the magazine alone would not cause an injury. The safety had to be disengaged. The bolt had to be cocked. The trigger had to be pulled. The gun had to be aimed. What was it Daisy's Ronald Joyce had said repeatedly in his deposition? "...A BB in the magazine that's trapped does not create a dangerous condition."

Becky told Tucker's story once again. Wilson listened this time without interruption. Periodically he jotted down a note on a clipboard, like a car mechanic doing a state inspection.

Specter said little throughout, knowing he would not make a convert out of Wilson or the woman he reported to. He simply asked that what he and Youman and Becky had presented to Wilson would be relayed to Gall. Wilson assured him it would be.

But so far, the vote was clear: 1–1.

NEXT THEY WENT to see Moore. If Moore had made up his mind how he would vote, it was impossible to tell. Even for Brown, who recently had had lunch with her fellow commissioner and couldn't get him to even hint at how he felt about a Daisy recall. On past votes Moore had ended up siding more often with Brown than with Gall. Moore, like Brown, was a Democrat and an appointee of President Clinton. Former legislative counsel to Sen. John Breaux of Louisiana, Moore was the father of two and had a one-year-old grandchild.

He met with Becky, Specter, and Youman not in his office but in a small nearby conference room. Neutral ground. He began not by asking Becky the details of what had happened to Tucker, but simply, "How's he doing?" Becky told him that Tucker was doing "okay," though her expression told a different story. She showed Moore various photos of her son, both before and after the mishap. Moore held the photos and sifted through them one by one, carefully, a slight smile on his face as he did so. He seemed sympathetic, but noncommittal.

"Well, from what we've seen, something ought to be done. It's a little late in your case," he said to Becky. "Maybe we can get some of these things off the market."

"Oh, thank you," she responded.

But then Moore said, "There might be a way to correct this problem, maybe not tomorrow, but with science and research in the years to come."

Specter didn't want to wait years. He wanted action with the commission's upcoming vote. What did Moore mean by this? Was he talking about the guns or Tucker's injuries? Was he planning to vote against a recall?

If action doesn't come soon, Becky implored, "Some other child is going to be hurt."

But again, Moore's reply expressed neither support nor opposition. "I certainly hope not," he said.

Moore said he found it "shocking" that the Daisy guns were so powerful that they could pierce the skull of a 16-year-old boy. "I had BB guns when I was a kid and they could barely kill a bird," he remarked.

When Becky related how Ty innocently shot and hurt Tucker, Moore's response was barely audible, a whisper. "My God."

Specter wondered whether Moore truly understood the issue, the lodging defect in the gun. He tried to focus his attention.

"We need to take this a step at a time, commissioner. This is the lodging defect with the gun. This would not have happened if not for the defect."

"Good point, good point," replied Moore.

Then the commissioner turned toward Becky and said, "Well, I hope you continue to hold on to hope."

"Oh," she said, "I couldn't get of bed every morning if I didn't."

Moore smiled at Becky and picked her photos up from the conference table. He looked at the photo of Tucker as a younger boy and chuckled faintly, then handed them back to Becky.

"We will look at this most thoroughly, most, most thoroughly," promised Moore's assistant. While government officials were notorious for leaking or at least indicating how they would vote, Moore did not. He provided not even a hint. Could it have been that he just hadn't decided yet?

Moore took Becky's hand as the meeting broke up. "Sorry you had to go through this," he said.

CHAPTER 21

LIES AND CONSEQUENCES

T HOUGH THE JURY WAS GONE and the verdict had been delivered in *Hall v. SEPTA,* Kline continued to drag witnesses
into court. This was the contempt hearing he had asked
Judge Massiah-Jackson to convene. She had complied. Leon Tucker
could scarcely believe it. He'd thought Kline had been showboat-
ing, that he'd shouted contempt to sway the jury to pump up its
award. But now?

"C'mon guys, you've already slain the dragon," Tucker pleaded.
"You've proven your point. What more do you want?"

Indeed, there was no more money to be won by Kline or his
client. Any contempt fine would be paid to the court. But Kline's
purpose was not money. Nor was it to get Tucker, whom he believed had been sandbagged by his own client. He wanted to
make sure the transit authority would never again do to another
person what it had done to the Halls. He wanted SEPTA cited for
failing to turn over all the appropriate documents to a plaintiff
trying to make a case. The Halls had been wronged, he felt, and
now the case was about principle, and Kline wanted to see it to
the end.

There were consequences for not playing fair. He also wanted
SEPTA to fix and properly maintain its escalators, all of its escalators.

(The escalator at Cecil B. Moore had been shut down for 18 months after Shareif's injury, but then had been put back into service after being upgraded and passing an inspection.)

Over the next several days, the same courtroom that provided the battleground for *Hall v. SEPTA* would look like a Mummer's parade, though instead of jovial, feather-bedecked marchers the participants would be grim-faced SEPTA executives in suits. The spectacle would have been funny, if the issue had not been so serious.

During the contempt hearing, the 44 pages SEPTA had provided at the start of the trial would grow into a mountain of documents. The yellow file that Figueira produced during the trial would become dozens of additional files packed with reports and drafts and memos and studies. So many, in fact, that Kline would ask the judge for an additional plaintiff's table just to hold it all. Forty-four pages would multiply into thousands.

Kline wanted to see how many documents existed referring to the Cecil B. Moore escalator and SEPTA escalators in general, how many people at SEPTA had them, and how easy it would have been to obtain them—that is, had SEPTA made the effort to submit them for discovery. The files, it seemed, were everywhere, in every nook and file cabinet in every SEPTA office—except that either nobody at SEPTA's headquarters had seen Leon Tucker's request for documents, or nobody had paid any attention to it.

Kline was out to demonstrate for Massiah-Jackson that one of two things had occurred: Either SEPTA and its lawyers had concealed documents, or they hadn't tried terribly hard to produce them. The lack of documents provided was not merely the result of a silly mix-up or bureaucratic bungling. SEPTA, he felt, had acted in bad faith and with bad intent.

For the proceedings, SEPTA hired a new outside attorney, Gino Benedetti, an expert in defending civil rights cases.

First up to testify was SEPTA's deputy general counsel, Eileen Katz, who headed the transit agency's claims litigation office, staffed by 29 litigators.

KLINE: *Now, in this case, in this case, there were discovery requests, correct?*

KATZ: *Yes, there were.*

Q: *And there are documents that are not turned over to the plaintiffs, correct?*

A: *So I understand.*

Q: *Is that something you just learned of in the courtroom?*

A: *That's something I just learned the other day.*

Q: *Are you embarrassed by it?*

A: *Yes, I am.*

Q: *It was wrong of SEPTA not to turn these documents over, correct?*

A: *Yes, it was.*

Q: *... You agree with me that SEPTA violated the letter and spirit of the discovery rules in failing to provide the accident investigation report dated May 15, 1997.*

Benedetti objected, but the witness was told to answer.

A: *Generally, yes.*

Katz said she had believed she had all the relevant documents that SEPTA possessed, and turned them over to Tucker. She said she hadn't known about the existence of the accident reports, even though one included the notation: "CC: E. Katz." She said she never got them. Kline made it known that he found that hard to believe. He used Katz to introduce a litany of documents that were produced late or not at all.

Q: *It's true that the failure to produce the documents, just like the failure to maintain the escalators, is a disgrace. Correct?*

A: *I think it's most unfortunate, and the documents should have been produced.*

Q: *Your answer is—correct?*

A: *Yes.*

Benedetti questioned Katz and made the point that SEPTA handled thousands of claims against it each year and that Katz had not intended to deprive the Halls of information for their suit. She had simply "overlooked it and made an innocent mistake," he told the judge.

Bull, thought Kline. Katz had to have been more aware of the suit. After all, he asked sarcastically, "How many other escalator accidents was she working on in which a little boy's foot was ripped off?"

Katz, like Figueira during the trial, was asked to go back to SEPTA and look for more pertinent documents. She, too, returned with a file of documents, though she claimed some were covered by attorney–client privilege. Expressing incredulity, Massiah-Jackson reviewed the documents and let SEPTA withhold only two pages. Further showing how much she trusted SEPTA, the judge during a lunch break ordered her staff to "stand guard" over the files. "I don't want them tampered with," she said.

The judge's disdain for SEPTA became increasingly evident as the hearing progressed. The next witness, Steve Krenzel, assistant director of maintenance, was greeted with an admonition. "We don't chew gum in my courtroom," she scolded. Krenzel, cringing like a chastised schoolboy, spit his gum into a piece of paper that he stuffed into a pocket of his suit jacket.

Kline now demanded all relevant files going back to 1991, including those from SEPTA police and SEPTA's computer banks. Leslie Hickman, director of the Broad Street Line, came to court with two thick orange files. She also had someone get from the computer system an "incident report," one authored after the accident, which, even at this late date, Kline had not seen before. Hickman said she had simply asked for it the night before, and after "whatever computer people do," there it was, on her desk by the time she arrived for work at 7:25 a.m. the next day.

> HICKMAN: *And I said, Bob, I need files that you guys have maintained . . . and I need them hand carried to me in the morning."*
> KLINE: *So, that's all it takes . . . .*

Among the new items was a June 24, 1999, memo that said "much of the work currently being done on SEPTA's escalators is being performed on a breakdown basis rather than on a preventative basis." This would have been useful during the trial.

Lt. John Wenke brought in a file retrieved from the SEPTA Police computer files. He said he hadn't brought them earlier for discovery before the trial for a simple reason: No one had asked him to.

A memo from September 23, 1999, more than two months before the trial, notified 20 SEPTA employees that they might be called as witnesses and should bring any pertinent documents with them. The memo from Leon Tucker asked for "any and all writings that mention or are related to the accident." Kline read the memo with some dismay. "So," he said, "they had two additional months . . . in which any of these documents which came to light should have been turned over." This proved conclusively to Kline that Tucker was indeed not a part of the problem.

New memos came in all shapes and sizes. One arrived in a clear, unmarked envelope. Who sent it? Nobody knew. Others mentioned attachments that no longer were attached. When Kline asked Hickman why she didn't have one such attachment she got testy, telling him that if he looked closely he would see there were no staple marks on her memo. That, she implied, made it obvious that there had been no attachment. Kline could have let it pass, but he wasn't in the mood.

KLINE: *In 1996, had the paper clip been invented yet?*
HICKMAN: *Yes, sir. It had.*

Trying to demonstrate how easy it would have been for SEPTA to dig up relevant documents, Kline asked Hickman to try to look for more. By Friday, she had uncovered another file an inch and a half thick. Where had these files been? Her secretary, Hickman said, "found them in my escalator–elevator file."

On December 17, Steve Krenzel came back to court yet one more time. He came with a department store shopping bag filled to the brim.

> KLINE: *Doing your Christmas shopping at Macy's?*
> KRENZEL: *No.*
> Q: *There are a lot more documents than we have previously seen that are in your possession. Correct?*
> A: *Yes.*
> Q: *. . . Sir, the amount of documents that you had to bring to the courtroom are so voluminous that you needed to bring them in a shopping bag. Correct?*
> A: *I chose to bring them in a bag.*

Cecil Bond, SEPTA assistant general manager, brought a brown manila envelope stuffed with more documents. One of them was a copy of the final accident report, which he had sent to GM Jack Leary. It too had never been offered up for trial.

> KLINE: *[It] could have been retrieved simply by somebody saying, "Mr. Bond, we need a copy of your file to see what's relevant in it." And then you would have given it to whatever lawyer asked you for it. Correct?*
> A: *Yes, that's correct.*

Figueira also made an encore appearance for the contempt hearing. This time he brought with him three more piles of documents, including escalator injury claims from 1991 to 1996. He agreed with Kline that it was no trouble getting the files, that they were available on the computer system simply "by pushing a couple of buttons."

AT LEAST ONE new document revealed during the hearing was of critical importance. The document could have greatly aided the plaintiffs during the trial. It surfaced only now during the testimony of a Robert Allman, SEPTA's director of system safety, a man whose real views Kline had previously known little—and for good reason. Allman was one of the SEPTA officials who had signed the final, May 15, 1997, accident report, which still cited Shareif Hall's shoelace as a "probable cause" of the accident. But the newly discovered document, a memo written by Robert Allman, had been intended for one person and one person only—Robert Allman.

It was what some people called a "conscience memo," Allman putting in writing, even if only to himself, that he had protested the accident report. Yes, he had signed off on the report but only after a verbal protest to his boss, Russell Figueira, and his boss's boss, Cecil Bond. Allman did not feel the accident had been investigated in an objective manner. The memo stated, in part: "Even after requesting, critical physical evidence was withheld from the investigating safety officers who were attempting to begin the initial phase of the investigation. Because of this, I informed Russ Figueira, chief officer, Safety and Risk Management, of my extreme displeasure with the events that transpired and that it would be hard to justify an objective investigation."

"Figueira," Allman now testified, "knew I was extremely angry with events."

Why hadn't any of this come out earlier? Said Allman, "For the record, sir, I had not been contacted for any documents until yesterday."

PATRICK NOWAKOWSKI, SEPTA's chief operations officer, who reported directly to Leary, brought in a bag filled with documents. He, too, had gotten a phone call just the day before. "I got together as much as I could . . . . I just brought everything," he said. Everything included the memo on the poor condition of SEPTA's escalators and the final accident report dated May 15, 1997. Had someone simply asked Nowakowski for the information earlier, he could have had it within a day. But no one had asked.

JAMES BAHN, THE SEPTA safety officer who had actually gone to the scene to investigate the accident on November 27, 1996, said he had requested the hardware from the accident and had been turned down by Leslie Hickman. Bahn was the one who had taken the photo of the white shoelace on Shareif Hall's shoe.

> KLINE: *Did you find it like that or did you put it like that?*
> BAHN: *No, sir. When I arrived on the scene, that was there.*

Kline ended the day's testimony by showing Shareif's black shoelace—the lace that was still tied—to Bahn. He also held up Shareif Hall's damaged boot. None of this had much to do with proving contempt, though it did show what could have been—that Kline could have had Bahn on the witness stand for the trial. He also wanted to hear Bahn, the actual investigator, say the words.

> KLINE: *Now that you look at the boot and the shoelace, would you agree with me, sir, that this boy's shoelace, now that we have had all of these years, all of this trouble, this entire trial, a jury verdict, as we sit here today, three days after a jury came in, will you admit to me that this boy's shoelaces were double-knotted, that they go to this boot, and that they did not get caught in the escalator?*

Kline handed Bahn the tied black shoelace and the shoe. He sought the simple answer he had not been able to get at trial.

> A: *From what I am looking at, it appears that this goes with this. Yes, sir.*
> Q: *That the boy's black tied shoelaces go with the black boot. Correct?*
> A: *It appears to be.*
> Q: *It's just that simple. Correct?*
> A: *Yes, sir.*

The day and the week ended with Kline having turned up 19 different files from various corners of the SEPTA bureaucracy. An avalanche of material was left stacked in piles in the front of the courtroom. The evidentiary phase of the hearing had concluded. But before the judge rendered a decision, Kline had two more fish to fry. They were very big fish at SEPTA. He asked that on Monday morning Gerald Bowers, SEPTA's legal chief, be called to the witness stand. And he wanted to publicly question GM Jack Leary. What Kline wanted, only Bowers and Leary could provide.

"And to this day," Kline said to Bowers, pointing out Deneen Hall in the courtroom, "nobody has apologized to her. Did you know that?"

Bowers didn't hesitate with a response. "Mom," he addressed Deneen Hall, "I apologize to you on behalf of myself and on behalf of SEPTA."

Bowers, a man of 70, had brought a red folder of documents to court to go with the canary yellow and orange and blue and beige that already sat like a paper rainbow atop Kline's table in court. Bowers claimed that he never saw the May 15, 1997, accident report. It was not part of his file.

In fact, Bowers testified that he hadn't seen much at all in the case. He said on this Monday morning that he hadn't even seen Robert Allman's memo, which had surfaced before the weekend break. Again, Kline wanted to know how Bowers could not have seen it when hundreds of thousands of people had by this time; the memo had been reprinted in both *The Philadelphia Inquirer* and *Daily News* the day after it was revealed in court the previous Friday. Bowers's answer: "I do not get either the *Inquirer* or the *Daily News* on Saturday."

Once he had authorized SEPTA to pay $250,000 to Shareif Hall, Bowers said he considered the case all but closed. That was, after all, the legal limit the authority could pay. After that, he hadn't paid much attention.

Kline wanted SEPTA to publicly condemn one of its legal practices, hoping to force the agency to change its ways. He got Bowers, who had been practicing law for 30 years, to admit that SEPTA's suit against Deneen had been virtually automatic. If SEPTA was sued in an injury case, it just naturally went on the offensive with a counterclaim, even if it lacked evidence that a parent or guardian was responsible.

"That's wrong, isn't it?" Kline asked.

Bowers agreed. "I have already issued orders that we are not to join anybody without an expressed approval," he said. His personal approval.

Yet the admission wasn't quite enough for Kline. He didn't want Bowers merely to make amends. He wanted him to repent. He asked the lawyer about SEPTA's false–claim hot line, an 800-number for riders to use if they believed someone was making a bogus injury claim against the transit authority.

> Q: *You planning to call that hot line about the claim of SEPTA versus Deneen Hall?*
> A: *No, I am not planning to call that line, sir. We would be calling ourselves.*
> Q: *Would be a good call to make, wouldn't it?*
> A: *Yes sir, I agree.*

Another thing.

> KLINE: *Will you admit in this courtroom that SEPTA was negligent and caused this boy's and his mother's injuries? Will you admit that today in this courtroom for SEPTA, finally?*
> BOWERS: *From what I have seen, it would appear that we were.*
> Q: *It would appear what?*
> A: *That we were.*
> Q: *Can you say the words—that we were negligent?*
> A: *I can say the words. We were negligent.*

And lastly . . . .

Jack Leary, a short man with white hair and a Boston accent, took the stand. Leary had previously managed the St. Louis and Boston transit authorities before moving to Philadelphia, which had the nation's fifth-largest mass transit system. He had had success, particularly when it came to coaxing city and state politicians to provide SEPTA with increases in government funding.

Kline knew that Leary hadn't been directly involved in the Hall case, yet he felt that SEPTA's top official needed to publicly acknowledge the wrong that SEPTA had wrought. Leary offered no excuses for SEPTA's actions. He was there to finally accept the blame.

> Q: *SEPTA sued the mom. Do you know that, Mr. Leary?*
> A: *Yes, sir.*
> Q: *You were wrong for doing so. Correct?*
> A: *Yes, sir.*
> Q: *SEPTA should be held accountable for having sued her improperly. Correct?*
> A: *I think that's fair.*
> Q: *Your answer is yes?*
> A: *Yes.*
> Q: *The handling of this case, sir, by SEPTA, has caused shame on the organization. Correct?*
> A: *That is correct.*

Leary conceded SEPTA's escalator preventive maintenance program had major deficiencies. He acknowledged that he had seen the final accident report and was shocked by it. He admitted that in this lawsuit SEPTA had violated the rules of discovery. And he agreed that heads should roll. "I believe there are people that are very nervous regarding being held accountable for this breakdown in the organization," he said. And he agreed with Kline that changes should be made to the way SEPTA operated and serviced its escalators.

Kline had one more thing before he let Leary go.

> Q: *And by the way, sir, Deneen Hall and Shareif Hall are owed an apology by SEPTA. Are you willing to give it at this time?*
> A: *Yes, sir. My heart goes out to the Hall family for this ordeal.*

Q: *That was due a long time ago, wasn't it, rather than a law-*
   suit against her?
A: *Yes, sir.*

When the testimony was over, Kline rose for one final speech—delivered in a manner that for the loquacious Tom Kline must have been excruciating. He kept it short.

Kline noted the importance of the case "not only to the public safety of SEPTA riders and the citizens of this region but also to us lawyers and professionals." Then he turned to Leary, who was still seated in the courtroom.

> *This, Mr. Leary, is a wake-up call to SEPTA. They have to un-*
> *derstand that these escalators are not fixed, that if they're not*
> *fixed, public safety will continue to be endangered. And, Mr.*
> *Leary and Her Honor, we are on your side. We are not the*
> *enemy like your PR people have tried to say. We are here to*
> *help. We want to help fix the system and make it safe.*
>
> *I told Miss Hall in a very sad moment during this trial that*
> *I believed something good can come out of something bad. And*
> *I hope that finally SEPTA will realize that something good can*
> *come out of something bad.*

Minutes later, Leary was in front of the TV cameras and newspaper reporters repeating Kline's very words. "Something good can come out of something bad," said the transit chief. "We will fix what is broken at SEPTA and it won't happen again."

Despite SEPTA's apologies and promises, Kline still demanded a real penalty, a monetary penalty. The case and SEPTA's behavior, he felt, demanded it.

Now there was no jury. Kline reminded the judge of "evidence tampering" in the case, pointing to the picture of the white shoelace positioned on the black shoe and the "sheared off screws" that magically became whole. He mentioned the memo of Robert Allman, a memo that he said showed the accident investigation "was a fraud and a phony and a fix." He urged Massiah-Jackson not so much to punish SEPTA as to create a catalyst to improve the agency.

> *And while it might be easier, Your Honor, for some judges and some lawyers to turn the other way, to, as they say, run with the money, sweep it under the rug, so much good is going to come when this court sanctions SEPTA, holds SEPTA in contempt.*

Benedetti's reply was brief. He told the judge that he offered not "a single excuse for what has unfolded in the courtroom" during the contempt hearing.

> *[It] is wrong and it shouldn't have happened. Documents should have been produced. Escalators and safety needs to be paid attention to. And for these things SEPTA is truly sorry and SEPTA expresses and has expressed its sorrow to the family.*

But, insisted Benedetti, SEPTA did not willfully withhold documents. It wasn't intentional. And, he said, SEPTA had already been punished, and severely. He noted that a jury had slapped the authority with a $51 million damages award, "which, I believe and I think the court would agree, was a clear message . . . ."

The Honorable Frederica Massiah-Jackson had her own message in mind. She spoke up about "a trial that was just incredible, and each day was more of an eye-opener than the day before." Her rebuke of SEPTA could not have been harsher.

> *First of all, I find that SEPTA's conduct did obstruct the administration of justice and prejudiced Shareif Hall's case. . . . The paper trail which was presented in this courtroom during the past week established without any doubt that SEPTA's management at the highest levels knew of Shareif Hall's accident, knew of the investigation reports and recommendations.*

Knew of the litigation, and yet failed to turn over the materials
to plaintiff's counsel before or during the trial . . . .

She noted that an improper action can be "a deliberate omission
or a deliberate failure to act" as was the case in SEPTA's failure to turn
over critical documents. Massiah-Jackson said that "the most devastating evidence," the May 4, 1994, memo depicting the poor shape
of SEPTA's escalators systemwide, had "remained hidden by SEPTA."
That memo, she said, "demonstrated to the jury and to the court
that SEPTA had actual knowledge of deteriorating escalators two and
a half years prior to Shareif Hall's accident." And yet the government-related agency took no action to improve those conditions.

> *In 1994, they were in "poor condition and getting worse at an*
> *ever-increasing rate." By 1996, Shareif Hall's foot was ampu-*
> *tated by SEPTA's escalator.*
> *SEPTA has shown gross indifference to its obligation to the*
> *court.*
> *SEPTA has demonstrated a cavalier disregard for the court*
> *process.*
> *SEPTA has demonstrated extraordinarily bad faith by fail-*
> *ing to acknowledge its responsibility to the court rules of civil*
> *procedure.*
> *SEPTA has not taken this litigation seriously and has dis-*
> *regarded the right of the other parties to the action.*
> *SEPTA obstructed the administration of justice and im-*
> *peded the judicial process.*
> *SEPTA hindered justice.*
> *Too many witnesses said they were never asked for files or*
> *never knew that their files were being sought. While Mr. Bow-*
> *ers has labeled this as purely bureaucratic bungling, I suggest*
> *the correct label is contempt of court.*

The judge mentioned differences in evidence, namely the condition of the comb-plate screws and the "white shoelace photo."

SEPTA's photograph shows a white shoelace on top of the pieces of the child's boot. Who tied that white shoelace? Who handled it? This court concludes that even while the child's blood was still wet on the ground, somebody from SEPTA was manipulating that physical evidence.

The next day, the *Philadelphia Daily News,* would run a red cover emblazoned with a two-word headline: "SEPTA'S SHAME." Reporter Chris Brennan's story followed:

SEPTA entered a personal injury trial two weeks ago, confident it could be held liable for only $250,000 in damages for a 1996 subway escalator accident that tore off a 4-year-old boy's foot.

What a difference two weeks and $52 million makes.

Among the lessons SEPTA learned in 14 days: Judges and juries don't like it when state agencies hide, lose and tamper with evidence or launch counterattack lawsuits on victims.

Common Pleas Judge Frederica Massiah-Jackson yesterday fined SEPTA $1 million, finding the agency in contempt of court.

CHAPTER 22

THE VOTE

SHANIN SPECTER, ANDY YOUMAN, and Tom Kline piled into Specter's black Audi sedan. Youman sat in the back with a dear companion, *The New York Times*. A headline in the national section announced: "Safety Panel Voting Today on a Recall of BB Guns." Youman scanned the article, then flipped to the crossword puzzle. He wished it were later in the week, Thursday or Friday. The Times crossword got harder as the week progressed, and this was only Tuesday. He wanted the puzzle to help him pass away a chunk of the two-plus–hour ride to Bethesda and the offices of the Consumer Product Safety Commission. Not that Youman was nervous but....

It had only been a few days since Becky Mahoney and her lawyers had met with the members—or in the case of Mary Sheila Gall, tried to—but it felt like much longer. It had been much longer, a full year, since Specter and Youman first brought the agency their evidence that Daisy's PowerLine BB guns were defective and dangerous. The trio of attorneys planned now to meet Becky at an afternoon news conference at which the CPSC would announce its vote and, they hoped, the filing of a lawsuit seeking to force Daisy to recall millions of the guns.

During the ride, Specter had someone on his staff stay in touch by telephone with someone on Ann Brown's staff to try to get the result of the vote as soon as it happened. "I'll be damned if I'll drive all the way down there if the vote goes against us. We'll just make a U-turn and come home," he told Kline. Specter seemed a little tense. Kline relaxed in the black leather passenger seat up front busily munching Necco Wafers.

About halfway to Bethesda, Specter's cell phone rang. He answered before it could ring a second time. Kline and Youman perked up, though they could hear only Specter's end of the conversation.

"Yes?"

"Yes."

"All right."

"Yes, I understand."

Specter was not smiling. He wasn't frowning, either. Kline poked his partner in the arm for a clue.

"Yes."

"Yes."

"All right. I've got it."

AN HOUR OR so later, Brown stood at a podium, seven television crews and a host of newspaper reporters waiting for her to announce the 2-1 decision:

> The U.S. Consumer Product Safety Commission today filed an administrative lawsuit against the Daisy Manufacturing Co., doing business as Daisy Outdoor Products, Rogers, Ark., seeking a recall of 7.5 million PowerLine Airguns. The lawsuit seeks to compel Daisy to notify consumers that the model 880 and the model 856 PowerLine Airguns are defective, and present a substantial risk of death or injury to anyone using the airgun.

In its lengthy investigation the commission had discovered horrors resulting from the Daisy PowerLine. Brown went on to the second paragraph:

CPSC's staff has learned of at least 15 deaths and 171 serious injuries that have been attributed to alleged design and manufacturing defects in Daisy's PowerLine airguns. About 80 percent of those who have been killed or injured by the airguns were children under the age of 16. Children have been killed after being shot in the head or chest. Other children have been seriously injured after BBs punctured the heart, spinal cord or skull, causing paralysis and brain damage.

The panel cited one case in particular, that of Tucker Mahoney. Brown mentioned an $18 million settlement. Then the facts of the case were recited by the most stalwart foot soldier against the Daisy PowerLine.

"He asked for a BB gun with a scope and that's what we found on the Kmart shelf. Little did we know ..., " said Becky Mahoney, standing out in a fuchsia jacket with a black flower in the lapel as she addressed the news media in a large press room at CPSC headquarters. She looked directly into the bright television lights and once again told Tucker's story, starting with the trip to Kmart and ending with Ty Weatherby pulling the trigger on May 24, 1999. "This could have been prevented," said Becky. The commission then showed a one-minute video of Tucker, his life before the shooting and afterward. The room fell silent while the tape played. Becky and Jay held hands as they watched.

After the news conference, Becky dutifully gave individual interviews with one reporter after another.

"We're very pleased with the decision of the commission."

"We're hoping to get the word out so that nobody else is injured."

"These guns are an accident waiting to happen."

Jay told reporters that he wished the commission had taken the action years earlier, before he walked into that Kmart store with $40 to buy Tucker's birthday present. Specter remained silent except when questioned directly, and then he held nothing back in his scorn for Daisy. "They killed and injured many people across the country. I hope this leads to a recall," he said. "Daisy for 30 years has shown reckless and outrageous conduct...oblivious to this carnage."

The commission's findings were even more damaging than what Specter had unearthed. The commission not only found defects other than the one that had led to BBs getting lodged in Daisy rifles, but also concluded that the changes made to the guns' baffles in 1998 and 1999 did not entirely fix the problem. BBs still got stuck in some of the guns. The CPSC sued for the recall of all the 880 and 856 models (plus their multiple offshoots—the 881, 882, 1880, 1881, 9072, 9082, 9083, 9093, 9393, 9382, 3305, 3480, 3933, 1455, 5150, 860, 2856, 7856, and 990) made since the first one rolled off the line in September 1972. The total through January 2001 was 7,279,151 guns, plus any others made since.

The CPSC was thorough. Its investigation had produced 50,000 pages of documents and conclusions, including findings from two independent experts. The proof of the Daisy defect was simple. Just as Youman had found he could demonstrate how BBs got stuck in the guns, so, too, the commission found the jamming occurred easily and often. "We were repeatedly able to replicate it," said one official. Jimmie Williams, picked to prosecute the case against Daisy in the courts, demonstrated the lodging defect at the news conference. Though anxious about being in front of the lights, he ably demonstrated how BBs got stuck in the gun. It took him only one try.

The commission didn't stop with the defect, though. It went on to cite other mechanical and design "defects," including the lack of an automatic safety. (Those devices were included in some BB guns made by other manufacturers, but not all. Some Crosman models had automatic safeties.) It also noted that the bolt tip, which Daisy had argued shooters could look at before pulling the trigger to see if there was a BB loaded for firing, was located at the top of the gun, not on the side. When a scope was attached, it had to be placed directly above the bolt tip, obscuring it from clear view. The commission's 10-page lawsuit noted: "Daisy's design relies unduly on consumers to see a BB in the loading port and then interferes with that ability....This design constitutes a defect." Also, Daisy BBs were coated with zinc and were silver in color, virtually the same color as the bolt tip. (Crosman's BBs were copper coated.) This could have added to a shooter's misperception that a gun was empty when it wasn't, even if he didn't take the time to check the bolt tip. And don't forget, the lawsuit added, these guns were being used primarily by children who were not likely to keep checking the bolt tip before firing each time—especially "with a gun they believe is not loaded."

The suit asked the court to require that Daisy halt future distribution of the guns. It sought that Daisy be forced to provide public notice about the hazard of using the product and a warning "to stop using the Daisy PowerLine airgun immediately." Notice also would have to be sent to every distributor who sold the gun and every person known to have bought one. For those who still had a gun, the company would have to repair it, replace it with another gun, or give the customer a refund. Not only that, but the CPSC wanted to be able to monitor what Daisy would do over the next five years, including access to company records. Plus, it demanded a 60-day notice in case Daisy decided to sell or seek bankruptcy, an action that would allow the government panel time to make sure Daisy complied with warning notices and the like before getting bankruptcy protection.

"Daisy has refused to recall the guns voluntarily or to take them off store shelves," Brown told the assembled crowd of about 100. She noted that Daisy had refused even to warn those who already owned the guns. "Even as we speak," said Brown, "parents and unsuspecting children can be buying these air guns."

To Brown, the case was horrific. Millions of children imperiled, and a company unwilling to do anything about it. The CPSC offered voluntary recall measures, but Daisy refused them. Generally, after a commission request, companies announced about 200 to 300 recalls each year, many of them for items with nowhere near the lethal repercussions of Daisy guns. Companies had agreed in the past to CPSC-recommended recalls of toys ranging from alphabet games to Zap Zap Racetrack sets and seemingly everything in between—baby rattles, baking sets, blocks, binoculars, a toy called

Bunny on a Stick, fuzzy puzzles, inflatable Snoopys, pull trains, toy chests, and xylophone mallets. The commission took pains to avoid even the most remotely possible injuries. A few months before filing its lawsuit against Daisy, it acted upon news that a 9-month old baby began to choke on a toggle that he pulled off cargo pants sold at Toys 'R' Us and Babies 'R' Us; the New Jersey–based company agreed to recall 7,000 pairs of the pants. *Pants.* And Daisy had refused to recall a powerful gun.

Easily more than a thousand recalls had been made during Brown's seven-year tenure. In all that time, the CPSC had to sue companies to force recalls only five times (and only about fifteen times in the commission's entire history). Daisy was now one of them.

At the news conference, Brown told reporters that the Daisy case was why the CPSC existed. She didn't realize herself the degree of coincidence at work here: The commission came into being under a measure signed into law by President Richard Nixon in October 1972, a month after the first Daisy PowerLine guns were manufactured for the Sears fall sales program. "This case," Brown said, "exemplifies the purpose of the Consumer Product Safety Commission: to reduce injuries and deaths among children."

Even though Specter knew the fight against Daisy was far from over, at least now the BB gun manufacturer was on the defensive. Because of the Mahoney case, Daisy could no longer keep secret that it had settled multimillion-dollar cases. That public–relations battle, felt Specter—who had already taken the case of another boy injured by a Daisy BB gun—had been lost by Daisy. Now the company would be forced to battle for its very survival to avert a recall of millions of guns from across the country and possible financial ruin in the process. It would take time to reach a conclusion. The CPSC lawsuit was estimated to take a year or more to be decided by an administrative law judge. Hearings had to be held, a ruling issued and, even then, any ruling could be open to appeal. And Daisy would undoubtedly appeal.

But that was for another day. Today had brought a victory for the Mahoneys and their attorneys.

Specter got behind the wheel of his car and headed back to Philadelphia, his cell phone ringing frequently with more reporters wanting a comment on the case. Specter turned on the radio listening for the news of the CPSC vote; then he clicked it off and drove the last half hour in silence. Tired, he drove slowly in the right lane as he crossed into Philadelphia, its skyline twinkling at dusk. Not once did he cheer out loud or pump a fist into the air over a victory that had been hard-earned and long in coming. That just wasn't Shanin Specter.

But he was happy. After parking in the garage across the street from his office, Specter rose from his car, stretched his legs and back, and allowed himself a smile and a brief congratulatory comment. "Today," he said, "was a good day to be a lawyer."

CHAPTER 23

APPEAL AND SETTLEMENT

S ORRY AS IT WAS, SEPTA WAS not so sorry that it simply paid
the jury award. It appealed the $51 million verdict, and its
arguments in the written post–trial motions varied greatly
from its public apologies. Gino Benedetti claimed that Massiah-
Jackson erred when she ordered—in front of the jury—Russell
Figueira to run over to his office and retrieve his files. The SEPTA
appeal also claimed that revealing documents in such a fashion in
open court constituted an "unfair surprise" that worked against
SEPTA. The appeal further insisted that SEPTA was legally liable to
pay only $500,000, the Pennsylvania cap of $250,000 each to
Shareif and Deneen Hall. It claimed, too, that the civil rights clause
did not apply, that the law "does not impose a duty to provide minimal levels of safety and security to the riding public."

Tom Kline anticipated the appeal. He never for a minute expected SEPTA merely to pull out its checkbook: *Pay to the order of
Shareif and Deneen Hall, $51,000,065.* It didn't have that kind of
money even if it wanted to.

A few days later, and not long after the verdict and contempt citation, Kline sat down with a new SEPTA attorney from yet another
outside law firm. SEPTA chose someone who knew Kline well.
Nina Gussack, a partner with the large Philadelphia law firm

Pepper Hamilton LLP, had been one of the defense attorneys in a major prescription drug case in which Kline had won two multi-million-dollar verdicts. Kline and Gussack agreed to agree. Although Kline felt it was doubtful the jury's verdict would be overturned, particularly on the question of negligence, it was also unlikely the $51 million verdict would stand as it was.

The post-trial negotiations were brief and without acrimony. SEPTA was willing to pay—and pay an amount far exceeding $250,000. Kline said he wanted enough money to ensure Shareif's future. He also had no desire to blow a gaping hole in the budget of the already financially strapped transit system. (The $51 million verdict represented 7 percent of SEPTA's $700 million annual operating budget.) Nor did he want SEPTA to use this case as an excuse for another fare increase for its 750,000 weekday train, bus, and trolley riders. "We recognized that the public interest had a place at the bargaining table. Our job in this case was not to destroy SEPTA. Our job was to effectuate change," he told one reporter.

Kline also added: "I'm proud that lawyers have been recognized, especially in the mainstream press, as instruments of social change instead of objects of derision."

Kline had SEPTA cornered for a good deal of money even if it didn't settle. Although half the $50 million awarded to Shareif Hall was for SEPTA's negligence and thus subject to the $250,000 limit under state law, Kline could ask the court for—and he would automatically have added—delay damages, or prejudgment interest on the entire $25 million dating back to one year from the time the claim was made. At prevailing rates, Kline calculated the sum at $4.1 million. The other $25 million had been awarded under the civil rights claim and was not eligible for delay damages. Although SEPTA could appeal, an appeal would cost it more time and more money.

"Plus," Kline told the lawyers on the other side of the negotiating table, "SEPTA acted badly in all of this. SEPTA owes this little boy."

Numbers were tossed back and forth. Someone from SEPTA worked a calculator. The meeting lasted not even two hours. A number was settled upon: $7.4 million. The amount was nowhere near the $51 million the jury had awarded, but it was—Kline did the math in his head—nearly 30 times the state-set "cap" of $250,000. Deneen would get a portion of the money, about one-sixth of the total. The rest would go to Shareif, with a small portion (nearly $100,000) for his brother Shaheed, who had been at the scene of the tragedy. The lion's share of the money (both from SEPTA and the confidential settlement with Schindler Elevator) would be deposited for Shareif by a court-appointed trustee, who would approve all expenditures and handle the boy's estate until he turned 18. Even after that, much of the money would remain in an annuity with a guaranteed interest and payments scheduled through 2047. The settlement ensured that there would easily be enough money to last Shareif the rest of his life. Kline was satisfied with the amount.

But this was about more than money. As *The Philadelphia Inquirer* put it in an editorial: "Tom Kline, the Halls' lawyer, called the monster $51 million award a wake-up call to SEPTA. He's right."

BESIDES PAYING DAMAGES to the Halls, in the final negotiation SEPTA also agreed again to change its ways, from improving the condition of its escalators to the way its legal department dealt with accident victims. It promised more regular inspections of escalators, better maintenance and repairs, a revamping of its legal department, and, in the future, the prompt production of trial documents. There would be no more lawsuits filed against mothers or fathers, unless there was evidence—real evidence—they were at fault.

To help in this endeavor, SEPTA established a blue-ribbon panel (at a cost of nearly $300,000) composed of an impressive threesome—D. Donald Jamieson, a retired state superior court judge; Edward N. Cahn, a retired chief federal judge; and Carl Singley, former dean of the Temple University Law School. The panel's attorney was David L. Cohen, who had been chief of staff and a close adviser to former Mayor Edward Rendell. The panel investigated the incident and interviewed about three dozen people before issuing a detailed, 109-page report about five months after the trial.

The panel had concluded, basically, that there had been no intentional wrongdoing in the Hall case and no conspiracy on the part of SEPTA officials, simply complacency and poor communication. Put simply, SEPTA wasn't bad, just stupid.

In its investigation, the panel was able to uncover many of the escalator inspection reports that SEPTA had claimed no longer existed. The records showed up in the old, now-abandoned office of Dan Duffy, the millwrights' foreman. Some were in boxes, some were scattered across the floor, some were in the trash.

While the panel found no hard evidence that records were intentionally withheld, it wrote that "some employees responsible for maintenance may have believed they would be held responsible for the accident if a full record were developed." It noted that Duffy, for one, had still worked in the Glenwood Avenue office during the discovery period and "presumably could have located the maintenance records, which were in his custody, with ease." The very fact that documents were found strewn about the old office, the panel wrote, "supports an inference that Operations Division employees did not seek to produce all relevant documents."

The legal department also was found to be systematically inept, both in general and in the Hall case in particular. The SEPTA lawyers had mistakenly assumed that Kline's main target in the lawsuit was the elevator manufacturer; they had missed the opportunity to move the case to the friendlier confines of federal court once Kline added the civil rights claim. The panel also criticized SEPTA's legal department's unwritten policy of virtually always— "automatically" was how one SEPTA official had put it—suing parents when a child was injured. Panel member Carl Singley noted that doing so "appears to add insult to injury." Overall, the panel faulted the legal department with a "culture of complacency" and suggested it totally revamp the way it conducted investigations of accidents, including a system to collect and store documents and provide information to opponents in lawsuits.

The blue-ribbon panel, in a section of its report titled "Analysis—What Went Wrong in *Hall v. SEPTA*," concluded that it wasn't any one thing. The panel decided: "The Hall case was not handled properly in many respects. In fact, this case represents a classic application of Murphy's Law—almost everything that could go wrong did go wrong."

Kline read the report and criticized the panel in the media. "They really did not have a strong backbone," he told the *Philadelphia Daily News*. "We must send a message that we will not allow the kind of conduct that occurred in the Hall case to happen again."

CHAPTER 24

RECALL RECALL

S PECTER WAS ABLE TO SAVOR his victory over Daisy with the CPSC—and the blissful notion that some 7.5 million dangerous guns would be removed from stores and kids' rooms all across the country—for about a year. Then hope for the recall crumbled.

About a year after the commission announced its lawsuit against Daisy, an administrative law judge was still compiling information and evidence in the case. Specter felt certain the judge would side with the commission and compel Daisy to recall the defective guns. Once that order was made, Daisy would have little wiggle room. The pricey recall could force the company into bankruptcy, though Specter hardly cared. Too many boys had been hurt for him to be concerned over the company's fate. Daisy could, of course, appeal a decision against it, but he knew the odds were long of its winning. Federal appeals courts didn't often reverse a lower court judge without an overwhelming reason to do so, and Specter didn't feel there was one in this case. He felt certain that the administrative law judge, after his review of the evidence, would hand down an order against Daisy. Soon.

But a ruling did not come soon enough. Judge William B. Moran's deliberations were terminated before he could render a decision in the case. The CPSC did not wait to see what the judge would decide but itself wrote the official ending to the case.

Things had changed at the CPSC in the year since it voted to sue Daisy. Ann Brown had left as a member and chairman, and George W. Bush, a conservative Republican, chose her replacement.

The new president had at first sought to name as chairman Mary Sheila Gall, the lone dissenter in the commission's 2–1 vote for the Daisy recall, but a Senate committee that considered her too probusiness to head the panel for consumers blocked her nomination. Then Bush tapped Hal Stratton for the job. Stratton, a former New Mexico politician and attorney general, had little track record on consumer issues, at least when compared to Brown, who had spent two decades as a consumer advocate and had served as vice president of the Consumer Federation of America before her appointment. Stratton had been cochairman of a group called New Mexico Lawyers for Bush in the 2000 presidential campaign. Stratton was probusiness and a longtime critic of government regulation. In New Mexico, he had founded a group called the Rio Grande Foundation, whose website said it "promotes public policy founded upon the principles of limited government, economic freedom and individual responsibility." Consumer groups opposed his nomination. "We're extremely concerned," said Consumers Union, expressing fear that under Stratton the CPSC would take a far less active role in removing faulty products. Stratton, consumer groups feared, would be a procorporate vote on an agency intended to protect the public from bad products and the companies that made them.

Specter didn't like the news. Would a new commission with Stratton aboard be so business-oriented and so emboldened that it would try to reverse the decision to file a recall suit against Daisy? It was a stretch, but not that big a stretch. It would seem too obvious a political move to snatch the case away from a judge already considering the case. But Specter had witnessed politics close-up, and he knew that in politics no maneuver was too brazen. Specter considered going to the Senate directly to urge its members to reject Stratton's nomination to head the CPSC. But he needed some ammunition. He decided to sound Stratton out on the Daisy recall. He called Stratton's office in New Mexico.

"My name is Shanin Specter, from Philadelphia," he said, resisting the temptation to invoke his father's name and position.

"I'm sorry, Mr. Stratton is not available...."

"I simply want to introduce myself and chat with the chairman for minute."

"I'm sorry...."

"It will only take a minute or two."

"Mr. Specter, Mr. Stratton is not talking to anybody."

"I understand."

Specter was pretty sure Stratton was talking to somebody. If George Bush called from the West Wing, Stratton would probably pick up the phone. Did he know who Specter was and what he wanted? Probably. Not getting on the phone was a smart move on Stratton's part. He deprived Specter of any evidence that might help block Stratton's confirmation in the U.S. Senate.

Specter had foreseen the possibility—the probability—of a commission shakeup, and he had been prepared to seek out a Senate ally willing to question Stratton's confirmation. Not his father, but Sen. Joseph Biden, an influential Democrat from Delaware and a family friend. But with nothing more than suspicion, albeit well founded, that Stratton would seek to drop the Daisy lawsuit, Specter was powerless to protest Stratton's nomination.

He was also aware that the Senate had its back up against a wall on the nomination. For one thing, it had already rejected the nomination of Gall as chairman. If it also rejected Stratton, the CPSC would be left with just two commissioners. The commission was created to have five members, though it could function with just three. With only two members, the panel lacked a quorum and would be powerless to make any decisions. The country would be left without an important check against hazardous products. So although some Democrats were wary that Stratton might give the CPSC a probusiness tilt, they felt his appointment was better than having no functioning commission at all—and, if Democrats blocked his appointment, better than taking the political heat for such a situation.

On July 25, 2002, Hal Stratton was confirmed as chairman of the U.S. Consumer Product Safety Commission.

"Maybe he'll leave Daisy alone," Specter said hopefully to Andy Youman, who was sitting in his office when Specter heard the news.

"You don't believe that."

"No, I don't."

But it was possible. The Daisy case was already in the hands of a federal administrative law judge. To stop that action, the CPSC, now with a 2–1 Republican edge, would have to be proactive and reverse its own vote. It might not look good.

Daisy made the first move. Silent for months, the company now went on the offensive. It offered a settlement. It proposed taking the matter away from the judge. It suggested further negotiations with the commission. Daisy also offered to spend $1.5 million on a safety campaign to help buyers more safely use its guns if the commission halted the suit seeking a recall. Opponents scoffed that the deal was no deal at all—that Daisy already spent money on promoting gun safety and essentially wanted the commission to drop the recall lawsuit.

Stratton considered the proposal and, in September 2003, rejected it for a variety of reasons. For one thing, he hadn't been on the CPSC when it considered the Daisy case, and he didn't feel he knew enough about it to make such a decision. Also, now that the matter was before a judge, the commissioners were prohibited by law from discussing the case directly with Daisy.

Daisy was undeterred. The following month it again appealed to the commission. It asked the commission to reconsider the settlement offer, as Stratton himself would later put it, "primarily on Daisy's financial condition." Daisy was hurting. It was, in the company's words, in "precarious" financial condition largely because of the government action against it. The settlement proposal was not significantly different, only now Daisy offered proof of its financial woes. It produced documents showing that it had had major legal expenses and had been unable to obtain liability insurance at a reasonable price. (Daisy's liability coverage had reportedly doubled to $2.4 million a year, thanks to the Mahoney case.) At this point Stratton agreed to waive the restriction on dealing with litigants while an administrative law judge had their case. Daisy supplied information about its finances to the commissioners, that is, to at least to two of them, Stratton and Gall. It did not provide the documents to Commissioner Thomas Moore, who had voted originally, along with Brown, to file the suit seeking a forced recall.

A settlement was, essentially, brokered among Stratton, Gall, and Daisy. Moore voted against the deal. Another 2–1 vote was taken, and this one favored Daisy. Nothing had changed over the years: The guns had not been found to be safe and free of defects. No court cases had exonerated Daisy. In fact, Specter would file suit on behalf of another injured child, a suit that would result in yet another monetary settlement from the company. Only one thing had changed—the makeup of the commission.

Instead of having to recall and fix its guns, Daisy would have to spend $1.5 million on safety programs, including a new warning label Daisy would place on packaging. It would read:

> WARNING: (1) Always point the gun in a safe direction; (2) Always treat every gun as if it were loaded; (3) Any gun may fail to load, feed or fire a BB for a variety of reasons. Even if the gun fails to fire a BB one or more times, do not assume it is unloaded; (4) A BB can seriously injure or kill you or other humans if it is fired in an unsafe condition; (5) Shoot safely.

And that was that.

Stratton said he made his decision for a number of reasons. First, he was "not at all sure" the CPSC would win its case on the merits. He said his analysis of the Daisy rifle convinced him that even though BBs might get lodged in the gun, "the link between lodging and injuries is not at all clear" and that the incidents were "relatively rare." Stratton was evidently not swayed on the issue of liability by the civil cases against Daisy—or the huge settlement it had paid the Mahoneys.

Stratton also noted that the recorded injuries were preventable. "They all involved either someone pointing the gun at someone and pulling the trigger or playing with the gun in an inappropriate manner—all in violation of widely known and accepted safety rules for the use of guns." Also, Stratton said he was bothered by the "animosity" among the parties in a case that had become "excessively adversarial"—even mentioning the administrative law judge's "attitude" against Daisy—and he felt it was "imprudent to let the parties and the [administrative law judge] go on fighting for years...." The chairman said he also considered Daisy's financial status. He reasoned that if Daisy were to go belly-up, consumers would get nothing, no additional safety campaign. He said: "...A settlement would provide certain immediate benefits to consumers, which they would not receive if Daisy becomes insolvent or this litigation drags on for years."

He said it was better to let Daisy run its safety campaign and refer the matter to another panel, the American Society for Testing and Materials (ASTM International), to come up with improved safety standards. Such standards would be voluntary.

Commissioner Gall noted in her written opinion that she believed the settlement "is in the public interest and represents an adequate resolution of this case." She noted that she had voted against the lawsuit seeking a recall and even chastised her colleagues for the decision: "The commission's actions have done serious and unjustified damage to the reputation and business prospects of a company whose product represents no substantial product hazard."

Gall ignored the many lawsuits (and the settlements paid out) against Daisy. She acknowledged that CPSC tests showed that BBs jammed in the Daisy rifles. "I concede, therefore," she wrote, "that a propensity of BBs to lodge in the magazine of a BB gun and remain there without the shooter's knowledge is an undesirable characteristic." But beyond that, she said, any injuries that might occur are the fault of the shooter. It is the shooter who checks the gun for the presence of BBs. It is the shooter who pumps the gun to provide the force that propels the BBs. And it is the shooter who aims the gun. Noted Gall: "Even if the shooter has failed to observe the loading of a BB and believes that pulling the trigger will result in a 'dry fire,' an injury will occur only if the shooter points the gun at another person at close range and pulls the trigger, an action violating every known rule of shooting safety and common sense."

THE COMMISSION'S DECISION set off a wave of protest, from consumer groups to Commissioner Thomas Moore, who dissented, and even the administrative law judge, William Moran, who had the case snatched from his hands before he could make a decision in the matter.

Moore's dissent was scathing.

> The bottom line is that we are not the Business Protection Agency; we are the Consumer Product Safety Commission. Our responsibility is to protect the public from dangerous consumer products. If we lose sight of that, we will get entangled in endless discussions of company finances while consumers are being put at risk of death or serious injury.

Moore decried the very manner in which the settlement had come about. For one thing, all such settlement offers, he noted, were supposed to go to the administrative law judge considering the case. But Moran never got it. He'd been blindsided. "We cannot just decide to steer the parties to mediation or to accept a settlement offer directly from the parties or to broker private settlement agreements," he wrote in his dissent.

Also, Moore protested Daisy's end run around him. He noted that Daisy representatives met with Stratton and Gall about the settlement, but not with him. They gave Stratton and Gall information about the company's financial status, but not his office. "This is completely outside of the agency's rules of practice," Moore wrote. "...This latest activity where representatives of the commission talked to only one side about the underlying merits of the motion and negotiated their own alternate settlement agreement was clearly inappropriate." He went further, saying that trouble lay ahead if his fellow commissioners continued to make such private deals. Wrote Moore: "We cannot just decide to steer the parties to mediation or to accept a settlement offer directly from the parties or to broker private settlement agreements. If parties, including the commission's Complaint Counsel, cannot rely on the commission to follow its own Rules of Practice, then chaos will reign."

He noted that the settlement was not substantially different than the first one offered by Daisy and rejected by Stratton, only that it recognized Daisy's monetary woes. "We should not allow this newly raised financial issue to be used as a device to reconsider a settlement proposal already rejected by the commission," he wrote, adding later, "our statutes do not put a company's finances above the public's safety."

Not only that, but Moore wasn't buying Daisy's argument about possible financial ruin. "This is not the first time a company has raised this argument," he noted, adding, "Most of these dire predictions never come to pass."

Perhaps worst of all, the settlement, said Moore, did nothing to remedy the danger of defective guns, millions of them, still out in the public's hands, in children's hands. Stated Moore: "It does not contain the major element sought by [CPSC's] Complaint Counsel—a retroactive corrective action plan." He said that Daisy's safety program was "basically an information and education campaign of safe airgun handling" that was "not much different" than the one Daisy had had for years. "Why should we expect this campaign to work any better than the past one?" he asked.

Moore said that no matter how many times you warned children, and children are the main users of the Daisy air rifles, they will sometimes fail to follow the rules. "Children will be children," said Moore. "They grow up pointing toy guns at each other. To expect them not to point BB guns at each other when they believe they are empty of BBs is to expect too much. In the incidents that would have been presented to the court in the administrative law proceeding, no one would have gotten hurt if the airguns had not unexpectedly had BBs in them, no matter where the guns were pointed."

"Quite apart from the procedural defects, the [settlement] offer must fail for the same reason that it failed last September—the plan does not do enough to protect the public from harm."

By snatching a decision from the administrative law judge before a hearing was even held, reasoned Moore, "The commission is deciding, in effect, that no substantial product hazard exists. I, for one, am not comfortable with such a decision."

JUDGE MORAN HAD previously, in May 2003, issued a statement of his own opposing the settlement. He warned the commission that to change its decision—after Brown's departure and the installation of a new, Republican–appointed chairman—would create a "public appearance" that the CPSC makes decisions based upon its political makeup. That perception alone, he said, was enough to reject the settlement.

Moran also cited "misgivings about the litigation tactics employed by Daisy." He called the settlement "highly unusual" and an "empty proposal" that would provide no warning to owners of the defective guns nor compel Daisy to make any real concessions. He termed what Daisy was offering as "negligible." The settlement, he said, "offers no more than Daisy was willing to do from the outset of the litigation."

What's more, he said, "It provides nothing in terms of any notification to those who may have purchased these guns. Nor is anything presented in terms of offering an exchange program or even a credit toward the purchase of a replacement airgun."

"The court does not recommend acceptance of the settlement," he said.

After the CPSC decision to approve the settlement, the Washington-based Consumers Union issued a public rebuke of the agency, or, more pointedly, of Stratton and Gall. In a statement by Sally Greenberg, its product safety counsel, it said:

> We regret that two of the three CPSC commissioners have agreed to settle this case by agreeing to a toothless education and information campaign that will do nothing to prevent the deaths and injuries to users of these air BB guns, the vast majority of whom are teenagers or younger children.
>
> CPSC has abdicated its responsibility to protect the public—in this case children—from a dangerous product, and given Daisy a free pass that allows them to escape recalling the product or fixing it in the future. This is a sad day for product safety.

Later, *The Wall Street Journal,* in its lead, front-page story, a story featuring a sketch of a smiling Tucker Mahoney from his days before the shooting, would sum the case up this way:

TRIGGERING LIABILITY

**Teenage Shooting Opens a Window on Safety Agency
U.S. Regulator Dropped Call for a Recall of BB Guns;
Daisy Defends Its Products**

Politics, Law and the NRA

WASHINGTON—In the fall of 2001, the Consumer Product Safety Commission sued Daisy Manufacturing Co., the best-known maker of air-powered BB guns. The CPSC, prompted by the accidental shooting of a teenage boy, sought to force Daisy to recall millions of allegedly defective guns.

Late last year, the same federal agency agreed in a settlement to drop its lawsuit. Daisy didn't recall a single gun.

Instead, it agreed to spend $1.5 million on publicity and la-
beling to promote safe BB-gun use.

The Daisy case illustrates how politics can influence important decisions at the supposedly independent CPSC,
the federal consumer-safety agency with the broadest
reach. One reason for the BB-gun reversal was a switch in
the CPSC's chairmanship: from a Democrat with a strong
regulatory record to a free-market Republican.

The story concluded with a note that the case wasn't over yet.
Specter would make one last-ditch effort to try to get the Daisy
guns recalled. He filed suit in federal court in Philadelphia to nul-
lify the CPSC settlement with Daisy, charging the agency with
"multiple violations" of its own rules and procedures. The suit
asked the court to review the "settlement." (Specter put the word
in quotes.) The suit termed the CPSC's action a "toothless remedy"
that required no corrective action by Daisy, a company that the Mahoney case had shown had known about the defect for at least two
years before Tucker's father bought his gun. Corrective action, the
suit claimed, was not only called for, but also required by, the Consumer Product Safety Act.

The suit also charged the two majority commissioners with holding improper ex parte meetings with Daisy representatives and
with "improperly bypassing" the administrative law judge and the
CPSC's own Complaint Counsel in reaching the Daisy deal. Daisy's
financial condition was improperly given consideration—and
never put before the commission's complaint lawyers or the administrative law judge—in reaching the settlement. On top of all
this, the deal was reached essentially behind closed doors, between
two commissioners and Daisy, without a hearing or any reviewable
official record.

Specter knew such a suit was a long shot.

Five more months elapsed before Federal Judge Robert F. Kelly
issued his opinion. It came as no surprise. He approved the CPSC's
motion to dismiss the suit seeking the massive Daisy recall.

Kelly's decision was two-pronged. First, he ruled that the Mahoneys, in appealing the CPSC decision, lacked standing to appeal the commission's decision. Specter had argued in the appeal on the Mahoneys' behalf that the CPSC had failed to take corrective action that would have allowed them—as the owners of two Daisy air rifles—either to have their guns repaired or replaced, or to receive a refund. But Judge Kelly found the commission was under no obligation to adopt a "corrective action plan," as the Mahoneys contended. "The commission is, therefore, free to accept or reject settlement offers, even those that do not provide for repair, replacement or refund of the purchase price. The Mahoneys are, thus, incorrect in their interpretation of the applicable law." Therefore, they couldn't claim they had suffered an injury—in this instance, lack of repair or replacement, or nonpayment of a refund. They did not possess the grounds for a lawsuit.

Second, and perhaps more important, Kelly ruled that the CPSC had discretion under the law to order any action that it considered appropriate if it found a product presented a substantial hazard. The court, his court, had no power to review commission decisions on the subject. Concluded Kelly: "The decision of the commission to settle its administrative action against Daisy is, therefore, unreviewable under the Administrative Procedure Act, and this court is without jurisdiction to review it."

SPECTER APPEALED KELLY's ruling to the U.S. Third Circuit Court of Appeals, another long shot. Almost a year after Kelly's initial ruling, the three-judge panel rejected Specter's appeal. It agreed with Kelly that the CPSC in such matters had the authority to make its own determinations. The appeals court noted that federal law stated only that the commission "may order action" in cases involving potentially hazardous products, but it isn't mandated to do so. The courts did not have a say in the matter. It ruled: "The decision of what, if any, corrective action is 'appropriate' is left to the sole discretion of the agency."

Specter could have appealed to the U.S. Supreme Court, but it would have been pointless. The case, with neither a dispute among lower federal courts nor novel questions of law, was not the sort that the nation's highest court would consider, never mind rule on in the Mahoneys' favor.

SO IT WAS over. Six years and four months after Tucker was shot in the head, a Daisy BB piercing his skull and damaging his brain, there was nowhere left to turn with the case. Daisy had paid a huge settlement to the Mahoneys—with their insurance companies' money—but not a steep price. It was still doing a brisk business and millions of its defective guns were still out there, still being played with by unsuspecting children. When would another one of these children pump the gun 10, 12, 20 times and, thinking it was empty, aim it at a friend and pull the trigger?

Specter let the appeals court decision fall from his hands and onto his desk. He removed his reading glasses, a reluctant capitulation to middle age, and rubbed his eyes. The Daisy settlement had been one of the largest ever for his firm. It had made him millions. Yet he considered the case a partial failure.

"Yes, I got the family financial compensation, which to them was somewhere between meaningless and next to meaningless. Yes, our law firm was enriched, also between meaningless and next to meaningless. The insurance company paid most of what Daisy had to pay, so Daisy wasn't harmed. We did rake Daisy over the coals through the legal process, so they have to at least give pause before doing this again in the future. But on the big issue, getting the guns recalled, Daisy escaped."

"I WONDER," JAY Mahoney said, discussing the CPSC decision long afterward, "how many others have been hurt since Tucker was injured with one of those guns."

CHAPTER 25

"SERIOUS ABOUT CHANGE"

I N THE MONTHS and years that followed the SEPTA trial, the transit agency made good, for the most part, on its promise to do better.

The legal department was revamped, starting at the top. Gerald Bowers, SEPTA's legal chief, was forced to retire. His subordinate, Eileen Katz, dubbed "The Ice Lady" by reporters during the trial for her distant and unemotional testimony, was not promoted to the job, as she might rightfully have expected in other circumstances. An outsider named James Jordan, a lawyer whom Kline knew and approved of wholeheartedly, was hired to head the department of systems safety, which included SEPTA's legal department. Jordan had previously been a high-ranking attorney with the Philadelphia city solicitor's office and also a medical malpractice lawyer at the firm Post & Schell. In the 1980s, he had defended two doctors in a case in which he handed Kline one of his rare defeats, a defense verdict delivered by a Philadelphia jury. Jordan reported directly to SEPTA's general manager. Years later, while still SEPTA's chief in-house counsel, he would reflect on the trial and remark: "To those who argue that what this country needs is a strong plaintiffs' bar to protect against abuses from government or large corporations, the Shareif Hall case is Exhibit A."

273

As a result of the case, SEPTA promised wholesale change in the way it handled claims: "We will stop the notion that this is a game to be won or lost." It pledged that in the future all relevant documents would be turned over to plaintiffs and that the transit authority would shed its "attitude problem," an attitude premised on the notion that it was protected by the $250,000 liability limit. If there were ever transgressions by lawyers in the future and a judge imposed a fine, pledged Jordan, the lawyer involved would be personally liable to pay it.

SEPTA itself fined a few employees as a result of the Hall case. Several others were dismissed, disciplined, demoted, or reprimanded for their behavior in the case. SEPTA refused to name names, but word leaked out that Steve Krenzel, who had testified at length about the escalator's "sheared off" screws, was among those fired. So was Dan Duffy, the millwrights' foreman. (SEPTA said both later appealed through their unions and were reinstated.)

SEPTA did more. Several months after the *Hall v. SEPTA* trial, *The Philadelphia Inquirer* ran the following story:

SEPTA CREATING FACILITIES DIVISION

The New Department to Manage Infrastructure— Such as Escalators—Is Part of Ongoing Restructuring

By Jere Downs
Inquirer Staff Writer

The fallout from last year's record jury verdict against SEPTA for the escalator incident that tore off a 4-year-old's foot continued yesterday when general manager John K. Leary Jr. announced the details of a major reorganization of the transportation authority.

A new department—created apart from transit operations—is intended to ensure the safety of escalators and the maintenance of all other infrastructure, a key feature of the SEPTA overhaul, Leary said.

"People making sure escalators were working were also making sure buses got out of the terminal on time," Leary said. The new department, he said, "will bring a direct focus on SEPTA's facilities."

In January, SEPTA's board commissioned an investigation after a jury in December awarded $7.4 million to Shareif Hall, who lost his foot in 1996.

... Tom Kline, the Philadelphia lawyer who represented Hall, applauded the changes yesterday but said he still sought a public accounting by SEPTA of who was disciplined for what actions in the Hall case.

"It is commendable that SEPTA has taken stock of itself and has decided to reorganize so that something can come out of the tragedy," Kline said.

The article went on to quote Jack Leary as saying that he had formed a task force to see to it that many of the changes called for by the blue-ribbon panel that investigated SEPTA after the Hall trial would be made over the next six months. He said that included creating a central system of investigating and tracking accidents as well as improved training for safety staff. He said the legal staff had already been meeting to come up with ways to improve coordination of legal claims and to review the progress of new lawsuits.

Leary said that within the next seven months the transit agency would be restructured into various units responsible for different functions—such as finance, legal operations, and human resources—and several other departments devoted to the operation of transit services. That would include a new department that would report directly to him on capital design and construction, for which SEPTA had designated $485 million—the largest budget ever—for the coming fiscal year.

Leary announced that he also planned to ask the state for more money to improve the system, but the SEPTA chief, once so influential with legislative leaders, found that the highly publicized Hall case had only soured the mood in Harrisburg. "I don't think we should be talking about giving them additional money," state Rep. Dwight Evans, a Philadelphian and the leading Democrat on the House Appropriations Committee, told *The Inquirer* in response to Leary's comments, adding, "...SEPTA's leadership has lost credibility with me. I'm waiting to see results on how they maintain their escalators and elevators."

HOWEVER, SEPTA's CHANGES, in both attitude and the structure of its legal department, did satisfy one important person. Judge Massiah-Jackson reduced her $1 million contempt fine to $100,000, a penalty that would be paid to the court system. SEPTA officials complained bitterly about having to pay even $100,000, but Massiah-Jackson refused to reduce the penalty to zero.

During the publicity surrounding the case, one organization of SEPTA commuters had urged the judge to direct that the fine somehow help the mass transit system or its riders. However, she could only order the penalty paid to the court system. But she thought that it was a grand idea if SEPTA's riders could somehow benefit from the case, and when the lawyers for both sides assembled before her to get the court's approval of the $7.4 million settlement, she said so. Perhaps, she said, if one of the parties in the case that stood to reap a percentage of the financial award.... Then she lifted her reading glasses to her forehead and said, "Mr. Kline?" He smiled at the judge. Kline & Specter later donated $100,000 to the city's Boys and Girls Clubs to buy subway tokens for lower-income high school students who needed transit fare to get to and from school.

After the case had concluded, Kline also noticed a difference in SEPTA. In a later suit he filed against the transit agency—this one for the family of another boy, Kyle Harris, who was killed—SEPTA was forthcoming, even fast, with documents. The agency also investigated whether it was at fault. It accepted part of the blame, even though the 12 year old had picked a lock to enter a motorman's booth; once inside, he then poked his head out the window and was struck by two poles. SEPTA immediately offered to pay the $250,000 cap to the boy's family. The agency also pledged to change all the locks on the booths. Jordan declared that this demonstrated SEPTA's legal department had changed course "180 degrees." He proudly told the news media, "We're not going to use litigation to beat down the other side or prolong this." SEPTA now appeared to be playing by the rules, at least when it involved one of Kline's cases.

Many months later, nearing the two-year anniversary of the trial, Leary, though just 58, decided to call it quits. His contract was almost up at year's end, and he wasn't interested in a new one. He'd had enough. He would retire to a new home he had built on Cape Cod. "Five years is a very respectable time in this job," he told reporters. "The gas tank runs empty." Though praised for streamlining SEPTA and producing balanced budgets, Leary had also had his troubles, including a 41-day mass transit strike and a 25 percent rate hike. And then there was *Hall v. SEPTA*. "That happened on my watch," Leary said as he headed for the door. "That was a low point."

It also was a hideous stain on an otherwise distinguished career in public transit. Instead of leaving to cheers for a job well done, Leary awoke the day after announcing his retirement to jeers. A column headline in the *Daily News,* which had called for his resignation after the Hall case, read: "It's Past Time for Jack Leary to Leave—Escalator Suit Marred Tenure." The headline on a parting editorial was more succinct: "Hit the Road, Jack."

The media and the public took Leary to task for the incident, but SEPTA's lawyer in the case escaped similar censure. Though SEPTA dropped Leon Tucker from its list of outside counsel, in November 2005 the Democratic Party would back him for a seat on Philadelphia Common Pleas Court, the same court in which *Hall v. SEPTA* had been decided. The *Philadelphia Daily News,* the same newspaper that had decried "SEPTA's Shame" in blaring headlines following the trial, would endorse Tucker and urge his election. It said in an editorial: "Leon Tucker feels that a term on the Common Pleas bench would be a fitting capper for a 30-year career in the law and in public service. We agree." Tucker was the top vote getter among 10 candidates.

SEPTA made moves to improve its escalators as well as its legal department. Not long after the Hall trial ended, the transit authority got back to doing daily escalator inspections and filing daily reports; the inspections were no longer carried out by six millwrights but by seventeen specially trained SEPTA employees who did nothing but escalator and elevator inspections and repairs. SEPTA also got back on schedule doing monthly preventive maintenance inspections and shutting down each escalator annually for complete inspections and servicing.

The authority hired a Long Island company to inspect its 38 escalators. It later put into place a $30 million, seven-year program to revamp its entire escalator system. Within two and a half years after the Hall trial, ten old escalators had been removed and replaced with brand new ones, each with a cost of about $1 million and each with automatic step-level and comb-plate shutoff devices. At least five more new escalators were scheduled to be installed, and many more were to be upgraded and modernized. "The new ones are above and beyond any others working anywhere else in the country," boasted Richard Maloney, SEPTA's spokesman.

"Escalators at this agency are now treated as a vehicle," he said. "Before *Hall,* the maintenance and servicing and replacement of escalators was, frankly, not going very well. Now it will be."

Kline, nevertheless, continued to be a burr in SEPTA's side. He monitored the transit agency's progress in making improvements to its escalators, checking them himself at certain subway stations—always with a TV reporter in tow—while sending staffers to check other stops. He called these his own "inspections." Some he found to be in unsatisfactory condition and others out of service, including the long-dormant escalator at City Hall. When he found a problem, Kline complained to SEPTA and the media. He wasn't out to harass the agency but to "keep on top of them," to make sure SEPTA kept its word and continued to improve its escalators. Said Kline, "I want the day to come when I declare total victory."

On April 19, 2002, at 8:30 a.m., a smooth swishing sound could be heard emanating from the subterranean confines at the intersection of the Cecil B. Moore Station. The sound, faint against the noise from arriving trains and college commuters, most of them unaware of the terrible thing that had happened on the very same spot five and a half years earlier, came as workers cranked into operation a glittering, spanking new Kone & Company 82-step escalator to carry passengers from the subway to the city streets above. This escalator had all the state-of-the-art features—brushes along the side to keep people's feet from bumping the edges, lighting along both sides, comb-plates at the top, and a bottom painted bright yellow. It also had all the latest safety and automatic-shutoff devices.

One sign with red letters, advising caution and listing the rules for safe riding, was installed on a concrete pillar at the base of the escalator. Another at street level announced the completion of the $1.4 million project. Both signs boasted the agency's long-standing—and now demonstrably accurate—slogan: "SEPTA—Serious About Change."

CHAPTER 26

"Seventy–Six Trombones"

IT WAS GOING ON THREE YEARS SINCE "the accident." Becky Mahoney was seated on a bruised and battered purple couch in the middle of the main foyer of the Wildwood Building, one of several at the Woods Services School, Tucker's latest address. She looked as fatigued as the furniture. Becky, who once sat straight and stiff-backed, allowed herself now to slide deep into the couch's cushions. Her voice was soft as she chatted with a first-time visitor, who accompanied her to the institution.

After a brief instant, a dark-haired young man noticed Becky and walked jauntily over to her. He was wearing jeans, a gray sweatshirt, and a puppy-dog smile. When he reached Becky, he held out his hands, palms down, about two inches from her face, though not saying a word.

"Hello, Lawrence," she said casually. Lawrence (residents' names have been changed to protect their privacy) was clean-shaven and handsome in an unusual way. He was about Tucker's age.

"See?" he said, holding out his hands.

"What?"

"See?"

"See what, Lawrence? Do you have a cut?" Becky glanced at the other visitor and forced a smile.

"No, silly!" said Lawrence, almost shouting, the second word coming out slurred, like *siwwy.*

"What am I looking at?"

"Looong. Wook at my naiwls."

"Ohhh," replied Becky, trying to match Lawrence's enthusiasm over the length of his fingernails. "They're growing. Is that it? Is that what you're trying to show me?"

"Yeah. Gwowing."

Delighted, Lawrence beamed. Then, without warning, he bent over the back of the couch and gave Becky's companion a hug. It was a warm, gentle embrace, one that belied the reason Lawrence was at the center and not at home with his parents: He beat them. This sweet man-child was capable, at a moment's notice, of turning vicious—especially against his parents. Becky knew this, so she was friendly but also wary of Lawrence and other patients at Woods. The center cared for young men suffering from brain injuries, mental illnesses, or emotional problems. A number were schizophrenic.

Next, Tommy came over, pushing the joystick control that directed his wheelchair toward Becky. It was a week before Christmas 2001, and the white walls of the lobby bore sparse signs of the holiday—a decorated tree off to one side, a haphazardly arranged string of lights against one wall, a strand of golden garland taped to another.

"Whatcha doin'?" Tommy wanted to know. An accident or an illness had left his face twisted on one side, which, when combined with the dark goatee he was growing, gave him a menacing look. His teeth were crooked and bunched together, his eyes looking off in different directions. He had a nasty bruise on the right side of his forehead. Yet he seemed happy. "Myyy...name...is...Sponge Bob...Squwaarre Pants," he announced, the words delivered with great effort, followed by a guttural laugh. The next second Tommy launched into song, "Wuuudolph...the wed-nosed weindeeer...." He insisted that Becky accompany him to the game room and the center's karaoke machine. He wheeled over to the machine and turned it on with help from an aide. Then he turned to Becky with a huge smile, raised a crooked arm, and contorted his hand to face palm up toward the ceiling. "C'mon, can I get a *whoop! whoop!?*" He laughed from one side of his mouth.

Becky smiled back at Tommy. It was a sad smile. Word had already spread throughout the institution: Tommy had tried to kill himself the previous night. Only 12 hours earlier, this young man had wrapped the wires from one of his video games around his throat and tried to hang himself in his room. An aide now followed Tommy everywhere he went.

As 3 p.m. and the center's employee shift change drew near, the place became very crowded. Some of the patients returned from attending school, real schools outside of Woods. The electric doors slid open, and a small battalion of wheelchairs glided inside, noiseless atop the carpeted lobby floor. Several drivers, their heads hanging lopsidedly, wandered off without apparent direction. A few moved straight for Becky Mahoney.

"Hi, Sandy."

"Hi Mitchell."

"Hi, Jimmy," she greeted them.

Her tone lacked emotion. Some of the youths said hello back. Some could not speak and began pointing, trying hard to smile. They were happy to see Becky, who had become a familiar sight at the Wildwood Building. She was there every day, one of the few adults who came visiting on weekdays, or at all for that matter. Last Christmas she gave a boom box as a gift to Jimmy, an undersized youth who had badly mangled legs and a scar that stretched nearly ear to ear across his scalp, through his crew cut, the apparent remnant of a surgical procedure. The boom box was stolen the next day. Now Jimmy was clutching a plastic bag full of candy, swinging it furiously at anyone who came too close. Jimmy, explained Becky, had a terrible temper.

Sandy walked by next, tripping over the wreckage of a soccer table game, whose legs had been broken and had collapsed onto the floor. A boy named Mario was off in a corner, using a stapler to add a green link to a long chain of paper loops, an arts and crafts project. Mitchell clutched for Becky's cell phone, which she wisely did not relinquish.

Lawrence returned with the board game Sorry! held against his chest, hoping Becky would play. Across the room someone was wailing, very loudly. From somewhere else a sharp yelp pierced the air every few seconds. One patient, a young man with a bushy head of red hair, pounded his chest with his fist, hard. Another sat quietly, staring at the ground, drooling, a crash helmet on his head. It was a strange scene, a large lobby filled with broken adolescents.

And Becky could only wish that her own son might achieve even their modest level of ability, that Tucker might some day be able to use a wheelchair or utter a single word.

Tucker, now 18, still could not move his arms or legs, except for the involuntary movements that kept his hands partially clenched. If he had never been paralyzed by that BB, that tiny ball of metal, Tucker would be in college now like the rest of his friends, maybe on a basketball scholarship, with a girlfriend.

Becky left the bedlam of the waiting area and walked into Tucker's room. She gave her son a cheery hello. "Hey, Tuck! How are ya?" He didn't respond. Didn't move, not even his eyes, which were focused straight ahead of him, somewhat to the left of a TV set showing a women's volleyball game between Stanford and Long Beach State. Becky smoothed the hair off Tucker's forehead, continuing to stroke his brow. He stared ahead, his mouth fixed in an odd overbite. Tucker barely resembled the pictures of him on the walls, pictures from before the accident.

Becky went to Woods Services School every day promptly at 9 a.m., getting relief late in the afternoon from her husband, Jay, after he finished work. She would leave only to travel with Tucker when he was transported to Crozer-Chester Hospital for therapy and other medical procedures, which Becky hoped would help him regain the use of his limbs, or learn to swallow again. She derived strength and hope from every improvement, no matter how small.

"He was able to chew and swallow a french fry last week and drink some soda," she related excitedly. Maybe if Tucker could eat regular food, then maybe some day he could be taken off the feeding tube; then maybe he could be moved to a different facility that would provide more rehab, less warehousing, for patients with traumatic brain injuries; then maybe....

Tucker had been in and out of several hospitals, with doctors trying various new therapies. He was treated for staph infection as well as pneumonia. He suffered from fatigue, muscle cramping, chronic diarrhea. A blue plastic diaper protruded from the top of his pants.

The whole experience was a drain on the Mahoney family, with Becky and Jay traveling nonstop from hospitals to therapy sessions to Woods. "Abby's life's been turned upside down," Becky said about her youngest child, now a sophomore in high school. "I'm not at home. Her dad's not there. Her grandparents have moved in, which is different for her. It's not normal. She doesn't like it." Becky's mother and father never returned to live in Florida after the shooting, instead staying at their daughter's house on a pull-out sofa all this time. Becky and Jay had not been on a vacation since the incident. Becky hadn't even had a chance to buy any Christmas presents yet this year. "Maybe there won't be Christmas this year," she said with a small laugh. "I guess I'll have to buy my presents at the hospital gift shop."

Ty Weatherby, a freshman at the University of Pittsburgh, would probably come by the Mahoneys' house during his Christmas break, Becky thought. He had stopped by over Thanksgiving, but he didn't have too much to say. He never apologized to the Mahoneys for the shooting. His parents moved from the neighborhood a few months after the shooting. Becky didn't know they were leaving until she saw the moving truck. Ty's parents hadn't called or come over in more than two years.

Becky had been back to the local Kmart, where she noticed Daisy PowerLine guns were still for sale.

And the toll mounted. The constant trips to the hospital, the never-ending worry, the daily visits to Woods surrounded by Lawrence and Tommy and Jimmy. No nights out, no letup. Becky, seated in one of those beat-up purple couches at Woods, looked down a moment at her folded hands when asked what it had been like. "It's a killer," she said.

Yet as long as there was hope she would press on. There was no choice. When he was healthy enough, the Mahoneys took Tucker home on weekends and several afternoons during the week. They built a wing onto their house they hoped could be his for good sometime in the future. For now, though, he needed too much help to stay at home. The Mahoneys had a private nurse with Tucker at all times as well as a privately paid aide from Woods, who was strong enough to help lift him from his wheelchair to a bed. Tucker had grown two inches since the shooting and was 6-foot-4 and 165 pounds. Since he was rarely outdoors, his hair turned from blond to a muted light brown. Most days Tucker stayed at Woods. Becky knew he did not like it because when he returned there once after a lengthy stay in a skilled nursing unit at Mercy Fitzgerald Hospital, his blood pressure soared and his pulse raced to 110 immediately after he was brought into the building. He would also became physically upset when Becky wheeled him out past the visitors' area and into the main corridor for his medication, a litany of drugs and vitamins he had to be given daily. Tucker was still able to smile at some things, and cry at others. The difference was imperceptible to visitors. Not to his mother. "He understands," she insisted. "That's what's so terrible about it."

Tucker's room at Woods was kept as cheerful as possible, its walls adorned with cards and posters signed by hundreds of former fellow students from his old high school. A bright red poster bearing the Nike "swoosh" was taped to a wall beside his bed. And there were visitors aplenty. Today, Becky was there and Jay arrived later. He walked into the room and bent over Tucker's bed, his face inches from his son's as he whispered a private thought. Tucker's grandmother was there. So was a neighbor. A private nurse hired by the Mahoneys was there as was Isaac, Tucker's aide, who came on at 3 p.m. But the get-together didn't last long. Not today.

At one point, Becky left Tucker's room to speak on her cell phone. She was on with a doctor, expressing concern over her son's persistent fever. The doctor agreed there seemed to be a problem, and he wanted Tucker returned as soon as possible to the hospital, where he would perform a spinal tap to check for bacteria. Within minutes, the Mahoneys had Tucker ready in his wheelchair, moving him down the hallway and outside to their specially equipped van. The van pulled out from a side exit. Puffs of smoke spewed from its exhaust as it made its way slowly from the Wildwood building, whose roof was rimmed with electrified icicles, its lawn adorned with sparkling reindeer and a smiling plastic Santa. Giant pine trees similar to the ones in the Mahoneys' backyard stood in a line behind the building, swaying in unison in the chill December wind. The van, with Tucker inside, pulled out of the driveway and disappeared down the highway.

IT WOULD BECOME a recurring hardship. Over the next year, Tucker would be transported back and forth to the hospital for a raft of maladies, his parents constantly catapulted into a state of fear until Tucker received treatment, rebounded temporarily, and finally returned to his room at Woods. Jay and Becky would grow dissatisfied with Tucker's care at Woods, worrying that not enough was being done there to repair his broken body and shattered life. Once when they missed visiting one day, they found that Tucker had not been moved out of his bed, his body not even turned. On another occasion they found Tucker hollering because a staffer was laughing and spraying Silly String on him.

The worst incident occurred at the hands of a psychologist. One day when Jay was sitting with his son, the psychologist entered Tucker's room and noticed the walls adorned with photos of Tucker with his friends from high school. The man came close to Tucker and told him the photos would have to be taken down. "That was your life *then*," he told the young man. The psychologist motioned toward the rest of the room and the sterile institution and added, "*This* is your life now." Jay ordered the man to leave the room. "And never come near Tucker again!" he shouted.

Jay, a large man with meaty arms and large, sad blue eyes, didn't want Tucker to forget. He wanted him to hold on to hope that he might get better, just as he and Becky held on to the special dream that their son would return to them. "Our hope is that one day he gets out of bed and says, 'Hi, Mom. Hi, Dad.' Our hope is that every day is the day," said Becky. "We're hoping for a miracle."

And the miracle began to come true. Slowly, incrementally, Tucker showed signs of improvement. He began eating food. One day a mashed french fry and a sip of Coke, then a bit more and more. After many months, Tucker could consume a menu of foods by mouth. All of it had to be mashed and pureed, but he managed to get it down—french fries, tacos, peaches. Becky dutifully chopped and pureed the food and watched in delight as her son was able to swallow the concoctions. Jay saw improvement of a more wondrous kind. He sensed that Tucker was comprehending more all the time. He "responded appropriately" to various stimuli, laughing at something funny, crying when he heard something sad. One time his private nurse, a woman named Kim, saw Tucker struggling with a task and said to him, "I know how frustrating this must be." He looked at her and a tear rolled down his cheek.

Tucker's arms and other extremities continued to cramp, but not his face. Tucker was able on occasion to reach and touch his mother or father. Once, while held up in a standing position, he placed his arm around Becky and stroked her back with his hand.

It was progress, however slow. If only Becky could get Tucker off that feeding tube, then he could leave Woods Services and get into Beechwood Rehabilitation Services, an affiliated program in nearby Langhorne, Pennsylvania, which dealt more with patients who could be helped and less with "hopeless cases." Beechwood had less of an institutional feel to it and was a community program where adult patients, most with brain injuries, lived on the grounds but also in independent homes and apartments in the surrounding area. Beechwood boasted a range of care and rehabilitation, from medical and nursing support to vocational services. Some of its patients even held jobs. Clearly, Becky felt, this would be a huge step up for Tucker. Such a place would move her son to an entirely new horizon in the recovery process. "While other parents were looking at colleges for their children, we were looking at getting him accepted into rehab," Becky would recall. Beechwood was a far stretch from college, but it had a reputation for helping patients, from young adults—patients had to be at least 18—to much older residents. Tucker now met the age requirement, but he was still getting some of his nutrients through a feeding tube. Beechwood mandated that patients be completely off feeding apparatus and be able to take their medicines orally. Some who visited and cared for Tucker doubted he would ever get to that point.

But not his parents. With hard work and diligence, the Mahoneys made it happen. Tucker got to the point where he could swallow his pills and eat his food through his mouth. Jay Mahoney remembered the exact day the feeding tube was removed. It was July 4, 2003, Independence Day. No sooner was the tube removed than Beechwood accepted him as a new patient.

Jay and Becky were overjoyed, even though their son remained in obviously poor shape. Finally, they thought, Tucker was on the road to recovery. And he did seem to flourish. The Beechwood staff was vigilant and friendly. One aide would get Tucker into a wheelchair and race him around the parking lot, while Tucker steered with his left hand, laughing. Other patients visited Tucker, sat with him, got him to laugh. They became his friends. The Mahoneys still came every day, and they felt more comfortable in the new surroundings. Though still plagued by physical ailments, particularly gastrointestinal problems, Tucker seemed to be getting better with every visit. Jay recalled a particular day, October 11, 2003, a Saturday, as "Tucker's best day." He and Becky took Tucker home with them and pushed him in a wheelchair outside so he could see the addition that was underway, being readied for regular visits, a few days a week at first and then perhaps some day for good. Jay stood his son up and held him tightly on one side. Becky stood on the other side, her arm around Tucker, his arm around her. Jay pointed to the addition. "You're going to get better, Tuck, and that's going to be yours." A wide smile formed on Tucker's face.

The next day, with Tucker back at Beechwood, Jay visited to find out that his son had vomited in his bed earlier that morning. It was a bad sign. Tucker was transferred to nearby St. Mary Medical Center, where Jay again sat beside his bed. Generally a silent man, Jay tried to talk to Tucker. He talked about a recent football game he had seen, about cars, about the upcoming holidays. He looked at Tucker, not certain if his son was listening to him. Tucker had become a little bit thinner in recent months. Suddenly, Jay heard small, shallow breaths coming from Tucker's mouth—choppy, hastened puffs. Tucker seemed short of breath, laboring. Jay dialed his cell phone. Becky picked up on the second ring. "Listen to this," Jay said, placing the phone near Tucker's mouth. When Jay got back on the phone, Becky was speaking loudly. "It's respiratory distress," she said. "Get someone in there, fast!" Jay jumped up and ran for help. He took a few steps down the hallway before he spotted a nurse.

"Tucker's in respiratory distress. Hurry!"

The nurse ran down the hall, to Tucker's side. She listened to his breathing and checked his pulse. Tucker was having a heart attack. She sounded a "Code Blue." Soon another nurse, then a doctor, ran into the room.

"Please step outside," one nurse asked of Jay, and he complied. For several minutes, Jay paced the corridor. After what seemed like forever, the doctor stepped out of the room. "I'm sorry," he told Jay. "There's nothing more we can do . . . ."

Just then another doctor came running down the hall. He had been finishing his rounds, his young daughter tagging along with him, when he heard the code sounded. They both ran into Tucker's room. This second doctor—whose name was Ben Solomon, Jay would find out later—started pressing on Tucker's chest, trying to revive him. And he did. Tucker's heart began pumping again, and he started to breathe. But he had fallen into a coma.

For several days, Tucker remained in an unconscious state. Then a week went by, then a week and a half. During all that time he was never alone. Becky sat by his side all day, every day. Jay came in the late afternoon or early evening and stayed until morning, usually sleeping in a chair bedside Tucker's bed in the Intensive Care Unit, where Tucker lay attached to a respirator, as well as various IVs and machines, the flickering lights and occasional beeps the only signs that he was still alive. Others visited as well, Tucker's grandparents, friends, neighbors, his private nurse, Kim. One day almost 30 friends of Tucker's from high school, home for the weekend from college, lined the hallway to wait their turn for a visit. At one point they helped a nurse move Tucker to another bed, one the staff felt would be more comfortable for him. His friends lifted Tucker, six on one side, six on the other. In quiet moments, Becky and Jay told Tucker how much they loved him. They told him he would re-bound from this setback, that he would get better. "You're a fighter, Tuck. You're going to beat this." Becky stroked her son's hair and begged him to "hang in there," to not give up.

The prognosis was not good. Tucker was experiencing bleeding, first from his mouth, then his nose, then from his eyes. The doctors thought it was because of drugs used to treat an infection Tucker had contracted. But they couldn't stop the drugs, and so they countered the bleeding with constant transfusions. "We're losing him," one of the doctors whispered to Becky one afternoon.

DURING THE SECOND week of the coma, on a Wednesday night, Tucker experienced a sudden drop in body temperature. A test showed internal bleeding. His kidneys were failing. The next morning, a nurse told Becky she thought that Tucker might have suffered a stroke. Becky gently pulled open his eyelids and noticed that his eyes were severely dilated. She let them drop closed again and peered into his face. He appeared somehow different to her. "There was just a different aura about him," she would recall. "He didn't seem to be there." Yet an electroencephalogram showed that Tucker still had brain activity. And by Saturday morning the internal bleeding had stopped. "A miracle," proclaimed one of the nurses. He's going to pull through, again, thought Becky. He's going to make it.

But the bleeding started again. And Tucker's vital signs worsened. "He's not going to make it through the weekend," one of the doctors told the Mahoneys. A second EEG exam found no brain activity.

On Sunday, Dr. Solomon and a pulmonary specialist came to the ICU to speak with the Mahoneys. They suggested removing the breathing tube to see if Tucker could breath on his own. If he could not, they would let him go. The Mahoneys agreed.

Jay and Becky stood by Tucker's side. Becky's parents were there, too. So was Kim, and neighbors Diane and Ernie Warner, and Tucker's aunt, Kathleen Clarke. Maggie and Abby were not present. As Solomon began to remove the breathing tube from Tucker's throat, another friend, Denise Nubani, fell to her knees and began to recite the rosary. The hospital chaplain started to sob. Jay and Becky, anxiety and fear etched on their faces, stood and watched.

The tube was removed. Tucker did not breathe. His face, still, began to darken, then turned a horrid grayish blue. At the sight, Becky turned and fled into the hallway. Jay followed her a few minutes later.

The cause of death was determined to be toxic megacolon, a condition in which a person's colon becomes hugely distended and can become perforated, leading to infection. The severe ailment can be caused by a number of things, including chronic diarrhea, common among patients on a feeding tube, as well as by blockages in the colon, which might have been triggered in Tucker's case by the introduction of food consumed orally. "It could have been his constant diarrhea. Or the very thing we thought would be good for him, getting off the feeding tube, could have been the problem. Probably a combination of the two," said Becky. The ailment resulted in Tucker's colon being distended and its walls becoming thin, the consistency of "tissue paper," was how one doctor had put it. No autopsy was performed. Tucker's body, largely immobile for years and subjected to all kinds of ailments and medicines and procedures for so long, had simply and finally given out.

November 1, 2003. It was 76 degrees, very warm for so late in the year. People were outside everywhere on this afternoon, jogging, bicycling, throwing Frisbees, walking their dogs. The sidewalks of

New Hope, Pennsylvania, with its quaint shops and storefront restaurants, were crammed with shoppers and tourists. Streets flooded with cars searching in vain for parking spaces, and leather-clad bikers inched their powerful machines along Route 32, the town's main drag.

Several miles north of town, sunshine filtered through trees in full fall regalia. Leaves speckled the pristine lawn at Trinity Episcopal Church, a stone structure built in the Bucks County countryside in 1876. Nearly 300 people packed into the church's pews, its balcony, aisles, and entrances, anywhere they could find room. A brilliant, searing light cast a triangular beam from a window directly onto the Mahoney family, Jay and Becky, Maggie and Abby. They stood silently, occasionally smiling as someone walked past them. Shanin Specter sat in the balcony.

So many of those in attendance were young, too many young people to be inside on such a beautiful day. The girls wore dresses, the boys appearing uncomfortable in dress shirts and ties on a Saturday. Some chatted in hushed tones. Most sat or stood in silence, occasionally glancing awkwardly at one another. Finally, the silence was broken.

"I swell with pride that I was able to spend so much time with someone so amazing," said Michael O'Donnell, one of those young people, as he stood at a lectern, his voice beginning to crack slightly. "I love you, Tuck, and I will never, ever forget you."

Jay and Becky Mahoney sat quietly during the memorial service for their son, whose four-year battle for life was finally over. His body, once athletic, had grown feeble, weary of fighting off infections and complications, of fighting fate. "You could see in his eyes how badly he wanted to live," O'Donnell told the teary-eyed assembly about the life of John Tucker Mahoney, a life ended at 20. Ty Weatherby and his parents were among the mourners at the church, though they stayed in the background.

The organist played a gleeful version of "Seventy-Six Trombones" as the service concluded. The song, from *The Music Man*, had been one of Tucker's favorites. Becky smiled slightly at the memory of Tucker when he was only four or five dancing around the family room with his little playmates as she had played the album from the musical.

Tucker's family, his parents, his grandparents, his two tall, blond sisters, walked slowly from the church. As the somber procession made its way to waiting black limousines, Becky, eyes glistening, greeted as many people as she could. Jay, as usual, was largely silent, walking in the middle of the throng, letting himself be swept along by it. The procession slowed even more as it reached the parking lot. Then the Mahoneys piled into the darkened interior of a limousine that took them home.

There would be no burial that day. Tucker's body was to be taken to a place near the home of his grandfather. The program for the memorial service stated simply: "Interment will take place at the Church of the Redeemer, Sarasota, Florida, at a future date."

A FEW YEARS later, Jay and Becky still could not bear the thought of parting with their son, not even his ashes. They had his body cremated after the memorial service in 2003 and placed in a miniature mahogany casket bearing a brass plaque and the inscription: "John Tucker Mahoney, 1983–2003." The box sat on top of a dresser in their bedroom.

"We know where he is. We know he's safe, not cold and under the ground," said Jay.

"It makes no sense but . . . ," said Becky, "I can't go through with a burial. I have to gather the strength to go through with that service. Someday we'll get to that point. Someday."

"You don't ever get used to losing a child," she said. "You put on a good face, but there's a hole in your life that's there forever."

CHAPTER 27

ON HORSEBACK

IT WOULD TAKE THE HALL FAMILY years, painful years, to get back on track.

Shortly after the $51 million verdict had been announced in *Hall v. SEPTA,* Deneen returned to her apartment in North Philadelphia to find it had been broken into and ransacked, some idiot burglar evidently reading the news and thinking Deneen had already cashed the check and stuffed the money under her mattress. It was, believe it or not, a common occurrence following large and widely publicized civil verdicts or settlements. The "winners" of those suits—many who had lost loved ones and didn't feel they had "won" anything at all—became victims anew. Charities beseeched them as if they had hit the lottery. Family members asked them for money, often turning nasty if they were refused. Friends asked for loans, no longer remaining friends if the money wasn't forthcoming. Employers assumed a plaintiff in a winning case wasn't going to return to work; Specter had represented one woman who lost her only child and won a large jury verdict, then returned to work to find her locker emptied out and her job given to someone else even though she had no money coming to her because her case faced years of appeals.

Eventually Deneen moved the family to a cozy middle-class neighborhood in the New Jersey suburbs, settling into a white aluminum-sided house with a bright red front door and a row of azalea bushes out front. Deneen remained suspicious and cautious and stayed away from the limelight, refusing phone calls from the news media or lawyers or people who wanted to be her friend. She had an unlisted number and address, and instructed her attorneys not to tell anyone where she had moved. If she wasn't sure who was ringing her doorbell, she sometimes would not come to the door, even though the cars parked in the driveway made it obvious she was home. She communicated little with Kline after the trial, but the following Christmas his office did receive a Christmas card bearing the depiction of a little boy, a black boy, holding an oversized candy cane and standing beside a puppy. "Just sharing special wishes for a holiday filled with sweet surprises," the card read. It was signed in an uneven scrawl, by someone obviously just learning to write script: "Love Shareif Hall and family."

Other than that, there was little communication from the Halls. They had gone from the headlines to virtual obscurity. And Deneen was fine with this. She just wanted to get accustomed to privacy and suburban tranquility, which wasn't as easy as it sounded for someone who'd only known life in the inner city.

A FEW YEARS later, in a place in the countryside, a place with rolling hills and verdant fields, Shareif bumps up and down on a trotting horse. Brilliant sunshine lights his face. He snaps the reins on his horse, urging her to go a little faster around the corral. Shareif feels in control, far from the city now, far from the littered streets of North Philly, far from the Cecil B. Moore Station. There are no clattering subways, not even many cars.

It seems like a dream, but it is not. Shareif's mother, with money from the SEPTA verdict, has enrolled him in a special school that caters to kids who have had unlucky breaks. It teaches children that they can do things they had thought impossible, things they had never envisioned themselves doing.

Shareif has become a decent rider for a nine year old, especially one with a plastic foot. This is "therapy," aimed at improving posture and balance—strength and muscle for the body, concentration and confidence for the mind. All Shareif knows is that it is fun. So is swimming. And ping-pong.

"He does everything," his mother says of the boy who only a few years ago had trouble making friends in kindergarten, trouble reciting his ABCs. At his new school, Shareif is doing well in his classes. He plays sports. "He is on the swim team. He has friends. He has lots of friends now."

As he rides his horse, a smile on his face, Shareif looks off into the azure horizon and inhales the sweet, fresh country air.

POSTSCRIPT

More than 11 years after suffering his injury at the Cecil B. Moore Station, Shareif Hall, months away from his 16th birthday, was still living in the same modest house in the suburbs, now attending public high school, playing sports, and making friends.

The little boy who had run wildly about Kline & Specter's offices during his trial now seemed respectful, even mature for his age.

"I heard you get good grades in school?" I asked him in a phone conversation.

"Yes, sir," he said, noting his last report card was all A's.

"Are you proud of that?"

"Yes, sir."

"What's your favorite subject?"

"Math."

Shareif said he played basketball and football and that even with his prosthesis he was pretty good at both. He played defensive end with a club football team named the Lions. He said that he still occasionally went horseback riding. And that he was happy.

Shareif jumped off the phone after a few minutes, but Deneen made him pick up a second time to properly finish our chat.

"Nice talking to you," he said.

"Nice talking to you, too, Shareif."

ACKNOWLEDGMENTS

I would like to thank a number of people for their time and their insights—and for sharing their memories, memories that were often painful for them.

In the SEPTA case, Judge Massiah-Jackson shared her views and recollections of the trial.

In the Daisy case, the Mahoney family untiringly discussed the events leading to Tucker's death and their personal feelings long afterward.

Thanks to those readers and critics of the early manuscript, which probably bears little resemblance to this book, including Russ Eshleman, Lori Yingling, Sue Houghtaling, and Susan O'Sullivan. And particularly to Tracy Leonardis, who let me use her high-speed printer, then started to read the pages, and eventually became an important sounding board. Thanks to Dawn Kudgis, who helped compile and edit the photos.

Thanks to Tom Kline and Shanin Specter, who hired me to write a book about their law firm and gave me the editorial freedom essentially to write what I wanted, and how I wanted to write it.

Special thanks to Avery Rome, who provided expert editing and friendly encouragement for this book.

GLOSSARY OF NAMES

THE HALL CASE

Robert Allman—director of system safety, Southeastern Pennsylvania Transportation Authority (SEPTA)

James Bahn—SEPTA's investigator for the incident

Gino Benedetti—outside counsel hired by SEPTA for contempt hearing

Cecil Bond—SEPTA assistant general manager

Gerald Bowers—SEPTA's legal chief

Paul Brady—defense attorney for Schindler Elevator Corporation

Chris Brennan—reporter for the *Philadelphia Daily News*

Thomas Brown—SEPTA station supervisor who spoke with the "mystery witness"

Edward N. Cahn—retired chief federal judge, member of SEPTA blue–ribbon review panel

David L. Cohen—former adviser to former Mayor Edward Rendell, counsel to SEPTA blue–ribbon review panel

Tom Dolan—Thomas Brown's supervisor

Dan Duffy—millwrights' foreman, whose memo cited problems with the escalator

Dwight Evans—Pennsylvania state representative, leading member of House Appropriations Committee

Michael C. Fagan—escalator expert hired by plaintiff

Russell Figueira—SEPTA director of safety and risk management

Jennaphr Frederick—Fox TV reporter, the first TV reporter at the trial

John Gregg—orthopedic surgeon who operated on Shareif

Deneen Hall—Shareif's mother

Shareif Hall

Sherrod, Sherrell, Shaneen, and Shaheed Hall—Shareif's siblings

Leslie Hickman—SEPTA's director of the Broad Street Line

David Hopkins—economic actuarial consultant, estimated total economic damages

D. Donald Jamieson—retired Pennsylvania superior court judge, member of SEPTA blue-ribbon review panel

James Jordan—attorney named after the trial to head SEPTA's department of systems safety, including its legal department

Eileen Katz—SEPTA deputy general counsel

Bill Kinkle—millwright for SEPTA

Tom Kline—lawyer for Shareif and Deneen Hall

Joe Kostkowski—Schindler Elevator Corporation's agent with the Zurich Insurance Company

Stephen Krenzel—assistant director of maintenance and construction, SEPTA Broad Street Line

Jack Leary—SEPTA general manager

Frederica Massiah-Jackson—Philadelphia common pleas court judge, presided at Hall case

Elizabeth Anne McGettigan—nurse who estimated costs for Shareif's health care

Ray Mosley—SEPTA millwright

S. Ross Noble—physician specializing in rehabilitative medicine, plaintiffs' expert

Patrick Nowakowski—SEPTA's chief operations officer

Vernon Odom—veteran reporter with ABC Channel 6

Rob Ross—Kline & Specter attorney

Carl Singley—former dean of Temple University Law School, member of SEPTA blue-ribbon review panel

Boyd Taggart—court crier

Leon Tucker—SEPTA outside counsel and lead defense attorney in the Hall trial

Jasen M. Walker—director of services for American Board of Vocation Experts, plaintiffs' expert

Eric Weiss—defense attorney for Schindler Elevator Corporation

John Wenke—SEPTA transit police officer

Carl J. White—patent holder for escalator safety devices hired by Kline as an expert